Chapter and Unit Tests
with Answer Key
··

THE HOLT AMERICAN NATION

HOLT, RINEHART AND WINSTON
A Harcourt Education Company

Austin • New York • Orlando • Atlanta • San Francisco • Boston • Dallas • Toronto • London

Cover: Maytag Company, courtesy PRC
Title Page: © CORBIS/Bill Ross

Copyright © by Holt, Rinehart and Winston

All rights reserved. No part of this publication may be reproduced or transmitted in any form or by any means, electronic or mechanical, including photocopy, recording, or any information storage and retrieval system, without permission in writing from the publisher.

Teachers using HOLT THE AMERICAN NATION may photocopy complete pages in sufficient quantities for classroom use only and not for resale.

Printed in the United States of America

ISBN 0-03-065323-1

3 4 5 6 7 8 9 082 04

Chapter and Unit Tests

UNIT 1 • BEGINNINGS

CHAPTER 1 • The World by 1500
Test Form A........................ 1
Test Form B........................ 4

CHAPTER 2 • Empires of the Americas
Test Form A........................ 5
Test Form B........................ 8

CHAPTER 3 • The English Colonies
Test Form A........................ 9
Test Form B........................ 12

UNIT 1
Test Form A........................ 13
Test Form B........................ 16

UNIT 2 • CREATING A NATION

CHAPTER 4 • Independence!
Test Form A........................ 17
Test Form B........................ 20

CHAPTER 5 • From Confederation to Federal Union
Test Form A........................ 21
Test Form B........................ 24

CHAPTER 6 • A Strong Start for the Nation
Test Form A........................ 25
Test Form B........................ 28

UNIT 2
Test Form A........................ 29
Test Form B........................ 32

UNIT 3 • GROWTH AND CHANGE

CHAPTER 7 • Nationalism and Economic Growth
Test Form A........................ 33
Test Form B........................ 36

CHAPTER 8 • Regional Societies
Test Form A........................ 37
Test Form B........................ 40

CHAPTER 9 • Working for Reform
Test Form A........................ 41
Test Form B........................ 44

UNIT 3
Test Form A........................ 45
Test Form B........................ 48

UNIT 4 • WAR AND REUNIFICATION

CHAPTER 10 • Expansion and Conflict
Test Form A........................ 49
Test Form B........................ 52

CHAPTER 11 • Sectional Conflict Increases
Test Form A........................ 53
Test Form B........................ 56

CHAPTER 12 • The Civil War
Test Form A........................ 57
Test Form B........................ 60

CHAPTER 13 • Reconstruction and the New South
Test Form A........................ 61
Test Form B........................ 64

UNIT 4
Test Form A........................ 65
Test Form B........................ 68

UNIT 5 • A NATION TRANSFORMED

CHAPTER 14 • The Western Crossroads
Test Form A........................ 69
Test Form B........................ 72

CHAPTER 15 • The Second Industrial Revolution
Test Form A.....................73
Test Form B.....................76

CHAPTER 16 • The Transformation of American Society
Test Form A.....................77
Test Form B.....................80

CHAPTER 17 • Politics in the Gilded Age
Test Form A.....................81
Test Form B.....................84

UNIT 5
Test Form A.....................85
Test Form B.....................88

UNIT 6 • A WORLD POWER

CHAPTER 18 • The Age of Reform
Test Form A.....................89
Test Form B.....................92

CHAPTER 19 • Progressive Politicians
Test Form A.....................93
Test Form B.....................96

CHAPTER 20 • America and the World
Test Form A.....................97
Test Form B.....................100

CHAPTER 21 • World War I
Test Form A.....................101
Test Form B.....................104

UNIT 6
Test Form A.....................105
Test Form B.....................108

UNIT 7 • PROSPERITY AND CRISIS

CHAPTER 22 • A Turbulent Decade
Test Form A.....................109
Test Form B.....................112

CHAPTER 23 • The Jazz Age
Test Form A.....................113
Test Form B.....................116

CHAPTER 24 • The Great Depression
Test Form A.....................117
Test Form B.....................120

CHAPTER 25 • The New Deal
Test Form A.....................121
Test Form B.....................124

UNIT 7
Test Form A.....................125
Test Form B.....................128

UNIT 8 • WORLD CONFLICTS

CHAPTER 26 • The Road to War
Test Form A.....................129
Test Form B.....................132

CHAPTER 27 • Americans in World War II
Test Form A.....................133
Test Form B.....................136

CHAPTER 28 • The Cold War
Test Form A.....................137
Test Form B.....................140

CHAPTER 29 • Society After World War II
Test Form A.....................141
Test Form B.....................144

UNIT 8
Test Form A.....................145
Test Form B.....................148

UNIT 9 • A CHANGING HOME FRONT

CHAPTER 30 • The New Frontier and the Great Society
Test Form A.....................149
Test Form B.....................152

CHAPTER 31 • The Civil Rights Movement
Test Form A.......................153
Test Form B.......................156

CHAPTER 32 • Struggles for Change
Test Form A.......................157
Test Form B.......................160

CHAPTER 33 • War in Vietnam
Test Form A.......................161
Test Form B.......................164

UNIT 9
Test Form A.......................165
Test Form B.......................168

UNIT 10 • MODERN TIMES

CHAPTER 34 • From Nixon to Carter
Test Form A.......................169
Test Form B.......................172

CHAPTER 35 • The Republican Revolution
Test Form A.......................173
Test Form B.......................176

CHAPTER 36 • Launching the New Millennium
Test Form A.......................177
Test Form B.......................180

UNIT 10
Test Form A.......................181
Test Form B.......................184

ANSWER KEY 185

Name _____ Class _____ Date _____

CHAPTER 1: The World by 1500

CHAPTER TEST • FORM A

■ **REVIEWING FACTS** *(3 points each)* In the space provided, write the name of the person or the historical term identified by each description. Choose your answers from the list below. There are two extra names or terms on the list.

Crusades	African Diaspora	the Aztec
Isabella of Castile	Prince Henry	Qur'an
Muhammad	the Maya	feudalism
Agricultural Revolution	King John	Renaissance

_____ 1. devised a number system that included zero well before the Europeans

_____ 2. holy book carried by Muslim merchants as they preached their religion

_____ 3. system of cooperation used by European rulers to combat invaders

_____ 4. series of military and religious expeditions conducted to control Palestine

_____ 5. signed a charter limiting the power of the English monarchy

_____ 6. built their capital on an island in Lake Texcoco

_____ 7. dramatic change that occurred worldwide as the biggest game died out

_____ 8. rebirth of European learning and artistic creativity

_____ 9. wanted to unify Spain by making the nation completely Catholic

_____ 10. relates to the displacement of 10 million people from their native lands

■ **UNDERSTANDING IDEAS** *(3 points each)* For each of the following, place the letter of the *best* choice in the space provided.

_____ 1. During the mid-1480s, Portuguese sailors charted the southwest coast of
   a. Asia.
   b. North America.
   c. Africa.
   d. Europe.

_____ 2. In what country did the Renaissance begin?
   a. Italy
   b. France
   c. Spain
   d. Portugal

Chapter and Unit Tests   Chapter 1 **1**

Chapter 1, Test Form A, Continued

_____ 3. Virtually all the important events during the Middle Ages took place
   a. at the manor.
   b. at the village church.
   c. in the fields.
   d. at the monastery.

_____ 4. How would you describe the Mesoamerican civilizations in North America?
   a. small and spread out over a wide area
   b. large and restricted to several large cities
   c. nonexistent
   d. very large societies

_____ 5. Most archaeologists believe the first people to enter the Americas came from
   a. Mesoamerica.
   b. Europe.
   c. Africa.
   d. Asia.

_____ 6. The first people in the Americas were the
   a. Mound Builders.
   b. Paleo Indians.
   c. Inca.
   d. Anasazi.

_____ 7. The Maya inherited much from which culture?
   a. Olmec
   b. Aztec
   c. Spanish
   d. Inca

_____ 8. China became the largest empire in the world during the
   a. Qin dynasty.
   b. Han dynasty.
   c. rule of Kublai Khan.
   d. rule of Genghis Khan.

_____ 9. The development of new farm equipment and the increased military strength of Christian kingdoms helped bring an end to
   a. feudal society.
   b. the Frankish kingdom.
   c. the Renaissance.
   d. nation-states.

_____ 10. Magna Carta guaranteed basic liberties for
   a. nobles.
   b. serfs.
   c. all people.
   d. all men.

■ **TRUE/FALSE** *(2 points each)* **Read each of the following statements, and then decide whether it is true or false. If the answer is true, place a *T* in the space provided; if the answer is false, place an *F* in the space.**

_____ 1. The Anasazi were probably ancestors of the Pueblo.

_____ 2. The climate in the Americas grew colder between 10,000 and 5,000 B.C.

_____ 3. An Arab merchant founded Islam.

_____ 4. Charlemagne ruled the Frankish kingdom.

_____ 5. Roger Bacon invented a printing press that used movable type.

Chapter 1, Test Form A, Continued

■ **PRACTICING SKILLS** *(5 points each)* Study the table below and answer the questions that follow.

Characteristics of North American Culture Areas Before Arrival of Europeans

Northwest Coast	• Coastal dwellers • Fishers • Developed complex cultures
Plateau	• River dwellers • Primarily fishers • Relatively low population
Great Plains	• Grassland dwellers • Nomadic buffalo hunters after introduction of the horse
Northeast	• Forest dwellers • Mostly hunter-gatherers; also farmers and fishers
Great Basin	• Desert basin dwellers • Mostly gatherers, due to barren surroundings • Low population
California	• Desert, mountain, river, or coastal dwellers • Farmers, nomadic hunters
Southwest	• Canyon, mountain, and desert dwellers • Farmers, nomadic hunters
Southeast	• River valley dwellers • Mostly farmers; also hunter-gatherers, fishers

1. Which culture areas at least partially depended upon agriculture for food?

2. Which culture area experienced changes after the introduction of a domesticated animal?

■ **COMPOSING AN ESSAY** *(20 points)* Write a brief essay on *one* of the following subjects. Remember to use examples to support your answer.

1. Define the Agricultural Revolution, and explain the effect it had on Native Americans.
2. Explain how the Crusades and Johannes Gutenberg contributed to the Renaissance.

Name _____ Class _____ Date _____

CHAPTER 1
The World by 1500

CHAPTER TEST • FORM B

■ **SHORT ANSWER** *(10 points each)* Provide brief answers for each of the following. Remember to use examples to support your answer.

1. How did the first people arrive in the Americas?
2. How did the rise of cities during the Agricultural Revolution affect Native Americans?
3. What were some of the advances Chinese civilization made in science and technology?
4. What did Magna Carta do?
5. What were some of the technological developments that improved sea exploration for the Europeans?

■ **PRIMARY SOURCE** *(10 points each)* In 1961 archaeologists discovered evidence of a Viking settlement built in the year 1000 at the northern tip of Newfoundland, Canada. They uncovered ruins of several houses, some old tools, and several other items. Other than that, not much is known about the settlement or why it was abandoned. Some people believe the settlement was the Vinland settlement that supposedly was established by Leif Eriksson and described in the *Greenlander's Saga*. The excerpt below is from that saga. Read the excerpt and answer the questions that follow.

> *They sailed to the land, reaching an island which lay to the northward of the country [Greenland].... They decided to stay for the winter and they built a large house. There was no shortage of salmon in the river or in the lake, and these were larger salmon than they had ever seen before. The qualities of the surrounding country were so good that they believed there would be no shortage of cattle fodder in the wintertime....*

> One of the settlers then discovered some grapevines. This surprised everyone because grapes generally do not grow well in cold climates. The story then continues with Ericksson saying:

> '*Hereafter we shall have two tasks. Every day we will either gather grapes and cut vines, or fell timber to make a cargo for my ship.*' *They cut a full cargo ... and sailed away. And Leif gave a name to the land, in keeping with its products, and called it Vinland.*

1. Why was Vinland an appropriate name for the land the Vikings discovered?
2. What types of resources did the area have?
3. What clue suggests that the settlement found by archaeologists was not Eriksson's Vinland?

■ **COMPOSING AN ESSAY** *(20 points)* Write a brief essay on *one* of the following subjects. Remember to use examples to support your answer.

1. Describe the factors that led to the end of fuedal society.
2. Define the Crusades and explain how they affected European economies.

Name _____ Class _____ Date _____

CHAPTER 2: Empires of the Americas

CHAPTER TEST • FORM A

REVIEWING FACTS *(3 points each)* In the space provided, write the name of the person that completes each sentence. Choose your answers from the list below. There are two extra names on the list.

Hernán Cortés	Christopher Columbus	Ferdinand Magellan
Moctezuma II	Francis Drake	Juan de Oñate
John Smith	John Cabot	Pocahontas
Francisco Vásquez de Coronado	Bartolomé de Las Casas	Vasco Núñez de Balboa

1. After returning to Spain in 1493, the queen and king gave _____ the title "Admiral of the Ocean Sea."

2. _____ wrote *Apologetic History of the Indies* in 1566.

3. _____ conquered the Aztec.

4. Queen Elizabeth II knighted _____ on the deck of his pirate ship.

5. _____ and his crew landed at Newfoundland in 1497.

6. _____ became an indispensable intermediary between the English and the Powhatan.

7. _____ died during a voyage in which his crew became the first to sail completely around the world.

8. The "Seven Cities of Gold" were sought after by _____.

9. _____ was elected the president of Jamestown in 1608.

10. _____ believed that Quetzalcoatl would one day return to rule over his people.

UNDERSTANDING IDEAS *(3 points each)* For each of the following, place the letter of the *best* choice in the space provided.

_____ 1. The Protestant Reformation can best be described as a
   a. political struggle.
   b. political, religious, and territorial struggle.
   c. religious struggle.
   d. territorial struggle.

_____ 2. The earliest challenges to Spain's American empire came in the
   a. early 1400s.
   b. late 1500s.
   c. early 1500s.
   d. late 1600s.

Chapter and Unit Tests   Chapter 2 5

Chapter 2, Test Form A, Continued

_____ 3. The great naval battle in a French port in 1588 ended in a major defeat for the
   a. Spanish.
   b. English.
   c. French.
   d. Portuguese.

_____ 4. Tobacco growing in Jamestown
   a. was a source of conflict with the Indians.
   b. was unsuccessful because of poor soil.
   c. was limited to low-lying areas.
   d. brought about the end of indentured servitude.

_____ 5. The people who had the highest social status in Spanish America were the
   a. mestizos and mulattoes.
   b. peninsulares and criollos.
   c. zambos and Indians.
   d. mulattoes and zambos.

■ **TRUE/FALSE** *(2 points each)* **Read each of the following statements, and then decide whether it is true or false. If the answer is true, place a *T* in the space provided; if the answer is false, place an *F* in the space.**

_____ 1. Most Spanish colonists protested the harsh treatment of American Indians.

_____ 2. Hernán Cortés was one of the most able and adventurous of the conquistadores.

_____ 3. The Inca Empire was centered in the Andes.

_____ 4. The Spanish established settlements in Texas before they established settlements in Florida.

_____ 5. *Crotoan* was the American Indian name for corn.

_____ 6. "The Lady Rebecca" was an Indian princess.

_____ 7. During Columbus's time, most sailors thought Earth was flat.

_____ 8. Queen Isabella objected to the system of *encomienda.*

_____ 9. The Northwest Passage does not exist.

_____ 10. Martin Luther believed that the Roman Catholic Church was corrupt.

Chapter 2, Test Form A, Continued

■ **PRACTICING SKILLS** *(5 points each)* Study the graph below and answer the questions that follow.

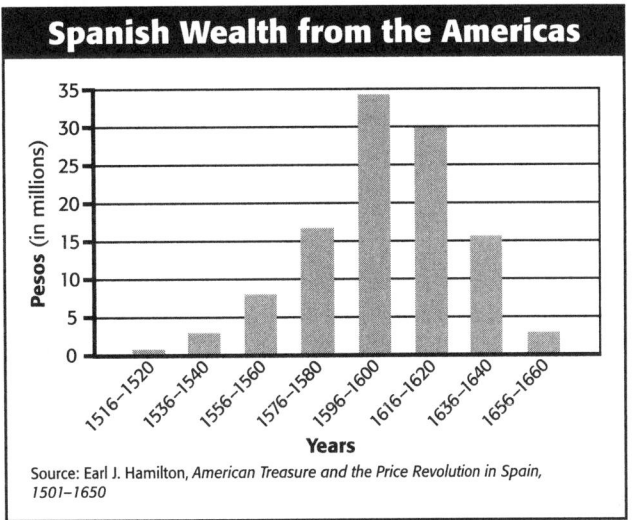

1. During which periods did Spain take 30 million or more pesos worth of gold and silver?

   _____

2. Approximately how many pesos worth of gold and silver was taken from the Americas during the 1500s?

   _____

3. During which period did Spain take the least amount of gold?

   _____

■ **COMPOSING AN ESSAY** *(20 points)* Write a brief essay on *one* of the following subjects. Remember to use examples to support your answer.

1. What was the *encomienda* system, and how did it affect the Spanish colonists and the American Indians?
2. Define the Protestant Reformation, and explain how it affected colonization.

Name _____ Class _____ Date _____

CHAPTER 2
Empires of the Americas

CHAPTER TEST • FORM B

■ **SHORT ANSWER** *(10 points each)* Provide brief answers for each of the following. Remember to use examples to support your answer.

1. Why did Columbus sail west from Europe?
2. In practice, what was the *encomienda* system?
3. Where in the present-day United States did Spain establish most of its settlements?
4. Why did so many explorers hope to find a Northwest Passage?
5. Why was the defeat of the Spanish Armada historically significant?

■ **PRIMARY SOURCE** *(10 points each)* In 1609 Captain James Smith, the leader of the Jamestown settlers, returned to England after becoming injured in a gunpowder explosion. The winter he was gone was a horrific one for the 500 settlers, recorded in history as "The Starving Time." Only 60 of the 500 lived through it. One of the survivors recorded the following account of that winter. Read the account and then answer the questions that follow.

> *Within six months after Captain Smith's departure, there remained not past 60 men, women, and children, most miserable and poor creatures; and those were preserved, for the most part, by roots, herbs, acorns, walnuts, berries, now and then a little fish.*
>
> *This was that time, which still to this day we called the starving time; it were too vile to say and scarce to be believed, what we endured. But the occasion was our own for want of providence, industry, and government, and not the barrenness and defect of the country, as is generally supposed. This in ten days more, would have supplanted us all with death.*
>
> *But God that would not this country should be unplanted, sent Sir Thomas Gates, and Sir George Sommers with 150 people to preserve us.*

1. What did the starving settlers eat to survive?
2. What event saved the remaining colonists?

■ **COMPOSING AN ESSAY** *(20 points)* Write a brief essay on *one* of the following subjects. Remember to use examples to support your answer.

1. Describe women's roles in Spanish America.
2. Who was Bartolomé de Las Casas? Describe the reforms he recommended to Spain's rulers.

Name _____ Class _____ Date _____

CHAPTER 3: The English Colonies

CHAPTER TEST • FORM A

REVIEWING FACTS *(3 points each)* For each of the following descriptions, place the letter of the *best* choice in the space provided.

_____ 1. Which of the following established a self-governing colony based on the majority rule of male church members?
   a. Mayflower Compact
   b. Toleration Act
   c. Albany Plan of Union
   d. Fundamental Orders of Connecticut

_____ 2. Who claimed to receive religious insights directly from God?
   a. Nathaniel Bacon
   b. Jonathan Edwards
   c. Anne Hutchinson
   d. William Bradford

_____ 3. What planter organized an army of Western settlers and attacked American Indians on the frontier?
   a. Edmund Andros
   b. Charles Whitefield
   c. William Pitt
   d. Nathaniel Bacon

_____ 4. What were the series of religious revivals that swept through the British colonies in the mid-1700s?
   a. Restoration
   b. Great Awakening
   c. Glorious Revolution
   d. Enlightenment

_____ 5. What era followed the death of Oliver Cromwelll, during which power of the English monarchy increased?
   a. Restoration
   b. Great Awakening
   c. Glorious Revolution
   d. Enlightenment

_____ 6. What is considered to be the world's first written constitution?
   a. Fundamental Orders of Connecticut
   b. Mayflower Compact
   c. Albany Plan of Union
   d. Toleration Act

_____ 7. What colony began as a "Holy Experiment"?
   a. New Amsterdam
   b. Delaware
   c. Pennsylvania
   d. Georgia

_____ 8. Who was referred to as King Philip by the English?
   a. William Penn
   b. Metacomet
   c. Squanto
   d. Jonathan Edwards

_____ 9. Who explored the Mississippi River in the late 1600s?
   a. Giovanni da Verrazano
   b. Jacques Cartier
   c. René-Robert de La Salle
   d. Louis-Joseph de Montcalm

_____ 10. Who was the cabinet minister who assumed full control of Great Britain's war efforts during the French and Indian War?
   a. Edward Braddock
   b. James Wolfe
   c. Jeffrey Amherst
   d. William Pitt

Chapter and Unit Tests

Chapter 3, Test Form A, Continued

UNDERSTANDING IDEAS (3 points each) Read each of the following statements and then decide whether you agree with it or disagree with it. If you agree, place an *A* in the space provided; if you disagree, place a *D* in the space.

_____ 1. Most large families in New England had little need for indentured servants or slaves.

_____ 2. Some historians believe the Salem witchcraft trials occurred because men did not want women to be independent.

_____ 3. Most of the men in the Virginia colony were married.

_____ 4. The Chesapeake planters preferred indentured servants to slaves.

_____ 5. The slaves on South Carolina's rice plantations retained more of their African traditions than did slaves in other areas.

_____ 6. The Georgia colony failed as a social experiment.

_____ 7. Most merchants supported the policy of mercantilism.

_____ 8. The Great Awakening sparked the growth of many new Protestant churches.

_____ 9. The Pilgrims were the least radical of the Puritans.

_____ 10. The Puritans believed in predestination.

TRUE/FALSE (2 points each) Read each of the following statements, and then decide whether it is true or false. If the answer is true, place a *T* in the space provided; if the answer is false, place an *F* in the space.

_____ 1. Rhode Island was founded by Roger Williams.

_____ 2. Virginia was referred to as the "best poor man's colony."

_____ 3. Georgia was planned by James Oglethorpe as a fresh start for English poor.

_____ 4. South Carolina's first colonists came primarily from Barbados.

_____ 5. The Duke of York gave the colony of New Jersey to two friends.

Chapter 3, Test Form A, Continued

■ PRACTICING SKILLS *(5 points each)* Study the table below and answer the questions that follow.

Colonial Populations in 1680 and 1750

	1680	1750
Connecticut	17,246	111,280
Georgia	*	5,200
Delaware	1,005	28,704
Maryland	17,904	141,073
Massachusetts	46,152	188,000
New Hampshire	2,047	27,505
New Jersey	3,400	71,393
New York	9,830	76,696
North Carolina	5,430	72,984
Pennsylvania	680	119,666
Rhode Island	3,017	33,226
South Carolina	1,200	64,000
Virginia	43,596	231,033

* Georgia did not become a colony until 1732.
Source: Historical Statistics of the United States

1. What were the most populous and least populous colonies in 1680 and 1750?

   _____

   _____

2. Which colony gained the largest number of settlers between the two dates?

   _____

■ COMPOSING AN ESSAY *(20 points)* Write a brief essay on *one* of the following subjects. Remember to use examples to support your answer.

1. Describe why some people chose to reject Puritan laws and ways and settle elsewhere.
2. Describe how the European desire for furs and land affected American Indians.

Name _____ Class _____ Date _____

CHAPTER 3: The English Colonies

CHAPTER TEST • FORM B

■ SHORT ANSWER (10 points each) Provide brief answers for each of the following. Remember to use examples to support your answer.

1. What were some of the problems faced by the Puritans in England?
2. What were some of the beliefs and characteristics of the Quakers?
3. Why did the colony of Georgia fail as a social experiment?
4. Why did the Great Awakening appeal to many people, particularly the poor and the enslaved?
5. What were the results of the French and Indian War?

■ PRIMARY SOURCE (10 points each) Jonathan Edwards is often credited with launching New England's Great Awakening. The native of Connecticut claimed that he felt a strong religious calling while still a child. During his youth, he recorded some of his feelings in a diary. The following is an excerpt from that diary. Read the excerpt and then answer the questions that follow.

"REMEMBER TO READ OVER THESE RESOLUTIONS ONCE A WEEK"

- *Resolved, never to do, be, or suffer any thing in soul or body, less or more, but what tends to the glory of God.*
- *Resolved, to live with all my might, while I do live.*
- *Resolved, never to lose one moment of time; but improve it in the most profitable way I possibly can.*
- *Resolved, never to do any thing, which I should be afraid to do if it were the last hour of my life.*
- *Resolved, to be endeavoring to find out fit objects of charity.*
- *Resolved, to maintain the strictest temperance in eating and drinking.*
- *Resolved, never to speak any thing that is ridiculous, or matter of laughter, on the Lord's day.*

1. How do these resolutions reject the idea of predestination (the idea that one's life course is decided by God)?
2. According to Edwards, what is the key to learning these resolutions?
3. What does Edwards's last resolution reveal about his attitude toward worship?

■ COMPOSING AN ESSAY (20 points) Write a brief essay on one of the following subjects. Remember to use examples to support your answer.

1. Describe family life in New England.
2. Define the Iroquois League and explain why it became so powerful after the Tuscarora joined it in 1712.

Name _____ Class _____ Date _____

UNIT 1 Beginnings

UNIT TEST • FORM A

REVIEWING FACTS *(3 points each)* In the space provided, write the name of the person or the historical term that completes each sentence. Choose your answers from the list below. There are two extra names or terms on the list.

French and Indian War	Crusades	Ferdinand Magellan
feudalism	Renaissance	Christopher Columbus
Toltec	Toleration Act	Agricultural Revolution
New England Way	Northwest Passage	Protestant Reformation

_____ 1. the explosion of creativity and new ideas in Europe in the 1500s

_____ 2. break from the Catholic Church that was started by Martin Luther's theses

_____ 3. battles over the Holy Land between Christians and Muslims

_____ 4. man whose ship and crew were the first to circumnavigate the globe

_____ 5. conflict in North America won by Great Britain

_____ 6. the cooperation used by the church and state to run a colony

_____ 7. much sought-after route from the Atlantic Ocean to the Pacific Ocean

_____ 8. change that made it possible for fewer humans on the planet to function as hunter-gatherers

_____ 9. Middle Ages form of society in which serfs served on manors owned by wealthy nobles

_____ 10. said that the first people he encountered called themselves Tainos

UNDERSTANDING IDEAS *(3 points each)* For each of the following, place the letter of the *best* choice in the space provided.

_____ 1. The world's first-known printed book was
   a. The Bible.
   b. *The Diamond Sutra.*
   c. The Qur'an.
   d. *The Reconquista.*

_____ 2. Spanish settlements in the Americas used all of the following EXCEPT
   a. haciendas.
   b. missions.
   c. casas.
   d. viceroyalties.

Chapter and Unit Tests

Unit 1, Test Form A, Continued

_____ 3. Prince Henry of Portugal led the way in the improvement and development of
  a. sailing.
  b. colonization.
  c. the slave trade.
  d. printing.

_____ 4. The Great Awakening was
  a. a rebirth of creativity and art in Europe.
  b. the division in the Catholic Church led by Martin Luther.
  c. the movement of many religious Europeans to the New World.
  d. a series of religious revivals in the British colonies.

_____ 5. The Aztec were conquered by
  a. Cortés.
  b. Pizarro.
  c. Atahualpa.
  d. Columbus.

_____ 6. King James licensed the organization of settlements in Virginia when he issued the
  a. Mayflower Compact.
  b. Fundamental Orders of Virginia.
  c. Charter of 1606.
  d. Chesapeake Charter.

_____ 7. The African Diaspora was the
  a. colonization of Africa by Europeans.
  b. Portugese control of African trading kingdoms.
  c. displacement of Africans from their native lands.
  d. transfer of African gold to European traders.

_____ 8. The Mesoamerican culture that controlled the Andes mountains was the
  a. Aztec.
  b. Olmec.
  c. Inca.
  d. Anasazi.

_____ 9. Bacon's Rebellion took place because
  a. white settlers demanded more indentured servants from England.
  b. the Virginia legislature was considering allowing slavery in the colony.
  c. white farmers wanted more American Indian lands for farming.
  d. wealthy planters were angry about treaties made with neighboring Susquehannock Indians.

_____ 10. The European country that claimed much of North America but settled very little of it was
  a. France.
  b. Great Britain.
  c. Portugal.
  d. Spain.

Unit 1, Test Form A, Continued

■ TRUE/FALSE (2 points each) Read each of the following statements, and then decide whether it is true or false. If the answer is true, place a *T* in the space provided; if the answer is false, place an *F* in the space.

_____ 1. In the Great Migration, people fled England for religious and economic reasons.

_____ 2. The Paleo-Indians were the first Americans.

_____ 3. The Middle Passage refers to the route Columbus took to cross the Atlantic Ocean.

_____ 4. The Pilgrims were called Separatists because they had broken with the Anglican Church.

_____ 5. American Indians refused to participate in the fur trade.

■ PRACTICING SKILLS (5 points each) Study the map below and answer the questions that follow.

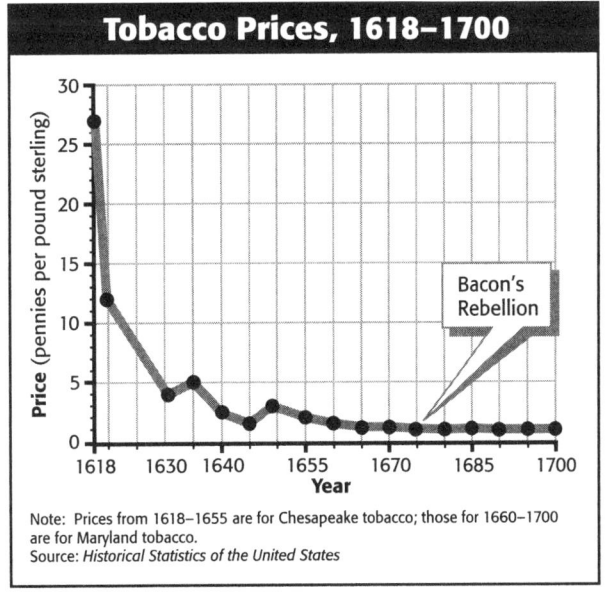

1. In what year were tobacco prices highest?
   _____

2. What was the price of tobacco in 1635?
   _____

■ COMPOSING AN ESSAY (20 points) Write a brief essay on *one* of the following subjects. Remember to use examples to support your answer.

1. Define the Agricultural Revolution, and explain the effect it had on Native Americans.

2. Define the Protestant Reformation, and explain how it affected colonization.

Name _____ Class _____ Date _____

UNIT 1

Beginnings

UNIT TEST • FORM B

SHORT ANSWER *(10 points each)* Provide brief answers to each of the following. Remember to use examples to support your answer.

1. How did the first people arrive in the Americas?
2. Why did so many explorers hope to find a Northwest Passage?
3. Why did the Great Awakening appeal to many people, particularly the poor and the enslaved?
4. What were the results of the French and Indian War?
5. Why was the defeat of the Spanish Armada historically significant?

PRIMARY SOURCE *(10 points each)* Olaudah Equiano described his Middle Passage ordeal in his autobiography, which was published in 1789. Read the statement, and then answer the questions that follow.

> There I received such a salutation in my nostrils as I had never experienced in my life: so that the loathsomeness [disgust] of the stench, and crying together, I became so sick and low that I was not able to eat, nor had I the least desire to taste any thing. I now wished for the last friend, death, to relieve me; but soon, to my grief, two of the white men offered me eatables; and, on my refusing to eat, one of them held me fast by the hands . . . and tied my feet, while the other flogged me severely.

1. According to Equiano, who was his "last friend"?
2. What happened to him when he refused to eat?

COMPOSING AN ESSAY *(30 points)* Write a brief essay on *one* of the following subjects. Remember to use examples to support your answer.

1. What was the *encomienda* system, and how did it affect the Spanish colonists and the American Indians?
2. Explain why some people chose to reject Puritan laws and ways and settle elsewhere.
3. Describe how the Renaissance changed Europe.
4. Describe how the European desire for furs and land affected American Indians.

Name _____ Class _____ Date _____

CHAPTER 4 Independence!

CHAPTER TEST • FORM A

REVIEWING FACTS *(3 points each)* For each of the following, place the letter of the *best* choice in the space provided.

_____ 1. Some of them held the belief that to resist the king was to rebel against God.
   a. Loyalists
   b. Patriots
   c. minutemen
   d. Hessians

_____ 2. In 1778 he led a group of 175 soldiers on a military expedition to secure the Illinois country.
   a. Nathaniel Greene
   b. Charles Cornwallis
   c. George Rogers Clark
   d. George Washington

_____ 3. He was known as the Delaware Prophet.
   a. Thayendanegea
   b. George Croghan
   c. Pontiac
   d. Neolin

_____ 4. His pamphlet *Common Sense* stirred up support for the Revolution.
   a. Thomas Paine
   b. Patrick Henry
   c. George Washington
   d. John Adams

_____ 5. Which battle is associated with Washington's crossing of the Delaware?
   a. Saratoga
   b. Yorktown
   c. Trenton
   d. Bunker Hill

_____ 6. This radical group protested British rule.
   a. Loyalists
   b. Olive Branchers
   c. Sons of Liberty
   d. The Opposition

_____ 7. The Second Continental Congress chose him to command the Continental Army.
   a. George Washington
   b. William Howe
   c. Nathanael Greene
   d. George Rogers Clark

_____ 8. Which battle effectively ended the war?
   a. Trenton
   b. Yorktown
   c. Saratoga
   d. Vincennes

_____ 9. This 33-year-old did most of the actual writing of the Declaration of Independence.
   a. Thomas Paine
   b. Thomas Jefferson
   c. Richard Henry Lee
   d. John Adams

_____ 10. This 19-year-old French nobleman became an important member of Washington's staff.
   a. Marquis de Lafayette
   b. Francis Marion
   c. John Burgoyne
   d. François de Grasse

Chapter and Unit Tests   Chapter 4 17

Chapter 4, Test Form A, Continued

■ UNDERSTANDING IDEAS *(3 points each)* In the space provided, write the name of the act, declaration, petition, proclamation, or treaty identified by each description. Choose your answers from the list below. There are two extra terms on the list.

Declaratory Act	Quartering Act	Stamp Act
Sugar Act	Proclamation of 1763	Townshend Acts
Tea Act	Intolerable Acts	Quebec Act
Olive Branch Petition	Declaration of Independence	Treaty of Paris

_____ 1. sent to George III to avoid a permanent break with Great Britain

_____ 2. required that colonies feed and shelter British soldiers

_____ 3. barred settlement west of the Appalachian Mountains

_____ 4. placed a tax on printed materials

_____ 5. main purpose was to win support for independence at home and abroad

_____ 6. placed import duties on common items such as tea

_____ 7. granted full religious freedom to French Roman Catholics

_____ 8. declared that Americans pay any debts owed to the British

_____ 9. passed to save the British East India Company from bankruptcy

_____ 10. closed the port of Boston and forbade town meetings

■ TRUE/FALSE *(2 points each)* Read each of the following statements, and then decide whether it is true or false. If the answer is true, place a *T* in the space provided; if the answer is false, place an *F* in the space.

_____ 1. The Battle of Trenton was a huge victory for the British.

_____ 2. The Battle of Saratoga was a turning point for Americans.

_____ 3. The First Continental Congress was a lawmaking body.

_____ 4. The Declaration of Independence inspired mixed reactions throughout the colonies.

_____ 5. The Tories were also known as the Patriots.

Chapter 4, Test Form A, Continued

■ PRACTICING SKILLS *(5 points each)* Study the map below and answer the questions that follow.

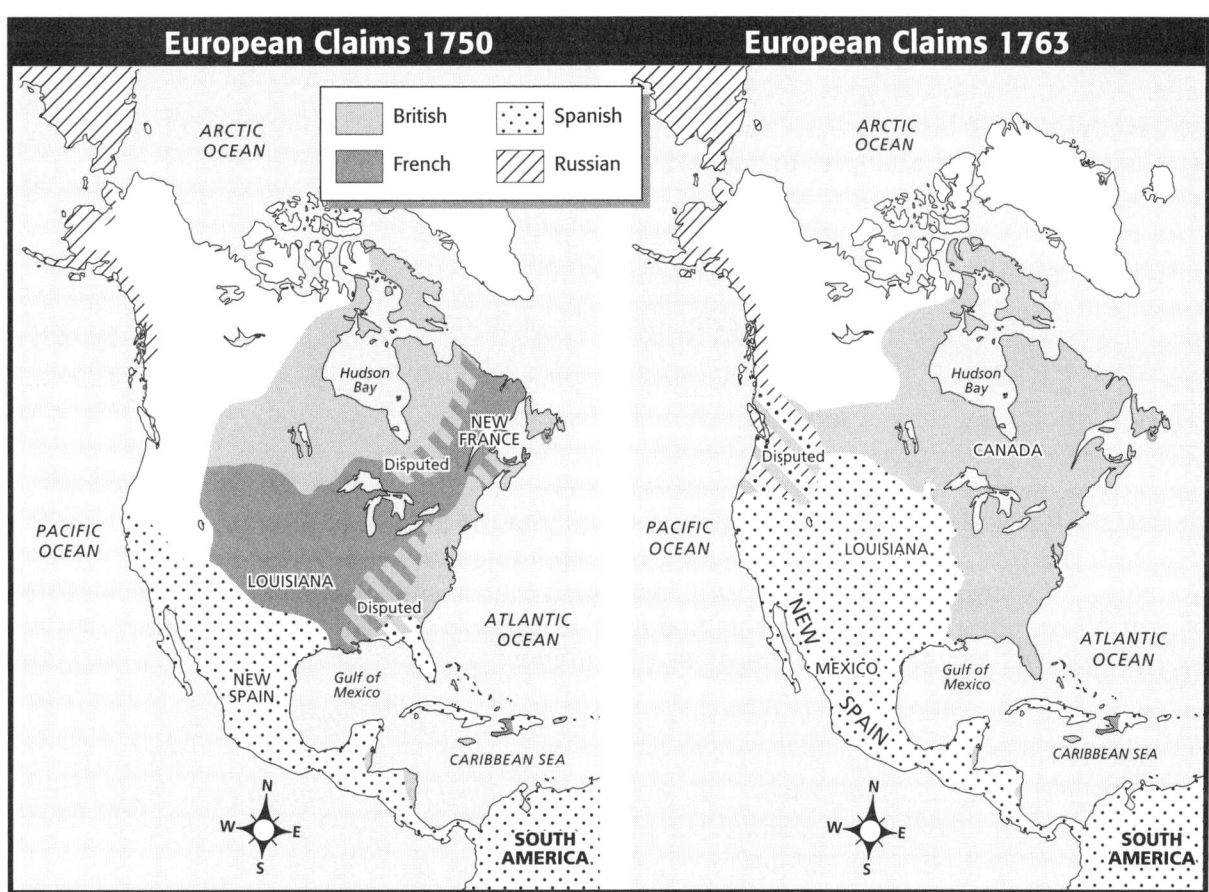

1. Which country claimed most of the land west of the Mississippi River in 1763?

   _____

2. Which country lost considerable land between 1750 and 1763? Which country gained the most land?

   _____

■ COMPOSING AN ESSAY *(20 points)* Write a brief essay on *one* of the following subjects. Remember to use examples to support your answer.

1. Describe the experiences of African Americans, American Indians, and women during the Revolutionary War.
2. Describe the importance of the roles played by Thomas Paine and Patrick Henry in gaining support for independence.

Name _____ Class _____ Date _____

CHAPTER 4: Independence!

CHAPTER TEST • FORM B

■ **SHORT ANSWER** *(10 points each)* Provide brief answers for each of the following. Remember to use examples to support your answer.

1. How did Great Britain respond to Pontiac's Rebellion?
2. Why did Britain pass the Sugar Act and the Stamp Act?
3. What events led to the battles at Lexington and Concord?
4. What were some of the purposes of the Declaration of Independence?
5. How did Patriot women serve the revolutionary cause?

■ **PRIMARY SOURCE** *(10 points each)* Several months before John Adams was to help draft the Declaration of Independence, his wife, Abigail Adams, wrote a letter to him with a few suggestions for the new Constitution that would later be written. An excerpt of this letter follows. Following that is John Adams's reply to his wife. Read the two excerpts and answer the questions that follow.

> *I long to hear that you have declared an independancy—and by the way in the new Code of Laws which I supposed it will be necessary for you to make I desire you would Remember the Ladies, and be more generous and favorable to them than your ancestors. Remember all Men would be tyrants if they could. If particular care and attention is not paid to the Ladies, we are determined to foment a Rebellion, and will not hold ourselves bound by any Laws in which we have not voice, or Representation.*

John Adams replied:

> *As to your extraordinary Code of Laws, I cannot but laugh. We have been told that our Struggle has loosened the bands of Government every where. That Children and Apprentices were disobedient—that schools and Colleges were grown turbulent—that Indians slighted their Guardians, and Negroes grew insolent to their Masters. But your Letter was the first Intimation that another Tribe more numerous and powerful than all the rest were grown discontented. —This is rather too coarse a Compliment but you are so saucy, I won't blot it out.*

1. What action did Abigail Adams want her husband to take?
2. What was John Adams's reaction to his wife's letter?
3. Which statement made by Abigail Adams unfairly labels men?

■ **COMPOSING AN ESSAY** *(20 points)* Write a brief essay on *one* of the following subjects. Remember to use examples to support your answer.

1. Describe how the participation of European powers affected the Revolutionary War.
2. Describe why it was advantageous for the United States not to include France and Spain in the negotiations that led to the Treaty of Paris.

Name _____ Class _____ Date _____

CHAPTER 5: From Confederation to Federal Union

CHAPTER TEST • FORM A

■ **REVIEWING FACTS** *(3 points each)* In the space provided, write the name of the person or the historical term identified by each description. Choose your answers from the list below. There are two extra names or terms on the list.

Benjamin Franklin	Judith Sargent Murray	John Locke
separation of powers	Federalists	elastic clause
James Madison	reserved powers	Daniel Shays
checks and balances	concurrent powers	supremacy clause

_____ 1. drafted the Virginia Plan

_____ 2. group that favored ratification of the Constitution

_____ 3. developed the theory of "natural rights"

_____ 4. gives each branch of government the means to restrain the powers of the other two

_____ 5. led farmers in a rebellion against the central government

_____ 6. prevents any one branch of the federal government from becoming too powerful

_____ 7. powers held jointly by the federal government and state governments

_____ 8. argued that men and women have equal intelligence

_____ 9. published the *Pennsylvania Gazette* and *Poor Richard's Almanack*

_____ 10. powers that are guaranteed by the Tenth Amendment

■ **UNDERSTANDING IDEAS** *(3 points each)* For each of the following, place the letter of the *best* choice in the space provided.

_____ 1. Which of the following was NOT a weakness of the Articles of Confederation?
  a. states had too little power
  b. no provisions for regulating international trade
  c. changes to articles required consent of all 13 states
  d. no provisions for taxing people directly

_____ 2. The depression that started in 1784 was caused in part by
  a. the extension of credit to too many farmers.
  b. the loss of British markets.
  c. a drought that destroyed cash crops.
  d. a flood of expensive British goods that hit American markets.

Chapter and Unit Tests

Chapter 5, Test Form A, Continued

_____ 3. Which of the following statements about women in the late 1700s is NOT true?
   a. The number of women attending private high schools declined.
   b. Many women opposed women's participation in politics.
   c. State constitutions denied women the right to vote.
   d. Some people believed women had an essential part to play in the creation of the new nation.

_____ 4. The Virginia Plan
   a. shifted power from the states toward the central government.
   b. rejected the idea of federalism.
   c. prohibited the Congress from overturning state laws.
   d. called for the federal government to be made up of two branches.

_____ 5. The Great Compromise
   a. was proposed by William Paterson of New Jersey.
   b. granted each state an equal voice in the upper house and representation in the lower house according to population.
   c. provided for a strong unicameral legislature.
   d. was rejected by a majority of delegates.

_____ 6. All of the following people were Federalists EXCEPT
   a. James Madison.
   b. Patrick Henry.
   c. Alexander Hamilton.
   d. John Jay.

_____ 7. Between 1776 and 1780 all but two states ratified new constitutions. Which of the following statements best describes them?
   a. Most rejected the ideas of John Locke.
   b. Most gave their governors extensive powers.
   c. Most increased the influence of the church on government.
   d. Most restricted the powers of their governors.

_____ 8. The Constitution gives all of the following powers to the national government EXCEPT the power to
   a. declare war.
   b. coin money.
   c. conduct elections.
   d. set standard weights and measures.

_____ 9. The Constitution gives all of the following powers to the states EXCEPT the power to
   a. create marriage laws.
   b. provide for public safety.
   c. establish foreign policy.
   d. establish and maintain schools.

_____ 10. An example of a concurrent power delegated by the Constitution is the right to
   a. establish courts.
   b. create marriage laws.
   c. admit states.
   d. establish post offices.

Chapter 5, Test Form A, Continued

TRUE/FALSE *(2 points each)* Read each of the following statements, and then decide whether it is true or false. If the answer is true, place a *T* in the space provided; if the answer is false, place an *F* in the space.

_____ 1. Abigail Adams agreed with her husband's viewpoints regarding women's rights.

_____ 2. The Northwest Ordinance banned slavery in the Northwest Territory.

_____ 3. Low unemployment usually accompanies a depression.

_____ 4. Continentals were backed by gold and silver.

_____ 5. Republican Motherhood fought for full citizenship for women.

PRACTICING SKILLS *(5 points each)* Study the chart below and answer the questions that follow.

1. Five states ratified the Constitution during which two-month period?

   _____

   _____

2. Which state was probably the most unsure about ratifying?

   _____

Ratification of the U.S. Constitution

Year	Month–Day	State
1787	12–7	Delaware
	12–12	Pennsylvania
	12–18	New Jersey
1788	1–2	Georgia
	1–9	Connecticut
	2–6	Massachusetts
	4–28	Maryland
	5–23	South Carolina
	6–21	New Hampshire
	6-25	Virginia
	7–26	New York
1789	11–21	North Carolina
1790	5–29	Rhode Island

COMPOSING AN ESSAY *(20 points)* Write a brief essay on *one* of the following subjects. Remember to use examples to support your answer.

1. Define Republican Motherhood, and then describe the opportunities as well as the limitations it placed on women of the late 1700s.
2. Define checks and balances, and then describe how this system can produce both positive and negative results.

Name _____ Class _____ Date _____

CHAPTER 5: From Confederation to Federal Union

CHAPTER TEST • FORM B

■ SHORT ANSWER *(10 points each)* Provide brief answers for each of the following. Remember to use examples to support your answer.

1. What political ideas were reflected in the new state constitutions that were ratified between 1776 and 1780?
2. What were some of the weaknesses of the Articles of Confederation?
3. How did the Virginia Plan allow for a stronger central government?
4. How did the Great Compromise balance the interests of large and small states?
5. What major objections did the Antifederalists have to the Constitution as written by the delegates of the Constitutional Convention?

■ PRIMARY SOURCE *(10 points each)* In 1732 Benjamin Franklin began publishing his witty and widely read *Poor Richard's Almanack,* in which he coined numerous clever proverbs. Some of these sayings appear below. Read the proverbs and then answer the questions that follow.

- *He that riseth late must trot all day, and shall scarce overtake his business at night; while Laziness travels so slowly, that Poverty soon overtakes him.*
- *The Sleeping Fox catches no poultry, and there will be sleeping enough in the grave.*
- *At the workingman's house hunger looks in, but dares not enter.*
- *It is true there is much to be done, and perhaps you are weak-handed; but stick to it steadily, and you will see great effects; for constant dropping wears away stones.*
- *Early to bed, and early to rise, makes a man healthy, wealthy, and wise.*

1. Which of the sayings suggests that people who work hard never have to worry about going hungry?
2. What do these proverbs tell you about Franklin's work ethic?
3. Which saying encourages people to be persistent?

■ COMPOSING AN ESSAY *(20 points)* Write a brief essay on one of the following subjects. Remember to use examples to support your answer.

1. Who is John Locke? How did his ideas influence American republicanism?
2. Describe how the separation of powers prevents each branch of government from becoming too strong.

Name _____ Class _____ Date _____

CHAPTER 6: A Strong Start for the Nation

CHAPTER TEST • FORM A

REVIEWING FACTS *(3 points each)* In the space provided, write the name of the person or the historical term identified by each description. Choose your answers from the list below. There are two extra names or terms on the list.

Anthony Wayne	Non-Intercourse Act	Aaron Burr
John Marshall	Alexander Hamilton	Thomas Pinkney
Zebulon Pike	Embargo Act	Treaty of Greenville
Treaty of Ghent	William Clark	John Jay

_____ 1. chief justice burned in effigy after negotiating a treaty with Britain

_____ 2. Revolutionary war hero known for his daring feats

_____ 3. President Washington's most trusted adviser

_____ 4. gave the United States much of present-day Ohio and part of Indiana

_____ 5. Republican who almost became president in 1800

_____ 6. his discoveries helped spur expansion into Texas and the Southwest

_____ 7. explored the Snake and Columbia rivers

_____ 8. officially ended the War of 1812

_____ 9. passed in response to the *Chesapeake* incident

_____ 10. prohibited trade with Britain and France

UNDERSTANDING IDEAS *(3 points each)* For each of the following, place the letter of the *best* choice in the space provided.

_____ 1. Which amendment guarantees a jury trial in most civil cases?
   a. Second
   b. Fourth
   c. Seventh
   d. Eighth

_____ 2. The Reign of Terror was conducted by revolutionaries from
   a. Italy.
   b. France.
   c. Spain.
   d. Portugal.

Chapter and Unit Tests

Chapter 6, Test Form A, Continued

_____ 3. Which amendment prohibits searches and seizures without a warrant?
   a. First
   b. Tenth
   c. Fifth
   d. Fourth

_____ 4. Most people blamed the Indian uprisings of the early 1800s on
   a. the French.
   b. the British.
   c. General William Henry Harrison.
   d. President Madison.

_____ 5. Which of the following terms or phrases is *NOT* associated with Alexander Hamilton's beliefs?
   a. federalism
   b. capitalism
   c. weak federal government
   d. loose construction

_____ 6. Which of the following did *NOT* play a role in causing the War of 1812?
   a. party politics
   b. desire for land
   c. economic concerns
   d. French economic policies

_____ 7. The Republicans believed in all of the following *EXCEPT*
   a. states' rights.
   b. French goals.
   c. individual liberties.
   d. strong national government.

_____ 8. Why was the United States ill-prepared for war in 1812?
   a. low morale
   b. poorly trained sailors and officers
   c. poorly equipped army
   d. indecisive Congress

_____ 9. Napoleon Bonaparte sold Louisiana because he
   a. did not have a base in the West Indies.
   b. was dying.
   c. had a strong friendship with President Jefferson.
   d. wanted to get even with the British.

_____ 10. Which amendment guarantees the right to a speedy trial?
   a. Sixth
   b. Tenth
   c. First
   d. Fourth

■ **TRUE/FALSE** *(2 points each)* Read each of the following statements, and then decide whether it is true or false. If the answer is true, place a *T* in the space provided; if the answer is false, place an *F* in the space.

_____ 1. Thomas Jefferson believed that the government could do only what the Constitution specifically allows.

_____ 2. George Washington could have run for a third term as president.

_____ 3. Sectionalism contributed to the emergence of two political parties.

_____ 4. The Alien and Sedition Acts received widespread support.

_____ 5. The purchase of Louisiana by the United States was good for France as well as the United States.

Chapter 6, Test Form A, Continued

■ PRACTICING SKILLS *(5 points each)* Study the graphs below and answer the questions that follow.

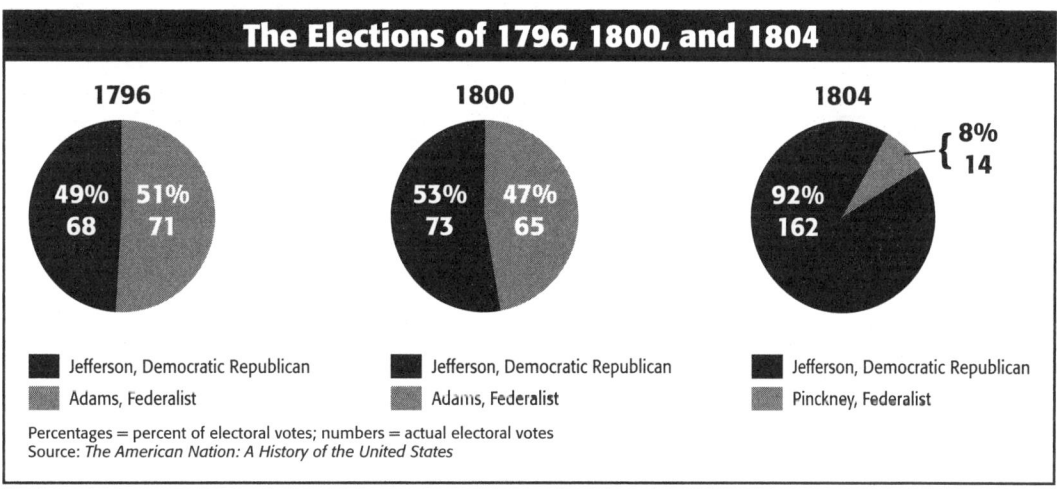

1. Which elections were captured by Jefferson?

   _____

2. Which political party slipped in popularity between 1796 and 1804?

   _____

■ COMPOSING AN ESSAY *(20 points)* Write a brief essay on *one* of the following subjects. Remember to use examples to support your answer.

1. Describe the importance of the Louisiana Purchase to the United States.
2. How did the War of 1812 affect the United States and Great Britain?

Name _____ Class _____ Date _____

A Strong Start for the Nation

CHAPTER TEST • FORM B

■ **SHORT ANSWER** *(10 points each)* Provide brief answers for each of the following. Remember to use examples to support your answer.

1. What key actions did the first Congress make?
2. How did Americans respond to the French Revolution?
3. How did the Federalists' and Republicans' main goals differ?
4. Why did Congress feel compelled to propose the Twelfth Amendment?
5. Why did Napoleon decide to sell Louisiana to the United States?

■ **PRIMARY SOURCE** *(10 points each)* During his more than 30 years as Chief Justice of the United States, John Marshall established many basic principles of United States constitutional law. In the excerpt below, from an opinion written in 1821, Marshall reflects on the role of the federal government. Read the excerpt and then answer the questions that follow.

America has chosen to be, in many respects, and to many purposes, a nation; and for all these purposes her government is complete; to all of these objects it is competent. The people have declared that in the exercise of all the powers for these objects it is supreme. It can, then, in effecting these objects, legitimately control all individuals or governments within the American territory. The constitution and laws of a State, so far as they are repugnant [incompatible] to the Constitution and laws of the United States, are absolutely void. These States are constituent parts of the United States. They are members of one great empire—for some purposes sovereign, for some purposes subordinate.

1. Do you think Marshall was a Federalist or a Republican?
2. According to Marshall, when are a state's laws not binding?
3. From which source does the federal government get its power?

■ **COMPOSING AN ESSAY** *(20 points)* Write a brief essay on *one* of the following subjects. Remember to use examples to support your answer.

1. Who was Alexander Hamilton? How did his strong belief in federalism shape his economic policy?
2. Define the Bill of Rights and describe some of its major rules and guarantees.

Name _____ Class _____ Date _____

UNIT 2: Creating a Nation

UNIT TEST • FORM A

■ **REVIEWING FACTS** *(3 points each)* In the space provided, write the name of the person or the historical term that completes each sentence. Choose your answers from the list below. There are two extra names or terms on the list.

Bill of Rights	veto	French Revolution
concurrent powers	Loyalists	Great Compromise
ratification	Olive Branch Petition	Sons of Liberty
Louisiana Purchase	Republican Motherhood	Three–Fifths Compromise

_____ 1. radical group opposed to British control of the colonies

_____ 2. allowed equal representation as well as representation based on population

_____ 3. vow of loyalty rejected by George III

_____ 4. influenced by the American Revolution; event that included beheadings of high officials

_____ 5. adoption of the Constitution by all 13 states

_____ 6. this greatly expanded the size of the United States

_____ 7. idea stating that women could best influence politics and society through their work in the home

_____ 8. powers held by both the states and the federal government

_____ 9. allows a president to override an act of Congress

_____ 10. the first 10 amendments to the Constitution

■ **UNDERSTANDING IDEAS** *(3 points each)* For each of the following, place the letter of the *best* choice in the space provided.

_____ 1. Thomas Paine's *Common Sense* stated that
  a. the colonists should remain loyal to Great Britain.
  b. war with Britain was wrong.
  c. fighting for independence from Britain was the right thing to do.
  d. it was logical for the colonies to seek help from France.

_____ 2. Delegated powers are powers
  a. granted to the states.
  b. granted to the federal government.
  c. shared by both the state and the federal government.
  d. that cannot be turned over to Congress.

Chapter and Unit Tests Unit 2 29

Unit 2, Test Form A, Continued

_____ 3. The president was able to imprison or expel all foreigners who were considered dangerous after passage of the
   a. Alien and Sedition Acts.
   b. Intolerable Acts.
   c. Non-Intercourse Act.
   d. Patriot Act.

_____ 4. The colonies were organized into a loose federation of states with the passage of the
   a. Constitution.
   b. Virginia Plan.
   c. Articles of Confederation.
   d. *Federalist Papers.*

_____ 5. The Three-Fifths Compromise allowed slave states to
   a. count all their slaves as part of their population.
   b. count two fifths of their slaves as part of their population.
   c. count three fifths of their slaves as part of their population.
   d. double their representatives in Congress.

_____ 6. All of the following laws passed by Britain angered the colonists EXCEPT
   a. the Stamp Act.
   b. the nonimportation agreements.
   c. the Sugar Act.
   d. the Declaratory Act.

_____ 7. George III ordered a British attack on the colonies after the
   a. First Continental Congress.
   b. Second Continental Congress.
   c. Boston Tea Party.
   d. repeal of the Stamp Act.

_____ 8. The Revolutionary War officially ended with the signing of the
   a. Treaty of Ghent.
   b. Treaty of Yorktown.
   c. Treaty of Paris.
   d. Treaty of Camden.

_____ 9. Most of the Declaration of Independence was written by
   a. George Washington.
   b. Samuel Adams.
   c. Alexander Hamilton.
   d. Thomas Jefferson.

_____ 10. Judicial review is the principle that states that
   a. the executive branch has supreme power over Congress.
   b. courts have the power to declare an act of Congress unconstitutional.
   c. power between the judicial and legislative branches must be separated.
   d. the Constitution can change over time.

TRUE/FALSE *(2 points each)* **Read each of the following statements, and then decide whether it is true or false. If the answer is true, place a *T* in the space provided; if the answer is false, place an *F* in the space.**

_____ 1. The XYZ affair made many Americans angry with Great Britain.

_____ 2. The Treaty of Ghent ended the War of 1812.

Unit 2, Test Form A, Continued

_____ 3. The philosophy of federalism stated that the central government must have absolute power.

_____ 4. The Constitutional Convention was called to fix problems in the Articles of Confederation.

_____ 5. The British army used guerrilla warfare in its fight against the Continental Army.

■ **PRACTICING SKILLS** *(5 points each)* **Study the map below and answer the questions that follow.**

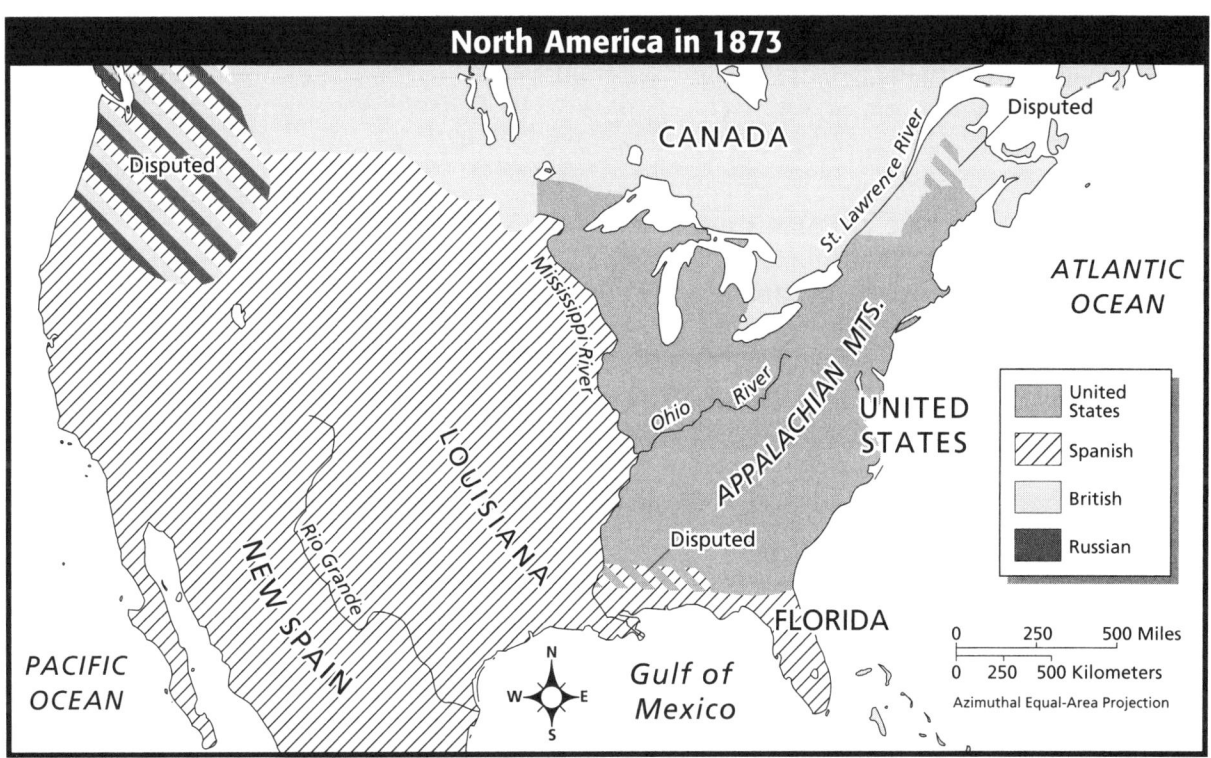

1. Which nation owned most of the land west of the Mississippi River?

   _____

2. Which nation controlled the land through which the Ohio River flows?

   _____

■ **COMPOSING AN ESSAY** *(20 points)* **Write a brief essay on *one* of the following.**

1. How did women, African Americans, and American Indians participate in the Revolutionary War?
2. Explain the system of checks and balances, and describe how it can produce both positive and negative results.

Name _____ Class _____ Date _____

UNIT 2: Creating a Nation

UNIT TEST • FORM B

■ **SHORT ANSWER** *(10 points each)* Provide brief answers to each of the following. Remember to use examples to support your answer.

1. What made Napoleon decide to sell Louisiana to the United States?
2. What important actions did the first Congress take?
3. What was Britain's response to Pontiac's Rebellion?
4. In what ways were the Articles of Confederation weak?
5. What did the Great Compromise accomplish?

■ **PRIMARY SOURCE** *(10 points each)* Thomas Paine's *Common Sense* was an influential document at the time when the colonies were considering rebelling against Britain. Read the passage below and answer the following questions.

> *Let a crown be placed theron, by which the world may know that, so far as we approve of monarchy, that in America the law is king. . . . But lest any ill use should afterward arise, let the crown at the conclusion of the ceremony be demolished and scattered among the people, whose right it is. . . . A government of our own is our natural right; and when a man seriously reflects on the precariousness of human affairs, he will become convinced that it is infinitely wiser and safer to form a Constitution of our own in a cool, deliberate manner while we have it in our power than to trust such an interesting event to time and chance.*

1. According to Paine, what reigns supreme in America?
2. What does Paine advocate in *Common Sense*?

■ **COMPOSING AN ESSAY** *(30 points)* Write a brief essay on *one* of the following subjects. Remember to use examples to support your answer.

1. What was Republican Motherhood, and how did it offer both opportunities and limitations for women of the 1700s?
2. How were the United States and Britain affected by the War of 1812?
3. Why was the Louisiana Purchase important to the United States?
4. Define checks and balances, and then describe how this system can produce both positive and negative results.

Name _____ Class _____ Date _____

Nationalism and Economic Growth

CHAPTER TEST • FORM A

■ **REVIEWING FACTS** *(3 points each)* In the space provided, write the name of the person or historical term that completes each sentence. Choose your answers from the list below. There are two extra names or terms on the list.

James Monroe	Simón Bolívar	Adams-Onís Treaty
Rush-Bagot Agreement	Henry Clay	Samuel Slater
Missouri Compromise	Andrew Jackson	Martin Van Buren
John C. Calhoun	Robert Fulton	Eli Whitney

1. Kentuckian _____, the architect of the Missouri Compromise, is considered by many historians to be one of the most important politicians of the 1800s.

2. The *Clermont*, which was designed by _____, was the first steamboat capable of carrying heavy loads upstream.

3. Under the _____, one slave state and one free state were created.

4. _____ received most of the popular votes in the election of 1824 but failed to capture the presidency.

5. In the _____, Great Britain and the United States pledged to limit the number of armed ships in the Great Lakes region.

6. _____ developed a British-style spinning mill that was a great financial success.

7. _____ wrote an essay expressing a viewpoint that became known as the doctrine of nullification.

8. Thomas Jefferson remarked that _____ was "a man whose soul might be turned wrong side outward, without discovering a blemish to the world."

9. _____ earned the nickname "the Liberator."

10. _____ used interchangeable parts in the manufacture of firearms.

■ **UNDERSTANDING IDEAS** *(3 points each)* For each of the following, place the letter of the *best* choice in the space provided.

_____ 1. The collapse of the Federalist Party coincided with a period of
   a. political harmony.
   b. economic turmoil.
   c. neutrality.
   d. political corruption.

_____ 2. The War of 1812 convinced many older Republicans to support
   a. states' rights.
   b. sectionalism.
   c. a stronger federal government.
   d. the doctrine of nullification.

Chapter and Unit Tests Chapter 7 33

Chapter 7, Test Form A, Continued

_____ 3. The Adams-Onís Treaty
   a. officially ended the Seminole War.
   b. gave the United States East Florida.
   c. gave Spain back the captured forts Andrew Jackson had seized in East Florida.
   d. put a limit on the number of British and U.S. warships in the Great Lakes.

_____ 4. Through the Monroe Doctrine, the United States declared its intention to
   a. defend the freedoms of other nations.
   b. expand its territory.
   c. make alliances with European nations.
   d. remain a neutral power.

_____ 5. Which of the following events was NOT caused by the decreased control of banks by the federal government in 1837?
   a. tight credit
   b. land speculation
   c. inflation
   d. a full-scale depression

TRUE/FALSE *(2 points each)* Read each of the following statements, and then decide whether it is true or false. If the answer is true, place a *T* in the space provided; if the answer is false, place an *F* in the space.

_____ 1. Simón Bolívar helped win independence for Venezuela in 1821.

_____ 2. Henry Clay created the economic plan called the American System.

_____ 3. "Clinton's big ditch" referred to the Panama Canal.

_____ 4. The Industrial Revolution began in the United States in the mid-1700s.

_____ 5. The Panic of 1819 weakened the Era of Good Feelings.

_____ 6. Andrew Jackson was nicknamed "Old Hickory" because his desk in the oval office was made from hickory wood.

_____ 7. The Cherokee wrote a constitution modeled after that of the United States.

_____ 8. The Second Seminole War was short-lived.

_____ 9. The United States gained much territory as a result of the War of 1812.

_____ 10. By the 1820s, many government officials wanted to move all American Indians to lands beyond U.S. borders.

Chapter 7, Test Form A, Continued

PRACTICING SKILLS *(5 points each)* Study the map below and answer the questions that follow.

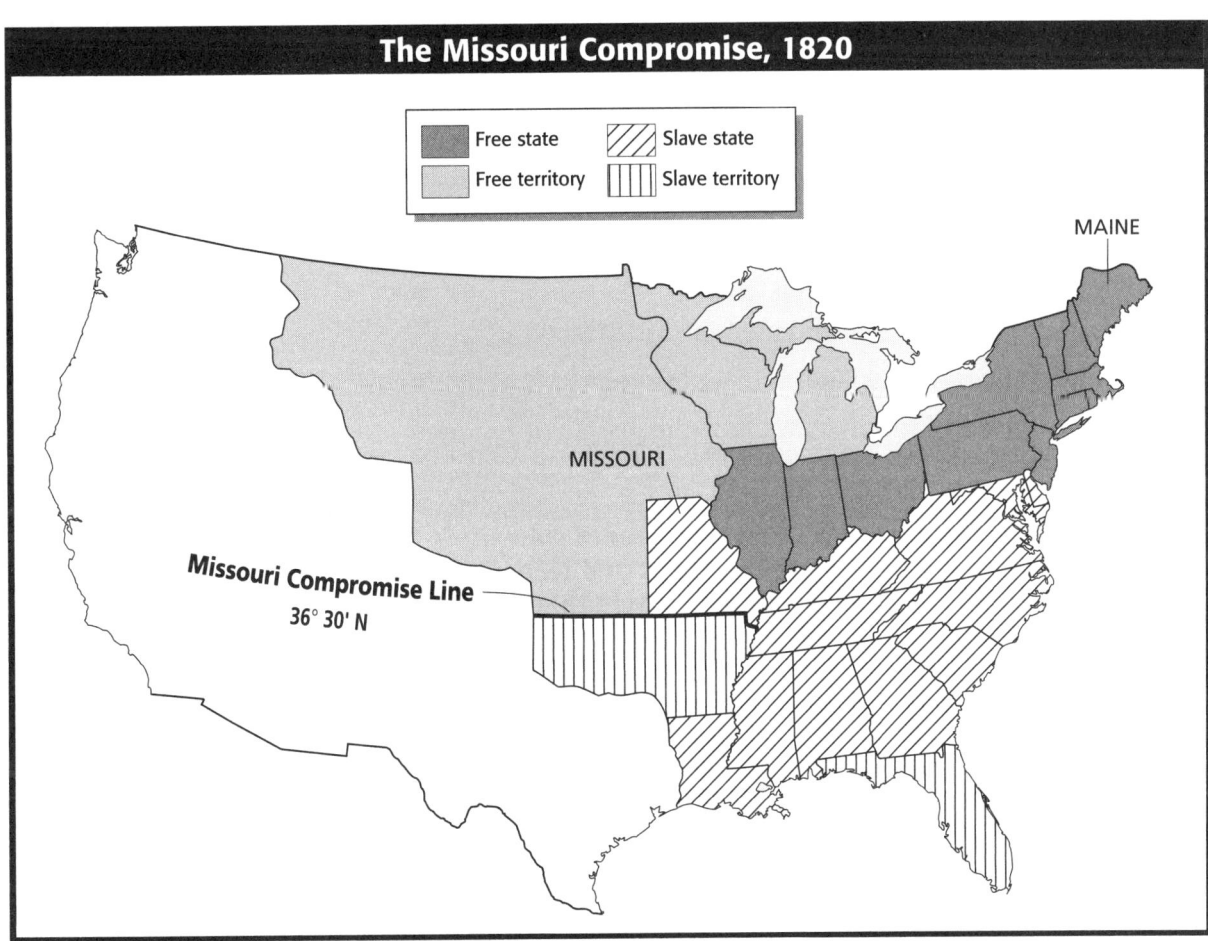

1. How many slave states were there after the Missouri Compromise?
_____

2. How many free states were there after the Missouri Compromise?
_____

3. How many slave states were north of the Missouri Compromise line?
_____

COMPOSING AN ESSAY *(20 points)* Write a brief essay on *one* of the following subjects. Remember to use examples to support your answer.

1. Describe how the Transportation Revolution affected the United States.
2. Explain why "Era of Good Feelings" was either an appropriate or inappropriate description of the period that followed the War of 1812.

Chapter and Unit Tests Chapter 7 35

Name _____ Class _____ Date _____

CHAPTER 7: Nationalism and Economic Growth

CHAPTER TEST • FORM B

SHORT ANSWER *(10 points each)* Provide brief answers for each of the following. Remember to use examples to support your answer.

1. Why did the Federalist Party lose power after the War of 1812?
2. What was the Monroe Doctrine?
3. What national weaknesses did the War of 1812 reveal?
4. What were some of the major accomplishments of the Transportation Revolution?
5. Why was Andrew Jackson considered the people's president?

PRIMARY SOURCE *(10 points each)* France's Alexis de Tocqueville observed the United States and its culture in the 1830s and recorded his findings in his book *Democracy in America*. Below is an excerpt from that book. Read the excerpt and then answer the questions that follow.

> *All free nations are vainglorious, but national pride is not displayed by all in the same manner. The Americans appear impatient of the smallest criticism, and insatiable of praise. . . . They increasingly harass you to praise them, and if you refuse, they praise themselves. . . . Their vanity is not only greedy, but restless and jealous; it will grant nothing, whilst it demands everything. . . .*
>
> *If I say to an American that the country he lives in is a fine one, "Ay," he replies, "there is not its equal in the world." If I applaud the freedom which its inhabitants enjoy, he answers, "Freedom is a fine thing, but few nations are worthy to enjoy it."*

1. What do you think the author meant with the statement "All nations are vainglorious"?
2. Do you think the author had a respect for Americans or a disdain?
3. Could the excerpt above be used to describe some Americans today? Why?

COMPOSING AN ESSAY *(20 points)* Write a brief essay on *one* of the following subjects. Remember to use examples to support your answer.

1. Define the Industrial Revolution. How did it change the United States?
2. What was the most significant effect of the War of 1812 on the United States?

Name _____ Class _____ Date _____

CHAPTER 8

Regional Societies

CHAPTER TEST • FORM A

REVIEWING FACTS *(3 points each)* In the space provided, write the name of the person or the historical term identified by each description. Choose your answers from the list below. There are two extra names or terms on the list.

Cyrus McCormick	Francis Cabot Lowell	Sarah G. Bagley
nativism	antebellum	yeoman farmers
Know-Nothings	spirituals	Nat Turner
William Ellison	Harriet Tubman	Denmark Vesey

_____ 1. designed and constructed a power loom to produce cotton textiles

_____ 2. favored native-born Americans over foreign-born Americans

_____ 3. nickname for the American Party

_____ 4. pre-Civil War

_____ 5. made up the majority of southern white society

_____ 6. textile mill worker who urged co-workers to form a union

_____ 7. led a violent slave uprising in Southampton County, Virginia

_____ 8. most famous conductor on the Underground Railroad

_____ 9. developed a mechanical reaper

_____ 10. free African American carpenter who planned a massive slave uprising in the Charleston area

UNDERSTANDING IDEAS *(3 points each)* For each of the following, place the letter of the *best* choice in the space provided.

_____ 1. In northern society, what new social class developed in the early 1800s?
  a. upper
  b. middle
  c. lower
  d. poor

_____ 2. In 1832, about what percentage of New England factory workers were children?
  a. 10
  b. 20
  c. 30
  d. 40

Chapter and Unit Tests

Chapter 8, Test Form A, Continued

_____ 3. Most Irish immigrants in the mid-1800s settled
   a. on farms.
   b. in city slums.
   c. on ranches.
   d. in small villages.

_____ 4. Most of the German immigrants in the mid-1800s came to the United States for
   a. political reasons.
   b. economic opportunity.
   c. religious reasons.
   d. adventure.

_____ 5. The Market Revolution
   a. increased the cost of manufactured products.
   b. decreased the cost of manufactured products.
   c. led to an increase in subsistence farmers.
   d. closed the gap between rich and poor.

_____ 6. Which of the following was NOT true about the southern economy?
   a. There was a strong reliance on agricultural products.
   b. There was a great demand for manufactured goods.
   c. Planters discouraged manufacturing.
   d. Factory workers were in short supply.

_____ 7. Central to the slaves' religion was their belief
   a. that they were God's chosen people.
   b. in more than one God.
   c. in reincarnation.
   d. that they would one day reach the "promised land" in Egypt.

_____ 8. Most of the German immigrants were
   a. Roman Catholic.
   b. Jewish.
   c. atheists.
   d. Protestant.

_____ 9. Southern farmers first began growing cotton in
   a. the late 1700s.
   b. the mid-1800s.
   c. the early 1800s.
   d. the late 1600s.

_____ 10. Before the Civil War, about what percent of southern whites owned slaves?
   a. 90
   b. 50
   c. 25
   d. 10

■ **TRUE/FALSE** *(2 points each)* Read each of the following statements, and then decide whether it is true or false. If the answer is true, place a *T* in the space provided; if the answer is false, place an *F* in the space.

_____ 1. Most southern slaveholders held more than 20 slaves.

_____ 2. Most white southerners lived on corn and pork.

_____ 3. Industrialization occurred at a faster pace in the South than the North.

_____ 4. Runaway slaves had a good chance of gaining their freedom.

_____ 5. Most enslaved African Americans lived and worked on plantations and farms.

Chapter 8, Test Form A, Continued

■ PRACTICING SKILLS *(5 points each)* Study the graph below and answer the questions that follow.

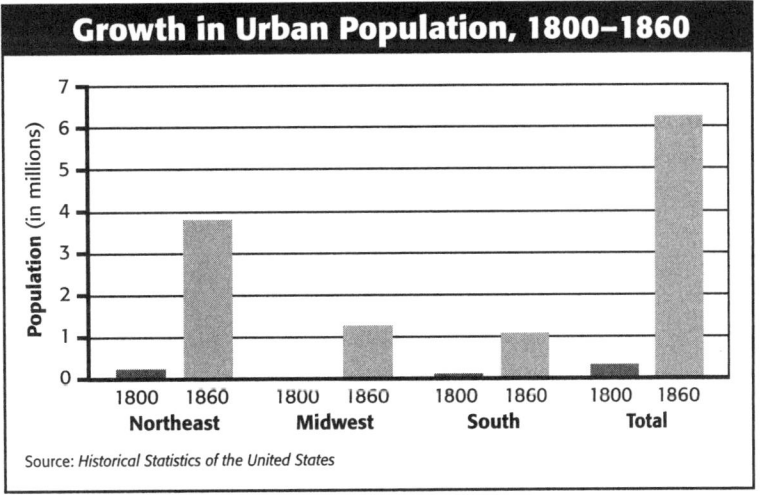

1. What were the approximate urban populations of the nation in 1800 and 1860?

   _____

2. Which region had virtually no cities in 1800?

   _____

■ COMPOSING AN ESSAY *(20 points)* Write a brief essay on *one* of the following subjects. Remember to use examples to support your answer.

1. Describe how life in the United States differed for Irish and German immigrants. Also explain how their lives were similar.
2. What were some of the factors that enabled the South to emerge as the Cotton Kingdom?

Name _____ Class _____ Date _____

CHAPTER 8: Regional Societies

CHAPTER TEST • FORM B

■ **SHORT ANSWER** *(10 points each)* Provide brief answers for each of the following. Remember to use examples to support your answer.

1. What were the roles of men and women in the new middle class?
2. How did the Irish and German immigrants differ?
3. What was life like for the typical planter in the antebellum South?
4. How did many white southerners justify slavery?
5. How did many slaves preserve and pass on their culture?

■ **PRIMARY SOURCE** *(10 points each)* The most tempting form of resistance to slavery was to run away. Chances of success were slim, and punishment, if caught, could be brutal. In the excerpt below, Henry Brown recalls how he made his daring escape to freedom in Philadelphia. Read the excerpt and then answer the questions that follow.

> *I went to the depot, and there noticed the size of the largest boxes . . . . I then repaired to a carpenter, and induced him to make me a box of such a description as I wished, informing him of the use I intended to make of it. He assured me I could not live in it, but as it was dear liberty I was in pursuit of, I thought it best to make the trial. . . .*
>
> *I took with me a bladder filled with water to bathe my neck with, in case of too great heat; and with no access to the fresh air, excepting three small . . . holes, I started on my perilous cruise. I was first carried to the express office, the box being placed on its end, so that I started with my head downwards, although the box was directed, "this side up with care." From the express office, I was carried to the depot, and from thence tumbled roughly into the baggage car. . . . But after a while the cars stopped, and I was put aboard a steamboat, and placed on my head. . . . I began to feel of my eyes and head, and found to my dismay, that my eyes were almost swollen out of their sockets . . . I made no noise however, determining to obtain "victory or death," but endured the terrible pain.*

1. What was Brown's destination?
2. What two precautions taken by Brown probably saved his life?
3. Which words and actions showed that Brown would rather lose his life rather than continue being a slave?

■ **COMPOSING AN ESSAY** *(20 points)* Write a brief essay on *one* of the following subjects. Remember to use examples to support your answer.

1. How did Eli Whitney's cotton gin affect the economy of the South?
2. How did the Market Revolution affect farming in the Midwest?

Name _____ Class _____ Date _____

Working for Reform

CHAPTER TEST • FORM A

■ **REVIEWING FACTS** *(3 points each)* In the space provided, write the name of the person or the historical term that completes each sentence. Choose your answers from the list below. There are two extra names or terms on the list.

Shakers	Mormons	Unitarians
Walt Whitman	Brigham Young	Dorothea Dix
Catharine Beecher	Frederick Douglass	Theodore Weld
Horace Mann	William Lloyd Garrison	Elijah Lovejoy

1. A New England journalist, _____, launched the newspaper *Liberator* in 1831.

2. The _____ are also known as members of the Church of Jesus Christ of Latter-Day Saints.

3. _____ was one of the most influential romantic writers.

4. The _____ rejected Puritan beliefs such as predestination.

5. Reformer _____ was one of the most famous members of her socially active family.

6. _____ championed the plight of the mentally ill.

7. _____ developed a model for free public elementary education.

8. A fugitive slave from Maryland, _____, published the anti-slavery newspaper the *North Star*.

9. Abolitionist editor _____ was murdered while trying to stop a mob from destroying his printing presses.

10. The leader of the American _____ claimed to be the messiah who would found a society free of sin.

■ **UNDERSTANDING IDEAS** *(3 points each)* For each of the following, place the letter of the *best* choice in the space provided.

_____ 1. All of the following are associated with the Mormons EXCEPT
   a. plural marriage.
   b. Mother Ann Lee.
   c. Brigham Young.
   d. golden plates.

_____ 2. The Second Great Awakening dealt with a renewed interest in
   a. impressionistic art.
   b. political activism.
   c. religion.
   d. territorial expansion.

Chapter and Unit Tests   Chapter 9   41

Chapter 9, Test Form A, Continued

_____ 3. Which of these schools was the first to admit both men and women?
  a. Harvard
  b. Troy Female Seminary
  c. Oberlin College
  d. Princeton

_____ 4. Increased support for abolition in the mid-1800s was driven by all of these factors EXCEPT
  a. religious principles.
  b. principles in the Declaration of Independence.
  c. political activism.
  d. new slavery laws.

_____ 5. The Seneca Falls Declaration of Sentiments laid the foundation for the
  a. temperance movement.
  b. women's rights movement.
  c. abolition movement.
  d. romantic movement.

_____ 6. The Protestant revivalists claimed that salvation could be attained
  a. by anyone who repented for his or her sins.
  b. only by those who were predestined.
  c. by shaking during worship.
  d. through a belief in the Holy Trinity.

_____ 7. Lyman Beecher preached extensively about
  a. transcendentalism.
  b. equal rights for women.
  c. the wrongs of slavery.
  d. the evils of alcohol.

_____ 8. Prison reformers argued that lawbreakers
  a. could be rehabilitated.
  b. need corporal punishment.
  c. could not be educated.
  d. should pay large fines.

_____ 9. By the mid-1800s, the temperance movement had led to
  a. lower liquor taxes.
  b. higher alcohol consumption rates.
  c. laws outlawing the consumption of alcohol.
  d. national prohibition.

_____ 10. The American Colonization Society wanted to
  a. send freed African Americans to Africa.
  b. rehabilitate lawbreakers.
  c. prohibit the consumption of alcohol.
  d. develop special reform colonies for the mentally ill.

■ **TRUE/FALSE** *(2 points each)* **Read each of the following statements, and then decide whether it is true or false. If the answer is true, place a *T* in the space provided; if the answer is false, place an *F* in the space.**

_____ 1. Most of the female reformers of the early 1800s were members of the lower class.

_____ 2. Catharine Beecher opposed women's participation in the public arena.

_____ 3. Most northern states had abolished slavery by the early 1800s.

_____ 4. Southerners generally did not support the establishment of public schools.

_____ 5. Many free African Americans wanted to leave the United States.

Chapter 9, Test Form A, Continued

PRACTICING SKILLS *(5 points each)* Study the graph below and answer the questions that follow.

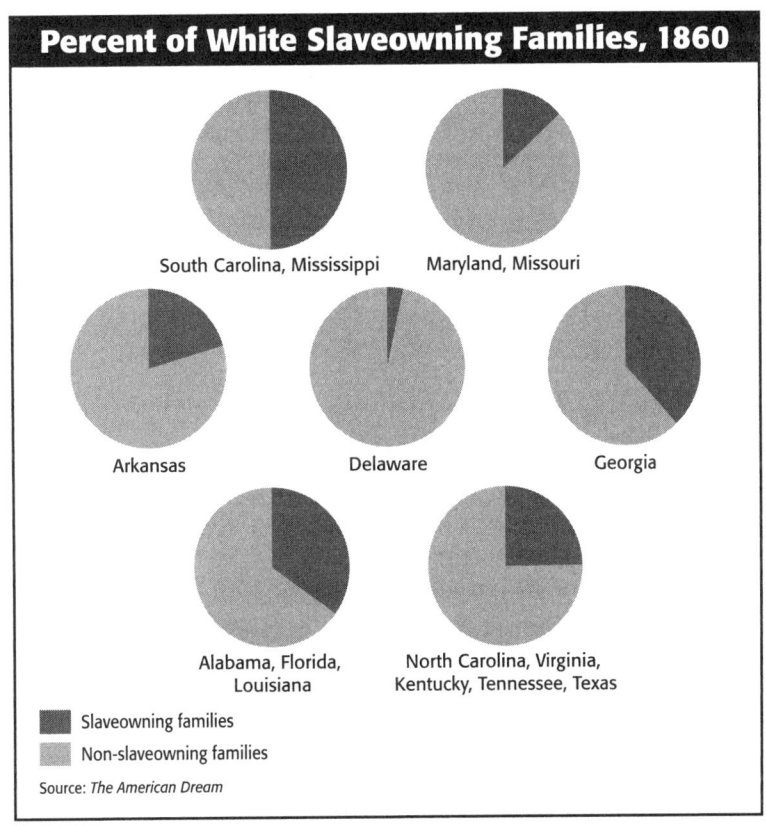

1. About what percent of the white families in North Carolina had slaves?

   _____

2. In which states did about half of the families own slaves?

   _____

COMPOSING AN ESSAY *(20 points)* Write a brief essay on *one* of the following subjects. Remember to use examples to support your answer.

1. How successful were women's rights activists in achieving their goals?
2. Define the Second Great Awakening and describe how it affected Protestant churches.

Name _____ Class _____ Date _____

CHAPTER 9
Working for Reform

CHAPTER TEST • FORM B

SHORT ANSWER *(10 points each)* Provide brief answers for each of the following. Remember to use examples to support your answer.

1. To what extent did women participate in the Second Great Awakening?
2. What was the philosophy of transcendentalism?
3. What were some of the effects of the temperance movement?
4. Why did educational reform have little impact on the South?
5. What new mood among abolitionists was reflected in Garrison's *Liberator* and Walker's *Appeal to the Colored Citizens of the World*?

PRIMARY SOURCE *(10 points each)* Dorothea Dix was one of the most influential reformers. She spent 18 months visiting jails and poorhouses throughout Massachusetts and discovered that mentally ill people were treated harshly. In January 1843 she collected her observations into a detailed report and delivered it to Massachusetts legislators. The following is an excerpt from that report. Read the excerpt and answer the questions that follow.

> *If I inflict pain on you, and move you to horror, it is to acquaint you with sufferings which you have the power to alleviate, and make you hasten to the relief of the victims of legalized barbarity. . . .* **Lincoln.** *A woman in a cage.* **Medford.** *One idiotic subject chained, and one in a closed stall for seventeen years.* **Pepperell.** *One often doubly chained, hand and foot; another violent; several peaceable now.* **Brookfield.** *One man caged, comfortable.* **Granville.** *One often closely confined; now losing the use of his limbs from want of exercise.* **Charlemont.** *One man caged.* **Savoy.** *One man caged.* **Lenox.** *Two in the jail, against whose unfit condition there the jailer protests.* **Dedham.** *The insane disadvantageously placed in the jail . . . two females in stalls, situated in the main building; lie in wooden bunks filled with straw; always shut up. One of these subjects is supposed curable.*

1. What do you think the boldfaced terms refer to?
2. How effective do you think her message is? Why?
3. What reforms does she ask for indirectly?

COMPOSING AN ESSAY *(20 points)* Write a brief essay on *one* of the following subjects. Remember to use examples to support your answer.

1. Describe some of the reforms that were initiated in education.
2. Explain why support for the abolition of slavery increased in the mid-1800s.

Name _____ Class _____ Date _____

Growth and Change

UNIT TEST • FORM A

REVIEWING FACTS *(3 points each)* In the space provided, write the name of the person or the historical term that completes each sentence. Choose your answers from the list below. There are two extra names or terms on the list.

Second Great Awakening	Frederick Douglass	American Colonization Society
American System	Industrial Revolution	Dorothea Dix
doctrine of nullification	Erie Canal	Monroe Doctrine
William Lloyd Garrison	Temperance Movement	Trail of Tears

_____ 1. the shift to machine production that started in Great Britain in the 1700s

_____ 2. wanted to send freed African Americans back to Africa to found new settlements

_____ 3. waterway that linked the East with the Midwest

_____ 4. worked to help the mentally ill in American society

_____ 5. the opinion that states could refuse or disobey federal laws they considered unfair

_____ 6. stated that the United States would help people seeking freedom

_____ 7. a renewed and passionate interest in religion that occurred in the late 1700s

_____ 8. forced relocation of the Cherokee Nation

_____ 9. prominent African American abolitionist

_____ 10. the crusade to limit alcohol consumption

Chapter and Unit Tests   Unit 3   45

Unit 3, Test Form A, Continued

UNDERSTANDING IDEAS *(3 points each)* For each of the following, place the letter of the *best* choice in the space provided.

_____ 1. The Missouri Compromise
   a. ended slavery in the North.
   b. admitted Maine and Missouri as slave states.
   c. admitted Maine as a free state and Missouri as a slave state.
   d. admitted both Maine and Missouri as free states.

_____ 2. The Indian Removal Act was designed to
   a. move American Indians from the fertile farmlands of the southeast.
   b. establish reservations on the East Coast for American Indians.
   c. bring American Indians into the urban centers of the east.
   d. help American Indians become assimilated into "white" culture.

_____ 3. Between 1830 and 1860, the largest group of immigrants to the United States was people from
   a. Germany.
   b. France.
   c. Ireland.
   d. Great Britain.

_____ 4. Nativism referred to
   a. appreciation for immigrants.
   b. fear of escaped African slaves.
   c. dislike of American Indians.
   d. dislike of immigrants.

_____ 5. Most northern middle-class children
   a. had to work to help support the family.
   b. were typically placed in East Coast boarding schools.
   c. usually did not attend school.
   d. did not need to work to help support their families.

_____ 6. Communities designed to create a perfect society were called
   a. unitarians.
   b. revivals.
   c. utopias.
   d. congregations.

_____ 7. All of the following came about because of education reform EXCEPT
   a. the establishment of free public high schools.
   b. college admission for women and minorities.
   c. an increase in free public education in the South.
   d. an increase in free public elementary schools in the North.

_____ 8. The Seneca Falls Convention was held to discuss
   a. women's rights.
   b. abolition.
   c. prohibition.
   d. prison reform.

_____ 9. The increase in the number of labor strikes in the 1830s coincided with
   a. rising numbers of labor unions.
   b. an increased number of working women.
   c. an increase in daily wages.
   d. improving work conditions in textile mills.

_____ 10. The antebellum South consisted of all of the following EXCEPT
   a. wealthy planters.
   b. rich industrialists.
   c. yeoman farmers.
   d. the very poor.

Unit 3, Test Form A, Continued

■ TRUE/FALSE *(2 points each)* Read each of the following statements, and then decide whether it is true or false. If the answer is true, place a *T* in the space provided; if the answer is false, place an *F* in the space.

_____ 1. Sojourner Truth ran the Underground Railroad.

_____ 2. Transcendentalists believed that material goods were the most important things to be attained in life.

_____ 3. Slave drivers were slaves themselves.

_____ 4. The Declaration of Sentiments outlined the wrongs and injustices of slavery.

_____ 5. The victory in the War of 1812 gave many Americans a strong feeling of nationalism.

■ PRACTICING SKILLS *(5 points each)* Study the map below and answer the questions that follow.

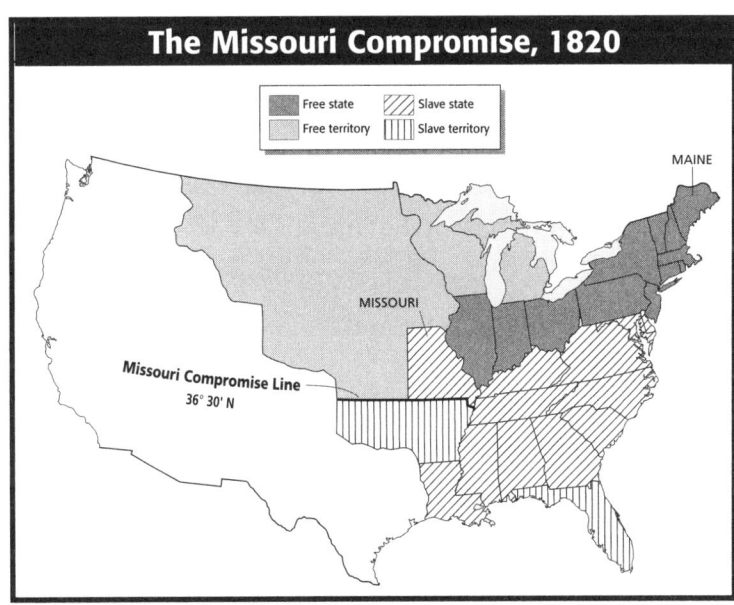

1. What was the land directly south of Missouri considered?
   _____

2. In which area of the country were most slave states?
   _____

■ COMPOSING AN ESSAY *(20 points)* Write a brief essay on *one* of the following subjects. Remember to use examples to support your answer.

1. Describe how the South became the Cotton Kingdom.
2. What was the Second Great Awakening, and how did it affect Protestant churches?

Chapter and Unit Tests   Unit 3   **47**

Name _____ Class _____ Date _____

UNIT 3

Growth and Change

UNIT TEST • FORM B

■ **SHORT ANSWER** *(10 points each)* Provide brief answers to each of the following. Remember to use examples to support your answer.

1. What were some of the major accomplishments of the Transportation Revolution?
2. What was life like for the typical planter in the antebellum South?
3. Why was Andrew Jackson considered the people's president?
4. What were some of the effects of the temperance movement?
5. How did many white southerners justify slavery?

■ **PRIMARY SOURCE** *(10 points each)* In 1831, Gustave de Beaumont and Alexis de Tocqueville wrote their observations of American prisons. Read the following excerpt and answer the questions below.

> *To sum up the whole on this point it must be acknowledged that the penitentiary system in America is severe. Whilst society in the United States gives the example of the most extended liberty, the prisons of the same country offer the spectacle of the most complete despotism [oppression]. The citizens subject to the law are protected by it; they only cease to be free when they become wicked.*

1. How do the writers describe American prisons?
2. When do Americans lose their freedom?

■ **COMPOSING AN ESSAY** *(30 points)* Write a brief essay on *one* of the following subjects. Remember to use examples to support your answer.

1. How successful were women's rights activists in achieving their goals?
2. Compare and contrast the lives of Irish and German immigrants.
3. Define the Second Great Awakening, and describe how it affected Protestant churches.
4. The period after the War of 1812 was called the "Era of Good Feelings." Explain why this was either an appropriate or inappropriate description of the period.

Name _____ Class _____ Date _____

Expansion and Conflict

CHAPTER TEST • FORM A

■ **REVIEWING FACTS** *(3 points each)* In the space provided, write the name of the person or the historical term identified by each description. Choose your answers from the list below. There are two extra names or terms in the list.

empresarios	Santa Fe Trail	Bear Flag Revolt
Donner party	manifest destiny	Tejanos
Mexican Cession	Antonio López de Santa Anna	Brigham Young
Juan Cortina	Oregon Trail	mountain men

_____ 1. a popular belief among Americans that God intended the United States to expand westward, all the way to the Pacific Ocean

_____ 2. native Mexicans who lived in Texas

_____ 3. people given generous land grants by the Mexican government in exchange for which they agreed to recruit and take responsibility for new settlers

_____ 4. an uprising in 1846 by American settlers in California against the Mexican government that led to the settlers' declaring California to be an independent republic

_____ 5. a member of a prominent Tejano family who engaged in skirmishes with Texas law enforcement officers in response to discrimination against Mexican Americans living in Texas

_____ 6. trappers who extended the fur trade into new areas of the Far West

_____ 7. a group of travelers that became snowbound in the Sierra Nevada Mountains during the winter of 1846–47, resulting in the loss of some 42 lives

_____ 8. the leader of thousands of Mormons to Utah

_____ 9. the vast territory acquired by the United States following the Mexican War

_____ 10. an overland route across the Great Plains and Rocky Mountains originally used by fur trappers but most heavily traveled by others headed west, such as farmers and missionaries

Chapter 10, Test Form A, Continued

UNDERSTANDING IDEAS *(3 points each)* For each of the following, place the letter of the *best* choice in the space provided.

_____ 1. The Bear Flag Revolt was led by
   a. Juan Cortina.
   b. James K. Polk.
   c. Brigham Young.
   d. John C. Frémont.

_____ 2. By 1830 the Mexican government was concerned about the huge migration into Texas by
   a. Spanish settlers.
   b. Americans.
   c. American Indians.
   d. Germans.

_____ 3. As part of the terms of the Treaty of Guadalupe Hidalgo, Mexico gave up all claims to
   a. San Jacinto.
   b. Texas.
   c. Mexico City.
   d. Salt Lake City.

_____ 4. Although Mexican lawmakers had banned slavery in 1829, Texans had negotiated a special law that classified their slaves as
   a. Tejanos.
   b. *empresarios*.
   c. indentured servants.
   d. Californios.

_____ 5. After Texas declared its independence from Mexico in 1836, many Americans opposed admitting Texas to the Union because
   a. Texas allowed slavery.
   b. so many Texans were of Mexican descent.
   c. Texas had a large German-speaking population.
   d. adding Texas would also mean increasing the number of American Indians living in the United States.

_____ 6. The Mexican Cession included all or part of present-day
   a. Florida and Louisiana.
   b. California, Nevada, Utah, Arizona, Colorado, New Mexico, and Wyoming.
   c. Oregon and Washington.
   d. Cuba and Puerto Rico.

_____ 7. The first Spanish settlers of California and their descendants were known as
   a. Tejanos.
   b. Californians.
   c. Mexicans.
   d. Californios.

_____ 8. In the 1830s and 1840s, before the Gold Rush, most non-Spanish settlers were drawn to California by
   a. cheap farmland.
   b. the discovery of oil.
   c. American Indian crops.
   d. religious freedom.

_____ 9. What was the Mariposa War?
   a. an attack on Californios by U.S. Army units
   b. a battle between the United States and Spain over land
   c. raids by American Indian tribes against white settlers
   d. the last battle of Santa Anna against Texas rebels

_____ 10. Faced with discrimination in the mining camps, many Chinese prospectors
   a. took jobs, settled in towns, and developed associations with other Chinese immigrants.
   b. moved to Mexico.
   c. became missionaries and ministered to American Indians.
   d. moved to Canada.

Chapter 10, Test Form A, Continued

■ TRUE/FALSE *(2 points each)* Read each of the following statements, and then decide whether it is true or false. If the answer is true, place a *T* in the space provided; if the answer is false, place an *F* in the space.

_____ 1. As a result of the Bear Flag Revolt, the United States gain about 80,000 Spanish-speaking citizens in land formerly held by Mexico.

_____ 2. The rights of Mexicans were supposed to be protected under the terms of the Treaty of Guadalupe Hidalgo.

_____ 3. President Polk campaigned aggressively to expand U.S. territory by annexing Oregon and Texas in 1844.

_____ 4. The defeat of Mexico at the Battle of San Jacinto won independence for Texas.

_____ 5. The first gold seekers in California were called "forty-niners" because that was the number of migrants who made the first overland trek on the California Trail.

■ PRACTICING SKILLS *(5 points each)* Study the graph below and answer the questions that follow.

1. Between which two consecutive years did the amount of gold mined make the biggest jump?

   _____

2. About how much more gold was mined in 1852 than in 1848?

   _____

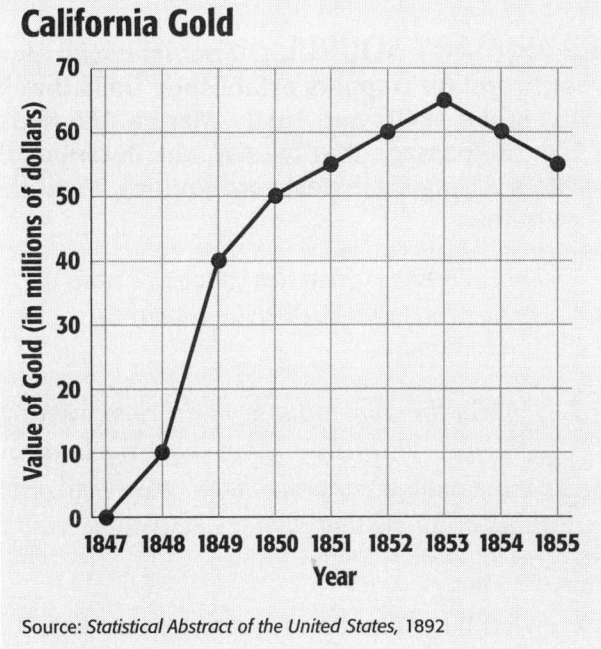

Source: *Statistical Abstract of the United States,* 1892

■ COMPOSING AN ESSAY *(20 points)* Write a brief essay on *one* of the following subjects. Remember to use examples to support your answer.

1. Describe the terms of the Treaty of Guadalupe Hidalgo, which ended the Mexican War in 1848.
2. Why did the forty-niners migrate to California, where did they migrate from, and how did they get there?

Chapter and Unit Tests   Chapter 10 **51**

Name _____ Class _____ Date _____

Expansion and Conflict

CHAPTER TEST • FORM B

■ **SHORT ANSWER** *(10 points each)* Provide brief answers for each of the following. Remember to use examples to support your answer.

1. Why did some members of Congress oppose the declaration of war on Mexico?
2. Why did Mexico close the Texas border to immigration from the United States and prohibit the importation of slaves to Texas in 1830?
3. Why, after Texas declared its independence from Mexico in 1836, did many Americans believe that Texas should be added to the Union as soon as possible?
4. What did the United States acquire from Mexico in the 1853 deal known as the Gadsden Purchase?
5. According to the Treaty of Fort Laramie, what were American Indians to receive in return for pledging not to interfere with settlers traveling westward on the Oregon Trail?

■ **PRIMARY SOURCE** *(10 points each)* During the early 1800s, American merchants and fur trappers established trails that brought waves of new settlers to the Far West in the 1840s and 1850s. Martha Ann Morrison traveled to Oregon at the age of 13. In the passage that follows, she describes the terrible hardships that befell many settlers during their westward journey. Read the passage and answer the questions that follow.

> *The men had a great deal of anxiety and all the care of their families, but still the mothers had the families directly in their hands and were with them all the time, especially during sickness.*
>
> *Some of the women I saw on the road went through a great deal of suffering and trial. I remember distinctly one girl in particular about my own age that died and was buried on the road. Her mother had a great deal of trouble and suffering. It strikes me as I think of it now that mothers on the road had to undergo more trial and suffering than anybody else.*

1. What hardship did men and women seem to have in common on the trail?
2. According to the writer, what made suffering worse for mothers?

■ **COMPOSING AN ESSAY** *(30 points)* Write a brief essay on *one* of the following subjects. Remember to use examples to support your answer.

1. What was the rendezvous system? How did it further the success of the fur trade in the Rocky Mountains and lead to settlers making their way to the Far West?
2. What effect did the Gold Rush have on American Indians living in California?

Name _____ Class _____ Date _____

CHAPTER 11: Sectional Conflict Increases

CHAPTER TEST • FORM A

REVIEWING FACTS *(3 points each)* In the space provided, write the name of the person or the historical term identified by each description. Choose your answers from the list below. There are two extra names or terms on the list.

Kansas-Nebraska Act	Confederate States of America	Compromise of 1850
John Brown	John C. Calhoun	Fugitive Slave Act
popular sovereignty	John Breckinridge	Harriet Beecher Stowe
Dred Scott	Wilmot Proviso	Frederick Douglass

_____ 1. an amendment that would have banned slavery in all lands acquired from Mexico

_____ 2. a proposal to allow the citizens of each new U.S. territory to vote on whether to permit slavery there

_____ 3. a law, included in the Compromise of 1850, that made it a federal crime to assist runaway slaves and authorized the arrest of escaped slaves even in states where slavery was illegal

_____ 4. an act, passed by Congress in 1854, that organized the territories of Kansas and Nebraska on the basis of popular sovereignty

_____ 5. abolitionist who led attacks against a pro-slavery settlement and a federal weapons arsenal

_____ 6. abolitionist and former slave who urged "forcible resistance" against slavery and wrote an autobiography detailing the harshness of slave life on a farm

_____ 7. a leading supporter of slavery and of southern rights; served as U.S. representative, U.S. senator, secretary of war, secretary of state, and vice president

_____ 8. various measures proposed by Henry Clay, and later passed by Congress, designed to satisfy both northern and southern interests, particularly concerning slavery

_____ 9. the formal name for southern states that seceded from the Union

_____ 10. a southern Democrat who ran unsuccessfully for president, believing, like many other southerners, that Congress had a duty to protect slavery in the territories

Chapter 11, Test Form A, Continued

UNDERSTANDING IDEAS (3 points each) For each of the following, place the letter of the best choice in the space provided.

_____ 1. In 1837, when citizens of Vermont presented a petition opposing slavery, southern members of Congress
  a. voted to turn Vermont into a slave state.
  b. refused to allow Michigan into the Union.
  c. drafted a so-called gag rule prohibiting slavery from even being discussed in Congress.
  d. refused to vote.

_____ 2. Harriet Beecher Stowe's *Uncle Tom's Cabin*, published in 1852,
  a. was used by southern politicians as a defense of slavery.
  b. fueled antislavery arguments.
  c. portrayed the hardships of life for early white settlers.
  d. offered a realistic picture of American Indian life.

_____ 3. The Lecompton Constitution failed to uphold the policy of popular sovereignty because it
  a. did not allow Kansas voters the right to outlaw slavery completely.
  b. outlawed the Republican Party.
  c. was unconstitutional.
  d. led to the Civil War.

_____ 4. Which political party was formed by antislavery settlers in Kansas?
  a. the Free State Party
  b. the American Party
  c. the Know-Nothings
  d. the Republican Party

_____ 5. Which group of southerners held extreme pro-slavery views?
  a. the Free-Soil Party
  b. the Democratic Party
  c. fire-eaters
  d. abolitionists

_____ 6. In the _____, the U.S. Supreme Court ruled that no African American could ever enjoy the rights of a U.S. citizen.
  a. Freedom Act
  b. Fugitive Slave Act
  c. Compromise of 1850
  d. *Dred Scott* case

_____ 7. Who is given credit for developing the Freeport Doctrine?
  a. Abraham Lincoln
  b. Stephen Douglas
  c. Frederick Douglass
  d. John C. Calhoun

_____ 8. The Confederate States of America chose _____ as the president of the Confederacy.
  a. Robert E. Lee
  b. John C. Calhoun
  c. John Breckinridge
  d. Jefferson Davis

_____ 9. Northerners opposed to _____ by the southern states argued that by ratifying the U.S. Constitution, a state did not have the right to withdraw from the Union.
  a. western expansion
  b. secession
  c. popular sovereignty
  d. democracy

_____ 10. Many feared that annexing the Republic of Texas would tip the balance of power in Congress in favor of
  a. Mexico.
  b. California.
  c. the slave states.
  d. Tejanos living in Texas.

54 Chapter 11

Chapter 11, Test Form A, Continued

TRUE/FALSE (2 points each) Read each of the following statements and then decide whether it is true or false. If the answer is true, place a *T* in the space provided; if the answer is false, place an *F* in the space.

_____ 1. The Free-Soil Party drew support in the 1848 election by encouraging western expansion with free land and proposing the end of expansion of slavery into the territories.

_____ 2. The Republican Party, organized in 1854, was initially formed for the purpose of supporting slavery in the South.

_____ 3. The *Dred Scott* decision concerned a slave who sued for his freedom following the death of his white owner.

_____ 4. Despite Abraham Lincoln's moderate stance on slavery, many southerners viewed his victory as a triumph for abolition.

_____ 5. A major feature of the Missouri Compromise was a ban on slavery north of 36°30′, Missouri's southern boundary.

PRACTICING SKILLS (5 points each) Study the table below and answer the questions that follow.

The Election of 1860			
	Electoral Vote	Popular Vote	% of Pop. Vote
Lincoln	180	1, 865, 593	39.8
Douglas	12	1, 382, 713	29.5
Breckinridge	72	848, 356	18.1
Bell	39	592, 906	12.6

1. What was the total number of electoral votes in the presidential election of 1860?

_____

2. Which candidate had the greatest number of electoral votes, and which candidate had the greatest percentage of the popular vote?

_____

COMPOSING AN ESSAY (20 points) Write a brief essay on *one* of the following subjects. Remember to use examples to support your answer.

1. Describe the Compromise of 1850. Explain why it was needed and discuss some of its measures.
2. Describe the circumstances that led to the *Dred Scott* decision by the U.S. Supreme Court. Why did the Court's decision anger abolitionists and other opponents of the expansion of slavery?

Name _____ Class _____ Date _____

CHAPTER 11: Sectional Conflict Increases

CHAPTER TEST • FORM B

■ SHORT ANSWER *(10 points each)* Provide brief answers for each of the following. Remember to use examples to support your answer.

1. Why did many northerners oppose the Compromise of 1850? Why did many southerners oppose the Compromise?
2. Why did the 1855 Kansas elections lead to escalating violence in 1855 and 1856?
3. Why did John Brown and his followers conduct their raid at Harpers Ferry, Virginia?
4. How did the results of the 1860 presidential election reflect the division between the northern and southern states?
5. How did southern secessionists use the doctrine of states' rights to justify their withdrawal from the Union?

■ PRIMARY SOURCE *(10 points each)* In the 1840s and 1850s the narratives of slaves who had escaped from the South were widely read in the North. In *Incidents in the Life of a Slave Girl,* Harriet Jacobs describes how, to escape extremely cruel conditions, she sought refuge in the attic of her grandmother's home. She remained there for the next seven years until she and her children could flee to the North. The following is an excerpt from her narrative. Read it and answer the questions that follow.

> *The garret [attic] was only nine feet long and seven wide. The highest part was three feet high, and sloped down abruptly to the loose board floor. There was no admission for either light or air.... The air was stifling; the darkness total.... The rats and mice ran over my bed; but I was weary, and I slept such sleep as the wretched may, when a tempest has passed over them. Morning came. I knew it only by the noises I heard; for in my small den day and night were all the same. I suffered for air even more than for light. But I was not comfortless. I heard the voices of my children. There was joy and there was sadness in the sound. It made my tears flow.*

1. Describe the air and light conditions in the attic.
2. What provided her with some comfort while she was hiding?

■ COMPOSING AN ESSAY *(30 points)* Write a brief essay on *one* of the following subjects. Remember to use examples to support your answer.

1. Explain the major principle of popular sovereignty. How did the Kansas-Nebraska Act reflect this principle?
2. Compare the reactions of many northerners to John Brown's raid on Harpers Ferry with the reactions of many southerners.

Name _____ Class _____ Date _____

The Civil War

CHAPTER TEST • FORM A

■ **REVIEWING FACTS** *(3 points each)* In the space provided, write the name of the person or the historical term identified by each description. Choose your answers from the list below. There are two extra names or terms on the list.

Elizabeth Blackwell	Richmond	Battle of Antietam
conscription	Ulysses S. Grant	Martin Delany
Copperheads	George B. McClellan	Anaconda Plan
Clara Barton	U.S. Sanitary Commission	Sally Louisa Tompkins

_____ 1. the capital of the Confederacy

_____ 2. a naval blockade of the South

_____ 3. the first professionally licensed female doctor in the United States; helped run the U.S. Sanitary Commission

_____ 4. a Union nurse who founded the American Red Cross

_____ 5. the military draft

_____ 6. organization that worked to battle the diseases and infections that killed twice as many soldiers as bullets alone

_____ 7. northern sympathizers of the South; most limited their antiwar activities to speeches and newspaper articles

_____ 8. led the Union to victory at the Battle of Shiloh and the Siege of Vicksburg; became commander of all Union armies in 1864

_____ 9. the first African American promoted to the rank of major

_____ 10. the Union victory that cost the Confederacy Britain's support and gave Lincoln the political strength he needed to move forward with his plans to free the slaves in the South

■ **UNDERSTANDING IDEAS** *(3 points each)* For each of the following, place the letter of the *best* choice in the space provided.

_____ 1. The North did not want to lose Fort Sumter to the Confederacy because
   a. it was a federal prison.
   b. it would be a sign that Lincoln could not protect federal property in the seceded states.
   c. it had great symbolic value.
   d. it was a meeting place for foreign diplomats.

Chapter and Unit Tests   Chapter 12 57

Chapter 12, Test Form A, Continued

_____ 2. The secession of _____ would have meant losing the U.S. capital to the Confederacy.
   a. West Virginia
   b. Maryland
   c. Kentucky
   d. Missouri

_____ 3. When West Virginia broke away from Virginia, it was admitted to the Union in 1863
   a. as a federal district.
   b. as part of Kentucky.
   c. as a slave state.
   d. as a border state.

_____ 4. Historians estimate that about 180,000 African Americans
   a. served in the Union army.
   b. were drafted into the Confederate army.
   c. fled to Canada.
   d. served the North as members of American Indian tribes.

_____ 5. In the aftermath of the First Battle of Bull Run,
   a. the Confederacy surrendered.
   b. France and Britain provided military help to the South.
   c. most people realized that the war would last longer than a few months.
   d. three southern states rejoined the Union.

_____ 6. The Confederacy was confident that France or Britain would come to the South's aid because
   a. both nations supplied the South with African slaves.
   b. so many southerners were of English or French descent.
   c. both nations' economies depended heavily on cotton.
   d. both nations hated the Union.

_____ 7. In the South, draft exemptions placed the major burden for fighting the war on
   a. teenage boys.
   b. German and Irish immigrants.
   c. poor farmers and working people.
   d. slaves and Cherokee Indians.

_____ 8. Capturing _____ led to the Union taking control of the Mississippi River.
   a. Chancellorsville
   b. Appomattox
   c. Washington
   d. New Orleans

_____ 9. Union victories at Vicksburg and Port Hudson were significant because
   a. Confederate troops were unable to transport their supplies.
   b. they gave the Union total control of the Mississippi River.
   c. Confederate general Thomas "Stonewall" Jackson was killed.
   d. the Union grew overconfident.

_____ 10. One of the Union's first all-black regiments, the 54th Massachusetts Infantry, was noted for
   a. being the first all-black outfit to be commanded by an African American officer.
   b. demonstrating to the South that African Americans were deserving of being allowed to serve in the armed forces.
   c. recruiting American Indians into its ranks.
   d. breaking the Confederates' hold on Fort Wagner.

Chapter 12, Test Form A, Continued

TRUE/FALSE (2 points each)
Read each of the following statements and then decide whether it is true or false. If the answer is true, place a *T* in the space provided; if the answer is false, place an *F* in the space.

_____ 1. When President Abraham Lincoln took office in 1861, seven southern states had already seceded from the Union.

_____ 2. The Confederate attack on Fort Sumter marked the beginning of the Civil War.

_____ 3. Robert E. Lee accepted President Lincoln's request to command the Union forces because he opposed slavery and secession.

_____ 4. From the beginning of the Civil War, the North's main goal was to restore the Union.

_____ 5. Despite the Union army's good showing at Antietam, President Lincoln fired George B. McClellan because he moved too quickly and took unnecessary risks.

PRACTICING SKILLS (5 points each)
Study the graph below and answer the questions that follow.

1. Which side suffered the greatest number of deaths in the Civil War?
   _____

2. Overall, did more Civil War soldiers die from battle causes or non-battle causes?
   _____

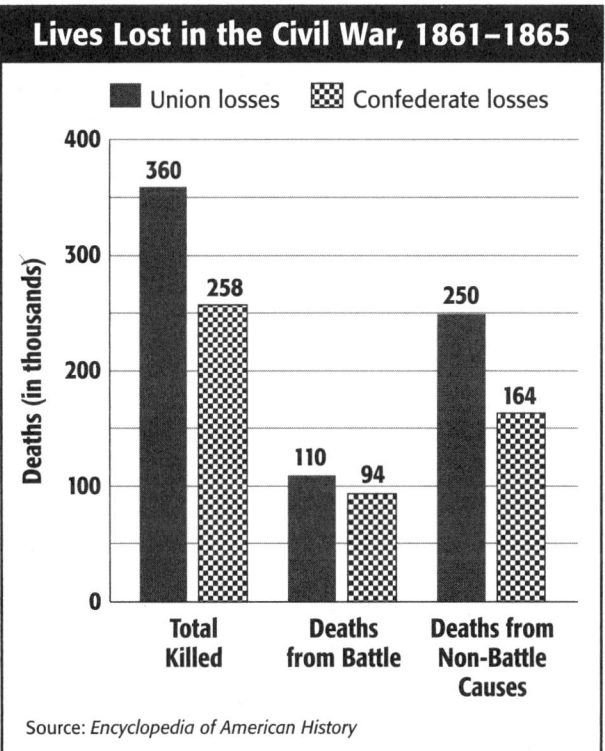

COMPOSING AN ESSAY (20 points)
Write a brief essay on *one* of the following subjects. Remember to use examples to support your answer.

1. Describe the Crittenden Compromise and the circumstances that led to its being proposed.
2. Describe the advantages that each side held at the beginning of the Civil War.

Name _____ Class _____ Date _____

CHAPTER 12

The Civil War

CHAPTER TEST • FORM B

■ **SHORT ANSWER** *(10 points each)* Provide brief answers for each of the following. Remember to use examples to support your answer.

1. Why did Confederate leaders believe that European nations such as France and Britain would aid the South in the Civil War?
2. Why was the Anaconda Plan an important strategy for the North?
3. How did the military strategies of the North and South differ from one another?
4. What were some of the responsibilities filled by northern women on the home front when men left for the battlefields?
5. What was the outcome of the Battle of Gettysburg and why was it important to the course of the war?

■ **PRIMARY SOURCE** *(10 points each)* Following the Union victory at Antietam, President Lincoln felt he had the political support he needed to free the slaves in the South. In July 1862 he informed his cabinet of his intention to issue the Emancipation Proclamation, which would take effect on January 1, 1863. Read the excerpts below and answer the questions that follow.

On the first day of January, A.D. 1863, all persons held as slaves within any state or designated part of a state, the people whereof shall then be in rebellion against the United States, shall be then, thenceforward, and forever free. . . .

Now, therefore, I, Abraham Lincoln, President of the United States . . . do order and declare that all persons held as slaves within said designated states . . . are, and henceforward shall be, free. . . .

And I further declare and make known that such persons of suitable condition will be received into the armed service of the United States to garrison forts, positions, stations, and other places, and to man vessels of all sorts in said service.

And upon this act, sincerely believed to be an act of justice, warranted by the constitution upon military necessity, I invoke the considerate judgment of mankind and the gracious favor of Almighty God.

1. What did the Emancipation Proclamation mean for slaves living in border states that remained in the Union?
2. What did Lincoln say would happen to such persons of "suitable condition"?

■ **COMPOSING AN ESSAY** *(30 points)* Write a brief essay on *one* of the following subjects. Remember to use examples to support your answer.

1. Discuss some of the reasons that people on both sides of the conflict opposed the war.
2. Describe General William Tecumseh Sherman's total-war strategy.

Name _____ Class _____ Date _____

Reconstruction and the New South

CHAPTER 13

CHAPTER TEST • FORM A

REVIEWING FACTS *(3 points each)* In the space provided, write the name of the person or the historical term identified by each description. Choose your answers from the list below. There are two extra names or terms on the list.

Civil Rights Act of 1866	Booker T. Washington	Ulysses S. Grant
Fifteenth Amendment	Black Codes	Compromise of 1877
carpetbaggers	Frederick Douglass	Jim Crow
Madame C. J. Walker	Ida B. Wells	amnesty

_____ 1. a civil rights activist, journalist, and teacher who fought against the practice of lynching and urged African Americans to leave the South

_____ 2. exchanged Democrats' acceptance of Rutherford B. Hayes for the removal of federal troops in the South

_____ 3. white and African American Republicans from the northern United States, who traveled south, hoping to influence the political process there after the Civil War

_____ 4. a policy promoted by President Abraham Lincoln to give a full pardon to all southerners who would swear allegiance to the U.S. Constitution and who would accept federal laws ending slavery

_____ 5. stated that everyone born in the United States enjoyed full civil rights, although it did not guarantee voting rights

_____ 6. a series of laws produced by state legislatures to ensure separation of the races, or segregation. These laws required schools, transportation, cemeteries, parks, and other public places to be segregated

_____ 7. laws passed by some states to limit the freedoms of former slaves and re-establish white control of African American labor

_____ 8. an amendment that ensured that citizens of the United States were allowed to vote regardless of "race, color, or previous condition of servitude"

_____ 9. a former Civil War general who ran for president in 1868

_____ 10. an entrepreneur who developed a hair preparations company and became one of the first female millionaires in the United States

Chapter and Unit Tests

Chapter 13, Test Form A, Continued

UNDERSTANDING IDEAS (3 points each) For each of the following, place the letter of the best choice in the space provided.

_____ 1. The Redeemers were
 a. a religious group.
 b. land radicals.
 c. supporters of white-controlled governments.
 d. suffragist.

_____ 2. Booker T. Washington believed that African Americans should react to discrimination by
 a. forming political parties.
 b. using violence against whites.
 c. leaving the United States.
 d. working to achieve economic independence.

_____ 3. Which of the following statements does NOT apply to the Fourteenth Amendment, passed in 1866?
 a. It guaranteed African American voting rights.
 b. It required states to extend equal citizenship to African Americans.
 c. It promised all citizens the "equal protection of the laws."
 d. It did not allow states to deprive anyone of "life, liberty, or property without due process of law."

_____ 4. A former slave, _____ became a leading abolitionist.
 a. Thaddeus Stevens
 b. Frederick Douglass
 c. Booker T. Washington
 d. James Madison Wells

_____ 5. President Andrew Johnson was impeached because he
 a. violated the Tenure of Office Acts.
 b. was involved in a scheme to sell federal lands containing oil.
 c. had tried to overturn Lincoln's financial policies.
 d. had lost control of his party.

_____ 6. In its ruling on _____, the U.S. Supreme Court ruled that "separate but equal" facilities were legal.
 a. the Civil Rights Cases of 1883
 b. the Reconstruction Acts
 c. Plessy v. Ferguson
 d. the Civil Rights Act of 1866

_____ 7. _____ were southern whites who had supported the Union cause.
 a. Abolitionists
 b. Scalawags
 c. Carpetbaggers
 d. Ku Klux Klan members

_____ 8. In the 1876 presidential election, _____ ran against Rutherford B. Hayes.
 a. Robert E. Lee
 b. Charles Sumner
 c. Thaddeus Stevens
 d. Samuel J. Tilden

_____ 9. The _____ were supposed to halt violence against African Americans.
 a. Tenure of Office Acts.
 b. Black Codes.
 c. Thirteenth and Fourteenth Amendments.
 d. Enforcement Acts.

_____ 10. President Abraham Lincoln's plan for beginning Reconstruction was
 a. to abolish slavery.
 b. to proclaim amnesty for most southerners.
 c. to have southern states renounce their acts of secession.
 d. to encourage former Confederate leaders to resign.

Chapter 13, Test Form A, Continued

TRUE/FALSE *(2 points each)* Read each of the following statements and then decide whether it is true or false. If the answer is true, place a *T* in the space provided; if the answer is false, place an *F* in the space.

_____ 1. President Lincoln issued the Proclamation of Amnesty and Reconstruction at the end of the Civil War.

_____ 2. Rutherford B. Hayes won the presidential election of 1876.

_____ 3. Few people in the North supported giving African Americans in the South the right to vote.

_____ 4. John Wilkes Booth assassinated Abraham Lincoln because Booth was part of a conspiracy organized by Confederate leaders.

_____ 5. The new African American vote was an important factor in Ulysses S. Grant's election as president.

PRACTICING SKILLS *(5 points each)* Study the table below and answer the questions that follow.

Cotton Production and Cotton Prices, 1876–1896

	Cotton Production (Acres of cotton harvested in millions)	Cotton Prices (Price per pound in cents)
1876	12	9.5
1880	16	9.8
1884	17	9
1888	19	8.2
1892	18	8.2
1896	22	6

1. In which year was the least amount of cotton produced? _____

2. In which year was the price of cotton highest? _____

COMPOSING AN ESSAY *(20 points)* Write a brief essay on *one* of the following subjects. Remember to use examples to support your answer.

1. What was the purpose of the Black Codes? Compare the reactions to the codes of white southerners, many northerners, and African Americans.

2. Discuss the advantages and disadvantages of the Fifteenth Amendment.

Name _____ Class _____ Date _____

CHAPTER 13
Reconstruction and the New South

CHAPTER TEST • FORM B

■ **SHORT ANSWER** *(10 points each)* Provide brief answers for each of the following. Remember to use examples to support your answer.

1. Besides freedom from slavery, what did many African Americans hope for at the end of the Civil War?
2. What did Thaddeus Stevens think breaking up the southern plantations would accomplish?
3. What were the purposes of the Freedmen's Bureau?
4. What were the goals of the Ku Klux Klan and what methods did they use to achieve their goals?
5. How did sharecropping keep workers tied to the same land and same jobs?

■ **PRIMARY SOURCE** *(10 points each)* Many African American writers of the post-Reconstruction period focused on the difficulties faced by African Americans after gaining their freedom, as well as on the more general African American experience. Charles W. Chestnutt's 1899 story "The Wife of His Youth" deals with the choice one man must make between the woman he married while still a slave and the young widow he is courting. Here is an excerpt from that story. Read it and answer the questions that follow.

> *Suppose that this husband, soon after his escape, had learned that his wife had been sold away, and that such inquiries as he could make brought no information of her whereabouts. Suppose that he was young, and she much older than he; that he was light, and she was black; that their marriage was a slave marriage, and legally binding only if they chose to make it so after the war. Suppose, too, that he made his way to the North, as some of us have done, and there, where he had larger opportunities, had improved them, and had in the course of all these years grown to be as different from the ignorant boy who ran away from fear of slavery as the day is from the night. Suppose, even, that he had qualified himself, by industry, by thrift, and by study, to win the friendship and be considered worthy. . . . And then suppose that accident should bring to his knowledge the fact that the wife of his youth, the wife he had left behind him, . . . was alive and seeking him, but that he was absolutely safe from recognition or discovery, unless he chose to reveal himself. My friends, what would the man do?*

1. What differences between the man and his first wife does the author describe?
2. In what ways had the man changed since his first marriage?

■ **COMPOSING AN ESSAY** *(30 points)* Write a brief essay on *one* of the following subjects. Remember to use examples to support your answer.

1. Describe how Reconstruction affected the South's economy.
2. Describe the major legislation that Congress passed to implement its plan for Reconstruction and President Johnson's reaction, if any, to those bills.

War and Reunification

UNIT TEST • FORM A

■ **REVIEWING FACTS** *(3 points each)* In the space provided, write the name of the person or the historical term identified by each description. Choose your answers from the list below. There are two extra names or terms on the list.

conscription	manifest destiny	Copperheads	Jim Crow
Clara Barton	Anaconda Plan	amnesty	Tejanos
John Brown	Ida B. Wells	Frederick Douglass	mountain men

_____ 1. a civil rights activist, she fought against the practice of lynching and urged African Americans to leave the South

_____ 2. a series of laws produced by state legislatures to create segregation of schools, transportation, cemeteries, parks, and other public places

_____ 3. he attacked a pro-slavery settlement and a federal weapons arsenal

_____ 4. abolitionist whose autobiography detailed the harshness of slave life on a farm

_____ 5. as a result of illnesses in the Civil War, she founded the American Red Cross

_____ 6. this required young men to serve in the armed forces

_____ 7. northerners who agreed with the South on Reconstruction issues

_____ 8. a popular belief among Americans that it was God's intent for the United States to keep expanding westward

_____ 9. offered by President Abraham Lincoln to all southerners who would swear allegiance to the U.S. Constitution and who would accept federal laws ending slavery

_____ 10. native Mexicans who lived in Texas

■ **UNDERSTANDING IDEAS** *(3 points each)* For each of the following, place the letter of the *best* choice in the space provided.

_____ 1. By 1830 Texas experienced a huge migration of
a. Spanish settlers.
b. American Indians.
c. Americans.
d. Germans.

_____ 2. Texans classified their slaves as
a. Californios.
b. *empresarios*.
c. indentured servants.
d. Tejanos.

Chapter and Unit Tests　　　　　　　　　　　　　　　　　　　　　　　　　　Unit 4　**65**

Unit 4, Test Form A, Continued

_____ 3. The Mexican Cession included all or part of present-day
   a. Oregon, Washington, and British Columbia.
   b. Cuba and Puerto Rico.
   c. Florida and Louisiana.
   d. California, Nevada, Utah, Arizona, Colorado, New Mexico, and Wyoming.

_____ 4. Harriet Beecher Stowe's *Uncle Tom's Cabin* was significant because it
   a. was used by southern politicians as a defense of slavery.
   b. fueled antislavery arguments.
   c. offered a realistic picture of the home life of certain American Indian tribes.
   d. portrayed the hardships of life for early white settlers.

_____ 5. The Supreme Court's ruling in the _____ stated that no African Americans were U.S. citizens.
   a. *Dred Scott* case
   b. Fugitive Slave Act
   c. *Brown* v. *Board of Education* case
   d. Freeport Doctrine

_____ 6. _____ was the provisional president of the Confederacy.
   a. Robert E. Lee
   b. Jefferson Davis
   c. John Breckinridge
   d. John C. Calhoun

_____ 7. Some 180,000 African Americans
   a. served the North as members of American Indian tribes.
   b. were drafted into the Confederate army.
   c. fled to the West Indies until the war ended.
   d. chose to serve in the Union army.

_____ 8. The Confederacy believed that France or Britain would assist the South during a naval blockade because
   a. both nations supplied the South with African slaves.
   b. so many southerners were of English or French descent.
   c. France and Britain depended on southern cotton.
   d. both nations supported slavery.

_____ 9. The Redeemers were
   a. suffragettes.
   b. supporters of all-white governments.
   c. liberals who hoped to give land to African Americans.
   d. a religious group.

_____ 10. Which of the following statements is false?
   a. The Fourteenth Amendment promised all citizens the "equal protection of the law."
   b. The Fourteenth Amendment guaranteed African American voting rights.
   c. The Fourteenth Amendment required states to extend equal citizenship to African Americans and anyone born or naturalized in the United States.
   d. The Fourteenth Amendment did not allow states to deprive anyone of "life, liberty, or property without due process of law."

Unit 4, Test Form A, Continued

TRUE/FALSE (2 points each) Read each of the following statements and then decide whether it is true or false. If the answer is true, place a *T* in the space provided; if the answer is false, place an *F* in the space.

_____ 1. The Republican Party, organized in 1854, was initially formed for the purpose of supporting slavery in the South.

_____ 2. Southern states began seceding from the Union after Lincoln was in office for one year.

_____ 3. The Union attacked Fort Sumter to discourage the South from fighting a civil war.

_____ 4. President Lincoln issued the Proclamation of Amnesty and Reconstruction at the end of the Civil War.

_____ 5. Most people in the North supported giving African Americans in the South the right to vote.

PRACTICING SKILLS (5 points each) Study the graph below and answer the questions that follow.

1. Which side suffered the greatest number of deaths in the Civil War?

   _____

2. Of the total number of lives lost by both sides, were more due to battle causes or to non-battle causes?

   _____

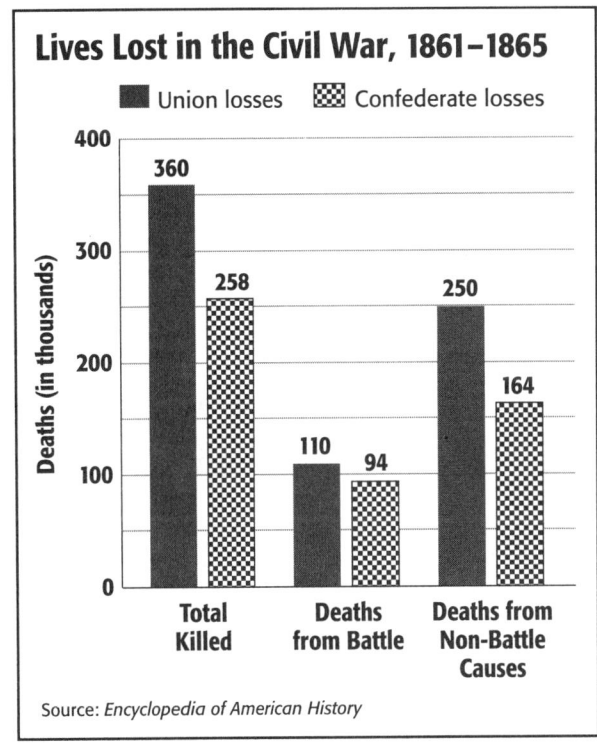

COMPOSING AN ESSAY (20 points) Write a brief essay on *one* of the following subjects. Remember to use examples to support your answer.

1. Explain why the South was so adamant about any attempts to end slavery.
2. What was the purpose of the Black Codes? Compare the reaction to the codes of white southerners, many northerners, and African Americans.

War and Reunification

UNIT TEST • FORM B

■ **SHORT ANSWER** *(10 points each)* Provide brief answers for each of the following. Remember to use examples to support your answer.

1. How did many abolitionists feel about the declaration of war on Mexico?
2. What was John Brown's motive in his raid at Harpers Ferry, Virginia?
3. Why did southern secessionists feel they were justified in withdrawing from the Union?
4. What kinds of things did women do during the Civil War?
5. What did the Ku Klux Klan want, and what were their methods?

■ **PRIMARY SOURCE** *(10 points each)* During Mexico's war with the United States, José Fernando Ramírez wrote several letters that examined changes in Mexican life and politics brought on by the war. The following is an excerpt from one of these letters. In it he describes the difficulties the Mexicans had fighting the better-funded and better-equipped U.S. forces. Read the excerpt and answer the questions that follow.

> *What happens then when a nation cannot count either upon a large army or upon patriotism? . . . [T]his is precisely the wretched condition we are in. Strictly speaking the army does not exist. What today bears that name is only a mass of men without training and without weapons. . . . The government has at last put all its hopes in a plan that is supposed to save the country. . . . This is one calling for guerrilla warfare, the last hope of peoples overwhelmed by superior forces. . . .*

1. What must the Mexicans turn to in order to have any chance against the Americans?
2. What two things, according to Ramírez, do the Mexicans lack?

■ **COMPOSING AN ESSAY** *(30 points)* Write a brief essay on *one* of the following subjects. Remember to use examples to support your answer.

1. What happened to American Indians in California during the Gold Rush?
2. Explain how the Kansas-Nebraska Act showed popular sovereignty at work.
3. Explain and give examples of Sherman's total-war strategy.
4. What was the South's economy like after the Civil War, and how did Reconstruction change it?

Name _____ Class _____ Date _____

The Western Crossroads

CHAPTER TEST • FORM A

REVIEWING FACTS *(3 points each)* In the space provided, write the name of the person or the historical term identified by each description. Choose your answers from the list below. There are two extra names or terms on the list.

Homestead Act	Sitting Bull	Pacific Railway Act
Dawes General Allotment Act	Sand Creek Massacre	Chief Joseph
Wovoka	Geronimo	Battle of the Little Bighorn
Klondike Gold Rush	Treaty of Medicine Lodge	Comstock Lode

_____ 1. one of the world's richest silver veins

_____ 2. when John M. Chivington and 700 volunteers murdered approximately 200 American Indians camping in Colorado Territory

_____ 3. allowed "any citizen or intended citizen to select any surveyed land up to 160 acres and to gain title to it" after living on the land and farming it for five years

_____ 4. a fight between an army of Sioux and other American Indian groups led by Sitting Bull and the U.S. Army's 7th Cavalry led by General George Armstrong Custer

_____ 5. led the last battle against the U.S. Army in resistance to the reservation system in the Far West

_____ 6. began when prospectors discovered precious metals in Alaska in 1896, and thousands of potential miners hurried there to make their fortunes

_____ 7. an agreement between the U.S. government and the southern Plains Indians whereby the Indians agreed to relinquish much of their land in exchange for a reservation in Indian Territory

_____ 8. divided former American Indian land and allotted 160-acre plots to American Indian families for farming; the remaining land could be sold to white settlers and developers

_____ 9. leader of the Nez Percé

_____ 10. a Paiute who began a religious movement known as the Ghost Dance

Chapter and Unit Tests   Chapter 14 **69**

Chapter 14, Test Form A, Continued

UNDERSTANDING IDEAS (3 points each) For each of the following, place the letter of the best choice in the space provided.

_____ 1. Basques, originally from Spain, immigrated to the United States to
   a. drive cattle from Texas to market towns.
   b. help build the railroads crisscrossing the West.
   c. herd sheep, especially in California.
   d. dig canals.

_____ 2. Author Willa Cather wrote
   a. about life in the mining camps.
   b. about discrimination experienced by African Americans.
   c. exposés about the meatpacking industry.
   d. novels about ordinary people on the Great Plains.

_____ 3. Thousands of people raced to _____, having heard of gold discoveries there.
   a. Deadwood
   b. Abilene
   c. Pikes Peak
   d. Tucson

_____ 4. Which mining technique used water to expose minerals beneath the earth?
   a. patio mining
   b. hard-rock mining
   c. strip mining
   d. hydraulic mining

_____ 5. Exodusters
   a. left the Great Plains area after the Dust Bowl storms.
   b. believed that American Indians should become assimilated into "white America."
   c. were miners who panned for gold dust in the Klondike.
   d. were African Americans fleeing violence in the South.

_____ 6. The _____ required states to build agricultural and engineering colleges.
   a. Morrill Act
   b. Homestead Act
   c. College and University Act
   d. Education Act

_____ 7. A Paiute Indian reformer, Sarah Winnemucca,
   a. urged American Indians to move to reservations.
   b. asked President Rutherford B. Hayes to allow the Paiute to return to their homelands.
   c. began the Carlisle Indian School in Pennsylvania.
   d. refused to move to a reservation.

_____ 8. In 1867, U.S. Secretary of State _____ negotiated with Russia to buy Alaska for the United States.
   a. Rutherford B. Hayes
   b. William H. Seward
   c. Richard Pratt
   d. Hamlin Garland

_____ 9. In 1864 the U.S. Army led the _____ nation on the Long Walk.
   a. Navajo
   b. Paiute
   c. Sioux
   d. Yakima

_____ 10. Which of the following people invented barbed wire?
   a. William Seward
   b. Benjamin Singleton
   c. Joseph Glidden
   d. Frederic Remington

Chapter 14, Test Form A, Continued

■ TRUE/FALSE *(2 points each)* Read each of the following statements and then decide whether it is true or false. If the answer is true, place a *T* in the space provided; if the answer is false, place an *F* in the space.

_____ 1. Because of their large staffs and division of labor into specialized tasks, bonanza farms were better able to handle boom-and-bust cycles of crop prices and unpredictable weather.

_____ 2. Texas longhorn cattle were famous for the flavor and tenderness of their beef.

_____ 3. Mining changed from an individual enterprise to a corporate endeavor.

_____ 4. The Ghost Dance combined elements of Christianity with aspects of American Indian religions.

_____ 5. The U.S. government honored most, if not all, of the treaties it made with American Indians.

■ PRACTICING SKILLS *(5 points each)* Study the graph below and answer the questions that follow.

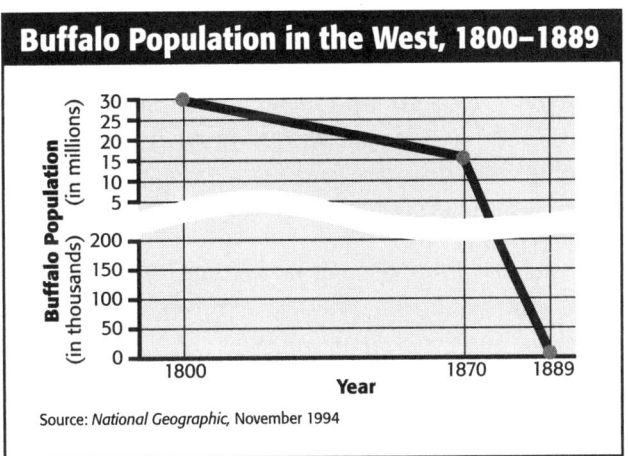

1. About how large was the buffalo population in 1800?

_____

2. How much did the buffalo population decline between 1870 and 1889?

_____

■ COMPOSING AN ESSAY *(20 points)* Write a brief essay on *one* of the following subjects. Remember to use examples to support your answer.

1. Describe life in the mining camps and how it changed.
2. How were the requirements for farming on the Great Plains different than traditional farming back East?

Name _____ Class _____ Date _____

The Western Crossroads

CHAPTER TEST • FORM B

■ **SHORT ANSWER** *(10 points each)* Provide brief answers for each of the following. Remember to use examples to support your answer.

1. Describe the relationship between railroad companies and prospective homesteaders.
2. Why were sod houses built on the Plains? What were the advantages and disadvantages of using this material?
3. What were the differences in treatment of African American, Mexican, and white cowboys?
4. What caused the end of the cattle boom?
5. How did unions help miners deal with large mining companies?

■ **PRIMARY SOURCE** *(10 points each)* By the end of the nineteenth century, a number of writers recognized the great beauty of the American West. An artist and writer who lived in California, Mary Hallock Foote, described the western landscape in her 1894 short story, "A Cloud on the Mountain."

Ruth Mary . . . paused often in her work and looked towards the high pastures with the pale brown lights and purple shadows on them, rolling away and rising towards the great timbered ridges, and these lifting here and there along their profiles a treeless peak or bare divide into the regions above vegetation.

She had no misgivings about her home. Fences would not have improved her father's vast lawn, to her mind, or white paint the low-browed front of his dwelling; nor did she feel the want of a stair-carpet and a parlor-organ. She was sure that they, the strangers, had never seen anything more lovely than her beloved river dancing down between the hills, tripping over rapids, wrinkling over sand-bars of its own spreading, and letting out its speed down the long reaches where the channel was deep.

1. After reading this passage, what can you presume about homes not located in the West?
2. How do you think the author felt about the area in which she lived?

■ **COMPOSING AN ESSAY** *(30 points)* Write a brief essay on *one* of the following subjects. Remember to use examples to support your answer.

1. What did the U.S. government gain by its treaties with American Indian tribes and what did those tribes hope to gain? Did the American Indians' hopes materialize? Explain.
2. What did different kinds of settlers hope to find in the West and what problems did they face?

Name _____ Class _____ Date _____

The Second Industrial Revolution

CHAPTER TEST • FORM A

REVIEWING FACTS *(3 points each)* In the space provided, write the name of the person or the historical term identified by each description. Choose your answers from the list below. There are two extra names or terms on the list.

Edwin L. Drake
social Darwinism
horizontal integration
Elijah McCoy
Knights of Labor
vertical integration
Eugene V. Debs
Bessemer process
American Federation of Labor
patent
Cornelius Vanderbilt
trust

_____ 1. a method of steelmaking that burned off impurities in molten iron with a blast of hot air

_____ 2. a guarantee to protect an inventor's rights to make, use, or sell his or her invention

_____ 3. the son of runaway slaves who made a major contribution to the industrial use of oil by inventing a lubricating cup that fed oil to parts of a machine while it was running

_____ 4. the theory that the "fittest" people, businesses, or nations would succeed, while the "unfit" would fail

_____ 5. a group of companies that turn control of their stock over to a common board, which then runs the companies as a single corporation

_____ 6. a method of reducing production costs by acquiring companies that provide the services and materials upon which an enterprise depends

_____ 7. an early pioneer in the railroad industry who extended his railroad system by purchasing smaller lines and combining them to make direct routes between urban centers

_____ 8. a means of business expansion in which one company controls other companies producing the same product

_____ 9. one of the earliest national unions; formed by a group of garment workers

_____ 10. head of the American Railway Union who supported the Pullman strikers by urging other union workers to boycott trains with Pullman cars

Chapter 15, Test Form A, Continued

UNDERSTANDING IDEAS (3 points each) For each of the following, place the letter of the best choice in the space provided.

_____ 1. In the late 1800s, a second period of industrial growth was spurred by
   a. the invention of the airplane.
   b. the creation of department stores.
   c. developments in processing steel and oil.
   d. the growth of labor unions.

_____ 2. The development of the horseless carriage was spurred by
   a. Thomas Edison's experiments in electricity.
   b. technology developed by the Wright brothers.
   c. the rise of corporations.
   d. innovations in oil refining.

_____ 3. The spread of the telephone required _____, thus providing new jobs for many women.
   a. engineers
   b. operators
   c. line repair workers
   d. insurance

_____ 4. Thomas Edison went into the "invention business" by
   a. proposing that the U.S. Congress grant patents.
   b. opening up a hardware store.
   c. opening a laboratory and doing research.
   d. teaching a course in electricity at a local college.

_____ 5. In a _____, organizers raise money by selling partial ownership of a company to stockholders, who then receive a percentage of the company's profits.
   a. communist state
   b. labor union
   c. corporation
   d. department store

_____ 6. A trust may become a monopoly if it
   a. gains exclusive control of an industry.
   b. reduces the cost of production.
   c. develops company towns.
   d. pays dividends to stockholders.

_____ 7. Some wealthy industrialists, such as Andrew Carnegie, believed that the rich had a responsibility to
   a. give away money on the street.
   b. give their wealth to society before their death.
   c. reinvest their money.
   d. employ many African Americans.

_____ 8. A year of labor unrest was known as
   a. the Haymarket Riot.
   b. the Great Upheaval.
   c. the Gospel of Wealth.
   d. the Trail of Tears.

_____ 9. The Sherman Antitrust Act outlawed
   a. all labor unions.
   b. all monopolies and trusts.
   c. the hiring of foreign workers.
   d. child labor.

_____ 10. Mary Harris Jones ("Mother Jones") was called "the most dangerous woman in America" by some opponents because
   a. her methods were violent.
   b. she encouraged workers to file lawsuits.
   c. her drive to educate and organize workers was so effective.
   d. she led a raid on a garment shop in Philadelphia.

Chapter 15, Test Form A, Continued

■ TRUE/FALSE *(2 points each)* Read each of the following statements and then decide whether it is true or false. If the answer is true, place a *T* in the space provided; if the answer is false, place an *F* in the space.

_____ 1. Poor working conditions in the new industries that emerged after the Civil War led many American workers to organize unions to improve their daily lives.

_____ 2. The steel industry depended on the mining of copper as a raw material out of which steel was processed.

_____ 3. John D. Rockefeller used vertical and horizontal integration to sell his oil for a cheaper price than his competitors.

_____ 4. In the late 1800s, the government's policies concerning business practices usually favored the industrialists, not the workers.

_____ 5. Most women and children in the labor force were allowed to work at slightly higher wages than adult white males.

■ PRACTICING SKILLS *(5 points each)* Study the map below and answer the questions that follow.

1. In which region of the United States was most industry and manufacturing concentrated in the late 1800s? Place a check in the space provided next to the correct answer.

   _____ the Great Lakes and Northeast

   _____ the Southeast

   _____ the Southwest

   _____ the Northwest

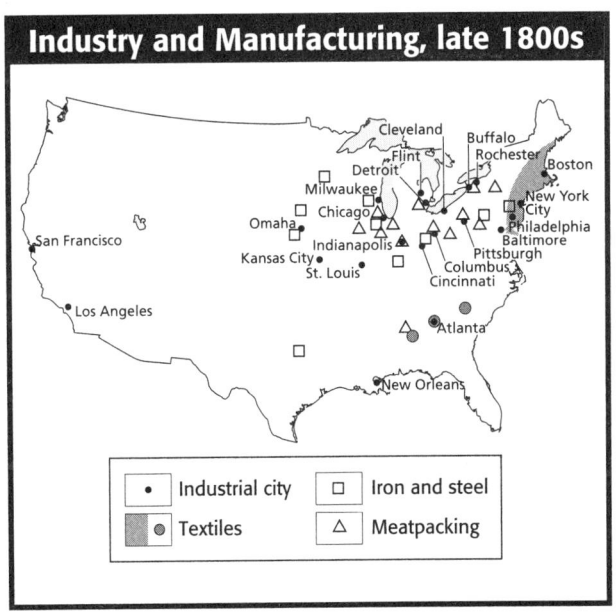

2. Which of the regions listed in the question above seems to have had the least amount of industry and manufacturing?

   _____

■ COMPOSING AN ESSAY *(20 points)* Write a brief essay on *one* of the following subjects. Remember to use examples to support your answer.

1. Discuss some of the ways in which the development and manufacturing of steel helped spur industrialization in the late 1800s.

2. Describe how Andrew Carnegie used vertical integration to control costs in his steel mills.

The Second Industrial Revolution

CHAPTER TEST • FORM B

■ **SHORT ANSWER** *(10 points each)* Provide brief answers for each of the following. Remember to use examples to support your answer.

1. Name five developments or innovations in the American rail system in the late 1800s that improved rail service.
2. In a capitalist economic system, according to Karl Marx, what is the basic difference between the bourgeoisie and the proletariat?
3. Why did George M. Pullman build a company town next to his factory?
4. What effect did the U.S. government's placing high tariffs on foreign imports have on American businesses?
5. Workers who lived in company towns were usually paid in the form of scrip. How did this affect their ability to make purchases?

■ **PRIMARY SOURCE** *(10 points each)* In 1871 visiting Austrian diplomat Joseph Alexander, Graf von Hübner, was impressed by the many opportunities Americans enjoyed in an industrialized society. He was also struck, however, by the fierce competition of American business and by the toll it took on working people. Read the excerpt from his account and answer the questions that follow.

> *In the New World man is born to conquer. Life is a perpetual struggle, . . . a race in the open field across terrible obstacles, with the prospect of enormous rewards for reaching the goal. The American cannot keep his arms folded. He must embark on something, and once embarked he must go on and on forever; for if he stops, those who follow him would crush him under their feet. His life is one long campaign, a succession of never-ending fights, marches, and countermarches.*
>
> *In such a militant existence, what place is left for the sweetness, the repose, the intimacy of home or its joys? Is he happy? Judging by his tired, sad, exhausted, anxious, and often delicate and unhealthy appearance, one would be inclined to doubt it. Such an excess of uninterrupted labor cannot be good for any man.*

1. According to von Hübner, what do workers experience far too little of?
2. Why does von Hübner say that so much work cannot be good for anyone?

■ **COMPOSING AN ESSAY** *(30 points)* Write a brief essay on *one* of the following subjects. Remember to use examples to support your answer.

1. Compare the government's role in business in capitalism and communism.
2. How did the growth of railroads stimulate the growth of other industries?

Name _____ Class _____ Date _____

The Transformation of American Society

CHAPTER TEST • FORM A

REVIEWING FACTS *(3 points each)* In the space provided, write the name of the person or the historical term identified by each description. Choose your answers from the list below. There are two extra names or terms on the list.

settlement houses   Elisha Otis   vaudeville
steerage   mass transit   Caroline Bartlett
Social Gospel   suburbs   Denis Kearney
ragtime   Jane Addams   conspicuous consumption

_____ 1. the poorest accommodations on ships carrying immigrants to the United States; located below deck on the ship's lower level

_____ 2. Irish immigrant and leader of the Workingmen's Party, which encouraged anti-Chinese sentiments in California during the 1870s

_____ 3. inventor of the elevator

_____ 4. public transportation, including subways, electric commuter trains, and trolleys

_____ 5. residential neighborhoods and towns on the outskirts of cities

_____ 6. the free and public spending of great wealth in order to impress others

_____ 7. community service centers that offered education, skills training, and cultural events to people living in poor neighborhoods

_____ 8. a type of variety show that featured a wide assortment of short performances

_____ 9. social reformer who helped found settlement houses and promoted women's suffrage

_____ 10. a type of music created by African American musicians, performed primarily on the piano

Chapter and Unit Tests   Chapter 16   77

Chapter 16, Test Form A, Continued

UNDERSTANDING IDEAS *(3 points each)* For each of the following, place the letter of the *best* choice in the space provided.

_____ 1. Charitable aid organizations that helped immigrants cope with problems were known as
   a. settlement houses.
   b. benevolent societies.
   c. Victorians.
   d. insurance companies.

_____ 2. The Immigration Restriction League tried unsuccessfully to impose _____ on all immigrants.
   a. a sobriety test
   b. a tariff
   c. conspicuous consumption
   d. a literacy test

_____ 3. Mass transit changed urban life by
   a. narrowing streets.
   b. encouraging the growth of cities and helping create suburbs.
   c. providing a way of getting to baseball games.
   d. encouraging the development of escalators.

_____ 4. In the late 1800s, accountants, clerks, engineers, managers, and salespeople became part of
   a. the labor movement.
   b. the upper class.
   c. benevolent societies.
   d. the growing middle class.

_____ 5. Much of the literature read by the nouveau riche in the late 1800s reflected the social standards of
   a. British Victorian culture.
   b. the American poor.
   c. the French elite.
   d. the middle class.

_____ 6. For poor, working-class Americans, city life
   a. was made worse by low pay, housing shortages, and high rent.
   b. held great appeal thanks to the advent of professional baseball.
   c. led to wealth.
   d. was an improvement over rural life.

_____ 7. The primary goal of the Social Gospel movement was
   a. to convert Jewish immigrants to Christianity.
   b. to provide jobs for women.
   c. to develop more priests.
   d. to apply Christian principles to social problems.

_____ 8. The primary objective of compulsory education laws was to
   a. create teaching jobs for women of the middle class.
   b. require parents to send their children to school.
   c. provide training for doctors.
   d. train children to operate industrial equipment.

_____ 9. The term *yellow journalism* refers to
   a. newspapers that featured color photography.
   b. a style of reporting that was sensationalistic.
   c. anti-Asian news reports.
   d. the color of the covers on many popular magazines.

_____ 10. _____ was one of the few sports played during the Victorian era in which women's participation was encouraged.
   a. Soccer
   b. Softball
   c. Basketball
   d. Baseball

Chapter 16, Test Form A, Continued

■ TRUE/FALSE (2 points each)
Read each of the following statements and then decide whether it is true or false. If the answer is true, place a *T* in the space provided; if the answer is false, place an *F* in the space.

_____ 1. Any immigrants passing through Ellis Island who were found to have contagious diseases or other serious health problems, like tuberculosis, were deported.

_____ 2. Improvements in technology led to people migrating out of the cities and onto farms.

_____ 3. Magazines like *Godey's Lady's Book* and *The Ladies' Home Journal* encouraged American women to leave their role as homemaker and strive to succeed in the business world.

_____ 4. In the late 1800s, the plight of poor city-dwellers was greatly relieved by government assistance programs.

_____ 5. Despite the attempts by educational reformers to improve the quality of education and to instruct students in proper behavior and American cultural values, children of different cultures in most public schools of the late 1800s remained segregated by race.

■ PRACTICING SKILLS (5 points each)
Study the chart below and answer the questions that follow.

1. What was the largest immigrant group in the period 1840–1860?

   _____

   _____

2. Which immigrant group experienced the greatest decrease between 1840–1860 and 1880–1900?

   _____

   _____

Shifting Patterns of Immigration

Where Immigrants Came From, 1840–1860: Northern and western Europe 93%, 1%, 3%, 1%, 2%

Where Immigrants Came From, 1880–1900: 61%, 31%, 6%, 1.5%, .5%

Place of origin: Northern and western Europe; Eastern and southern Europe; North and South America; Asia; All other areas

Source: *Historical Statistics of the United States*

■ COMPOSING AN ESSAY (20 points)
Write a brief essay on *one* of the following subjects. Remember to use examples to support your answer.

1. Describe the nativist response to new immigration. What were some of their reasons for this response?

2. Explain how rapid urban growth, the rise of big business, and new industries and technologies affected women.

Name _____ Class _____ Date _____

CHAPTER 16: The Transformation of American Society

CHAPTER TEST • FORM B

■ SHORT ANSWER *(10 points each)* Provide brief answers for each of the following. Remember to use examples to support your answer.

1. What were some of the reasons that immigrants came to the United States?
2. What were some of the differences between the *old immigrants*—the wave that came to the United States from 1800–1880—and the *new immigrants*, who arrived between 1891 and 1910?
3. How did the Chinese Exclusion Act, passed in 1882, affect Chinese immigration to the United States?
4. What improvements in technology helped further the development of skyscrapers?
5. What were some of the ways in which city-dwellers sought leisure as a relief from their hard work, crowded living conditions, and other daily struggles?

■ PRIMARY SOURCE *(10 points each)* In her memoir, *Twenty Years at Hull-House*, Jane Addams describes the vision and goals behind the settlement house she had founded. Read the excerpt from her memoir and answer the questions that follow.

> *The Settlement casts aside none of those things which cultivated men have come to consider reasonable and goodly, but it insists that those belong as well to that great body of people who, because of toilsome and underpaid labor, are unable to procure [aquire] them for themselves.*

1. What are the words that Addams uses to describe the cultural opportunities she wants poorer people to be able to take advantage of?
2. Why do people who have less money have a difficult time taking advantage of cultural opportunities?

■ COMPOSING AN ESSAY *(30 points)* Write a brief essay on *one* of the following subjects. Remember to use examples to support your answer.

1. Describe the social values that were expressed by the new class of wealthy city-dwellers known as the nouveau riche.
2. Compare the goals and methods of settlement houses with those of the Social Gospel. Include examples of the types of programs and services offered by each.

Name _____ Class _____ Date _____

CHAPTER 17: Politics in the Gilded Age

CHAPTER TEST • FORM A

REVIEWING FACTS *(3 points each)* In the space provided, write the name of the person or the historical term identified by each description. Choose your answers from the list below. There are two extra names or terms on the list.

Gilded Age
Charles Guiteau
graft
mugwumps
Mary Elizabeth Lease
Half-Breeds
political machines
Stalwarts
William Marcy Tweed
graduated income tax
cooperatives
James Pendergast

_____ 1. Kansas City political boss who gained political support by providing special services to his African American, Irish American, and Italian American constituents

_____ 2. the acquisition of money or political power through illegal or dishonest practices

_____ 3. from a novel by Mark Twain and Charles Dudley Warner; a description of American society in the late 1800s that is based on the image of corruption and greed lurking beneath superficial politeness and prosperity

_____ 4. a faction of the Republican Party that strongly opposed reforming patronage, or the spoils system

_____ 5. a faction of the Republican Party that, although it did not completely oppose patronage jobs, generally supported reform

_____ 6. assassinated President James A. Garfield less than four months after Garfield's inauguration, hoping that killing Garfield would hurt the cause of civil service reform

_____ 7. Algonquian word for "big chiefs"; Republican reformers who backed the Democratic candidate for president, Grover Cleveland

_____ 8. organizations in which groups of farmers pooled their resources to buy and sell goods

_____ 9. a tax that taxed higher incomes at a higher rate

_____ 10. spread the cause of the Alliance movement among farmers by speaking out against monopolies

Chapter 17, Test Form A, Continued

UNDERSTANDING IDEAS *(3 points each)* For each of the following, place the letter of the best choice in the space provided.

_____ 1. The rapid growth of cities in the late 1800s placed huge demands on utilities and public services, leading
   a. cities to raise utility rates.
   b. local politicians and ward bosses to be placed in charge of running their city governments.
   c. volunteers in charge of providing public services.
   d. to an end to public services.

_____ 2. The real strength of political machines lay in the relationship between urban voters and
   a. their elected representatives.
   b. prominent newspaper publishers.
   c. precinct captains.
   d. voters in rural areas.

_____ 3. Which of the following is *NOT* an example of the types of corruption used by political bosses?
   a. "voting early and often"
   b. kickbacks
   c. providing voters with transportation to the polls
   d. bribes

_____ 4. Republican leaders felt that Ulysses S. Grant would be a good presidential candidate because
   a. he had an understanding of government.
   b. he was wealthy.
   c. his fame as a Civil War general made him a popular candidate.
   d. he was a lawyer.

_____ 5. Many critics viewed the corruption in President Grant's administration as a result of
   a. the spoils system.
   b. the Pendleton Civil Service Act.
   c. an angry Congress.
   d. the Populist movement.

_____ 6. In the 1888 presidential race, Grover Cleveland won the popular vote, but Benjamin Harrison became president because
   a. Cleveland cheated.
   b. Harrison's supporters bribed election officials.
   c. Harrison won the electoral vote.
   d. Cleveland resigned.

_____ 7. To lower their costs, some farmers
   a. moved to Canada to find work.
   b. became tenant farmers.
   c. pressed Congress for reforms.
   d. organized cooperatives.

_____ 8. As the urban population grew farmers responded by
   a. raising more crops and animals.
   b. moving to the cities to work.
   c. hoarding livestock and cutting back on growing crops.
   d. exporting their products overseas to increase demand.

_____ 9. Of the following organizations, which was *NOT* formed for the purpose of helping farmers?
   a. the National Grange
   b. the National Farming Cooperative
   c. the Colored Farmers' Alliance
   d. the Southern Alliance

_____ 10. Which of the following would a member of the Populist Party reject?
   a. a longer workday
   b. restrictions on immigration
   c. voting reforms
   d. government ownership of the railroads

Chapter 17, Test Form A, Continued

■ TRUE/FALSE (2 points each) Read each of the following statements and then decide whether it is true or false. If the answer is true, place a *T* in the space provided; if the answer is false, place an *F* in the space.

_____ 1. Because English was their primary language, Irish Americans had slightly easier access to American political processes than did many other immigrant groups.

_____ 2. A congressional investigation into the Black Friday scandal revealed that President Grant had led a scheme to influence government spending.

_____ 3. The Civil Service Commission established the policies for examining and hiring based on merit rather than political patronage.

_____ 4. In the late 1800s, increases in crops grown in the United States and abroad raised the market price of fruit, vegetables, and other farm products.

_____ 5. The Interstate Commerce Act prohibited railroads from giving special rates, rebates, or refunds to shippers or charging more for short hauls than for long hauls over the same line.

■ PRACTICING SKILLS (5 points each) Study the chart below and answer the questions that follow. Remember to use examples to support your answer.

1. Compare the number of farms and the total farmland that existed between 1900 ("Then") and today ("Now"). Which of the following statements is true? Circle the letter that matches your response.
   a. There are more farms on more land today.
   b. There are more farms on less land today.
   c. There are fewer farms on more land today.
   d. There are fewer farms on less land today.

2. If the trend shown in the illustrations continues, will there be more or fewer farms 100 years from now?

   _____

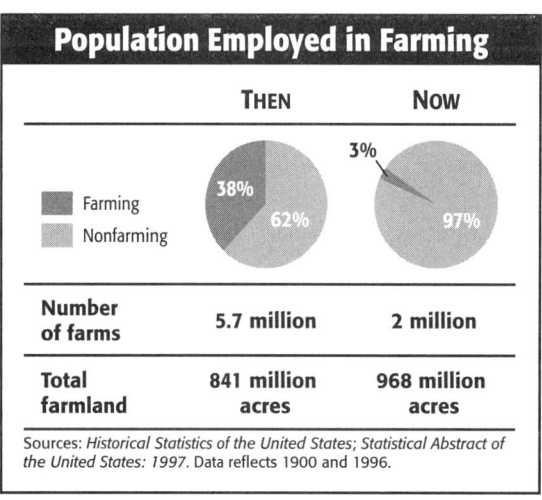

■ COMPOSING AN ESSAY (20 points) Write a brief essay on *one* of the following subjects. Remember to use examples to support your answer.

1. Describe the methods New York City's powerful Democratic political machine, known as Tammany Hall, used to win the support of new immigrants. Did Tammany Hall use its power to improve these people's lives?

2. Compare the goals of the National Grange with those of the Farmers' Alliance. In what ways were they similar? In what ways were they different?

Name _____ Class _____ Date _____

CHAPTER 17: Politics in the Gilded Age

CHAPTER TEST • FORM B

■ SHORT ANSWER (10 points each) Provide brief answers for each of the following. Remember to use examples to support your answer.

1. Why were well-organized political parties called political machines in the late 1800s?
2. How did Thomas Nast help bring about the downfall of corrupt political boss William Marcy Tweed?
3. Following President James A. Garfield's assassination, how did President Chester A. Arthur alter his stand on civil service reform?
4. When Benjamin Harrison became president, how did he deal with the reform efforts of Grover Cleveland?
5. What was the purpose of the so-called Granger laws passed during the 1870s in Iowa, Wisconsin, Illinois, and Minnesota?

■ PRIMARY SOURCE (10 points each) Despite the efforts of many journalists and political reformers to expose and put an end to corrupt machine politics, some bosses went to great lengths to defend their practices and personal financial gain. One of these was George Washington Plunkitt, who defended his practices as examples of "honest graft." Read the following excerpt by Plunkitt and answer the questions below.

> There's an honest graft, and I'm an example of how it works. My party's in power in the city, and it's goin' to undertake a lot of public improvements. Well, I'm tipped off, say, that they're going to lay out a new park at a certain place. . . . I go to that place and I buy up all the land I can in the neighborhood. Then the board of this or that makes its plan public, and there is a rush to get my land. . . . Ain't it perfectly honest to charge a good price and make a profit on my investment and foresight? . . . Well, that's honest graft.

1. What advantage does Plunkitt have over other citizens who might want to buy land in the area of a new park?
2. How do we know that he plans to sell the land at a far higher price than he bought it for?

■ COMPOSING AN ESSAY (30 points) Write a brief essay on *one* of the following subjects. Remember to use examples to support your answer.

1. What issues did President Grant's critics raise as a result of the increasing scandals that came to light during his administration? How did these scandals affect the way the public felt about politics?
2. What issues in the Populist Party's platform might have frightened business leaders into contributing millions of dollars to the campaign of Republican William McKinley, who subsequently defeated the populist Democrat, William Jennings Bryan?

Name _____ Class _____ Date _____

UNIT 5: A Nation Transformed

UNIT TEST • FORM A

REVIEWING FACTS *(3 points each)* In the space provided, write the name of the person or the historical term identified by each description. Choose your answers from the list below. There are two extra names or terms on the list.

Chief Joseph   horizontal integration   patent
vertical integration   graft   Geronimo
settlement houses   Jane Addams   conspicuous consumption
cooperatives   social Darwinism   trust

_____ 1. he eluded capture by the U.S. Army, which hoped to place him on a reservation

_____ 2. Nez Percé leader who said, "From where the sun now stands, I will fight no more forever"

_____ 3. protected an inventor's rights to make, use, or sell his or her invention

_____ 4. the theory that the "fittest" people, businesses, or nations would succeed, while the "unfit" would fail

_____ 5. a way to reduce production costs by owning businesses that provide the services and materials upon which an enterprise depends

_____ 6. the lavish spending of money to impress others

_____ 7. community centers that offered education, skills training, and cultural events

_____ 8. established Hull House and fought for women's rights

_____ 9. illegal or dishonest way of gaining money or political power

_____ 10. a way for farmers to work together to cut costs and increase profits

Unit 5, Test Form A, Continued

UNDERSTANDING IDEAS (3 points each) For each of the following, place the letter of the best choice in the space provided.

_____ 1. Paiute Indian reformer Sarah Winnemucca
  a. considered armed attacks on the United States Congress.
  b. asked President Rutherford B. Hayes to allow the Paiute to return to their homelands.
  c. demanded money from the United States government.
  d. urged American Indians to move to reservations.

_____ 2. In 1867 U.S. Secretary of State William H. Seward negotiated with Russia to buy
  a. the Klondike.
  b. Alaska.
  c. the Yukon.
  d. Canada's west coast.

_____ 3. In 1864 the U.S. Army led the Navajo nation on the Long Walk to _____, a reservation in New Mexico.
  a. Bosque Redondo
  b. Wounded Knee
  c. San Carlos
  d. Yakima

_____ 4. The invention of the telephone created new _____ for women.
  a. responsibilities
  b. jobs
  c. problems
  d. roles

_____ 5. A monopoly is when one company
  a. gains exclusive control of an industry.
  b. reduces production costs.
  c. develops company towns.
  d. pays dividends to stockholders.

_____ 6. The Sherman Anti-Trust Act outlawed
  a. sobriety testing.
  b. all labor unions.
  c. all monopolies and trusts.
  d. child labor.

_____ 7. Most poor, working-class Americans
  a. became middle class.
  b. moved to the country.
  c. usually gave up trying to "get ahead."
  d. usually remained poor.

_____ 8. The term *yellow journalism* refers to
  a. a style of reporting that was sensationalistic.
  b. reports about Asians.
  c. a style of reporting that tried not to offend anyone.
  d. focusing on news that people like hearing.

_____ 9. Which of the following was NOT used by political bosses to gain power and wealth?
  a. providing jobs in return for votes
  b. demanding kickbacks
  c. refusing to associate with politicians
  d. contracting with city governments

_____ 10. Populists would fight for all of the following EXCEPT
  a. a longer workday.
  b. restrictions on immigration.
  c. voting reforms.
  d. government ownership of the railroads.

Unit 5, Test Form A, Continued

■ TRUE/FALSE *(2 points each)* Read each of the following statements, and then decide whether it is true or false. If the answer is true, place a *T* in the space provided; if the answer is false, place an *F* in the space.

_____ 1. The U.S. government violated most treaties it signed with American Indians.

_____ 2. Unionizing was a way for American laborers to fight for better working conditions.

_____ 3. As industrialization increased, most upper- and middle-class American women chose to leave their role as homemaker and enter the business world.

_____ 4. The Civil Service Commission established the policies for examining and hiring based on merit rather than political patronage.

_____ 5. Most farmers protested the Interstate Commerce Act.

■ PRACTICING SKILLS *(5 points each)* Study the map below and answer the questions that follow.

1. In which region of the United States was most industry and manufacturing concentrated in the late 1800s? Place a check in the space provided next to the correct answer.

   _____ in the Northeast

   _____ in the Southwest

   _____ in the Northwest

   _____ in the Southeast

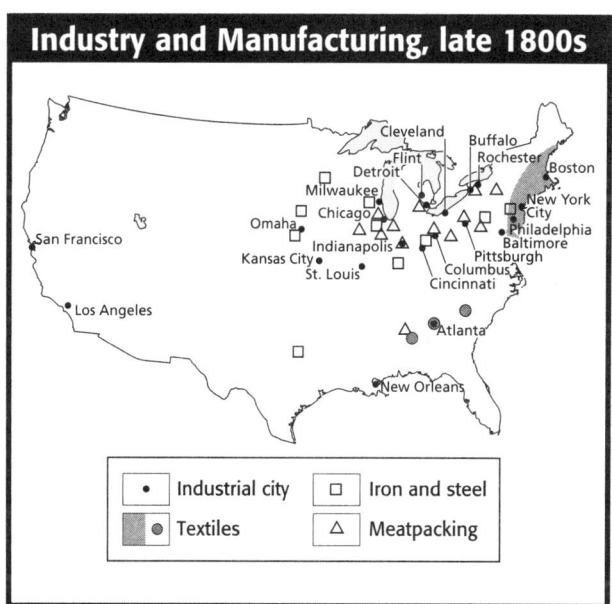

2. Which of the regions listed in the question above seems to have had the least amount of industry and manufacturing?

   _____

■ COMPOSING AN ESSAY *(20 points)* Write a brief essay on *one* of the following subjects. Remember to use examples to support your answer.

1. Describe life in the mining camps and how it changed.
2. Describe the methods New York City's powerful Democratic political machine, known as Tammany Hall, used to win the support of new immigrants. Did Tammany Hall use its power to improve these people's lives?

Name _____ Class _____ Date _____

UNIT 5: A Nation Transformed

UNIT TEST • FORM B

■ **SHORT ANSWER** *(10 points each)* Provide brief answers for each of the following. Remember to use examples to support your answer.

1. Describe how railroad companies helped prospective homesteaders.
2. What effect did the U.S. government's placing high tariffs on foreign imports have on American businesses?
3. Workers who lived in company towns were usually paid in the form of scrip. How did this affect them economically?
4. What allowed architects to build skyscrapers?
5. Why did political machines stay in power so successfully?

■ **PRIMARY SOURCE** *(10 points each)* By the end of the nineteenth century, a number of writers recognized the great beauty of the American West. An artist and writer who lived in California, Mary Hallock Foote, described the western landscape in her 1894 short story, "A Cloud on the Mountain."

> *Ruth Mary . . . paused often in her work and looked towards the high pastures with the pale brown lights and purple shadows on them, rolling away and rising towards the great timbered ridges, and these lifting here and there along their profiles a treeless peak or bare divide into the regions above vegetation.*
>
> *She had no misgivings about her home. Fences would not have improved her father's vast lawn, to her mind, or white paint the low-browed front of his dwelling; nor did she feel the want of a stair-carpet and a parlor-organ. She was sure that they, the strangers, had never seen anything more lovely than her beloved river dancing down between the hills, tripping over rapids, wrinkling over sand-bars of its own spreading, and letting out its speed down the long reaches where the channel was deep.*

1. After reading this passage, what can you presume about homes not located in the West?
2. How do you think the author felt about the area in which she lived?

■ **COMPOSING AN ESSAY** *(30 points)* Write a brief essay on *one* of the following subjects. Remember to use examples to support your answer.

1. Why did the U.S. government sign its treaties with American Indian tribes? Did the Indians get what they wanted?
2. What were the different kinds of settlers in the West and what problems did they face?
3. Compare the arguments that the theories of laissez-faire capitalism and communism made about the role of government in business.
4. Describe the lifestyles of the new class of wealthy city-dwellers known as the nouveau riche.

Name _____ Class _____ Date _____

The Age of Reform

CHAPTER TEST • FORM A

■ **REVIEWING FACTS** *(3 points each)* In the space provided, write the name of the person or the historical term identified by each description. Choose your answers from the list below. There are two extra names or terms on the list.

National Association of Colored Women
populism
progressivism
John Dewey
muckrakers
Ida Tarbell
Triangle Shirtwaist Fire
National Association for the Advancement of Colored People
Eighteenth Amendment
W. E. B. Du Bois
Daniel Burnham
Samuel Gompers

_____ 1. an architect who promoted the ideas of the city planning movement by creating plans to redesign such cities as Chicago, Washington, D.C., and San Francisco

_____ 2. investigative journalists and writers who exposed corruption and social problems

_____ 3. author of the "History of the Standard Oil Company," which exposed that company's unfair business practices

_____ 4. the 1911 workplace event that prompted the New York legislature to enact stricter fire-safety codes

_____ 5. the law that made alcoholic beverages illegal

_____ 6. a largely urban reform movement that worked to improve living and working conditions and to fight corrupt political machines in the cities

_____ 7. a largely rural reform movement that protested unfair and corrupt business practices and called for greater voter control of government

_____ 8. co-founder of the NAACP and editor of its widely read monthly magazine, *The Crisis*; organizer of a series of Pan-African congresses, and author of *The Souls of Black Folk*

_____ 9. a national organization that fights racial discrimination and has won a number of important legal rights for African Americans by arguing before the Supreme Court

_____ 10. leader of the American Federation of Labor

Chapter and Unit Tests

Chapter 18, Test Form A, Continued

UNDERSTANDING IDEAS *(3 points each)* For each of the following, place the letter of the *best* choice in the space provided.

_____ 1. Progressives' goals included
   a. less help for the poor.
   b. an eight-hour workday, minimum wage, safety in the workplace, and an end to child labor.
   c. increased profits for wealthy businesses in the cities.
   d. increased immigration.

_____ 2. Ray Stannard Baker's *Following the Color Line* was about
   a. company-owned towns.
   b. immigrant Americans working in the garment industry.
   c. a lynching in Springfield, Ohio.
   d. the temperance movement.

_____ 3. The American Federation of Labor
   a. was a labor union.
   b. was a communist organization.
   c. organized working immigrants to build playgrounds.
   d. was a federal government program created to help workers.

_____ 4. The Industrial Workers of the World (IWW) opposed
   a. cooperation with business owners.
   b. closed shops.
   c. women in the workplace.
   d. including unskilled workers in its membership.

_____ 5. An open shop refers to
   a. a factory that operates at night.
   b. a government business.
   c. a factory or business that does not allow its workers to belong to a union.
   d. a male-only workplace.

_____ 6. Most progressives were
   a. middle or upper class.
   b. working class.
   c. immigrants.
   d. high school dropouts.

_____ 7. The *Great Train Robbery* was
   a. a huge theft.
   b. committed by immigrants.
   c. the first movie to tell a story.
   d. a muckraking novel.

_____ 8. The _____ was founded to improve job and housing opportunities for African Americans.
   a. AFL
   b. National Grange
   c. National Urban League
   d. Opportunity Council

_____ 9. Which of the following people was an American Indian Olympic gold medalist?
   a. Carlos Montezuma
   b. Jim Thorpe
   c. Billy Sunday
   d. Herbert Croly

_____ 10. In 1911 American Indians formed the _____ to help deal with their loss of land and way of life.
   a. Bureau of Indian Affairs
   b. Native American League
   c. Society of American Indians
   d. Land Cooperative

Chapter 18, Test Form A, Continued

■ TRUE/FALSE *(2 points each)* Read each of the following statements and then decide whether it is true or false. If the answer is true, place a *T* in the space provided; if the answer is false, place an *F* in the space.

_____ 1. The Gilded Age, with its industrial development and great business profits, raised wages and improved living conditions for the average worker.

_____ 2. The National Tuberculosis Association, founded by a group of physicians and reform-minded citizens, was unable to lower the death rate from tuberculosis because they could not find a cure.

_____ 3. Many businesses ignored child labor laws, claiming that they needed cheap child labor in order to make a good profit.

_____ 4. Although women enrolled in colleges in increasing numbers in the 1900s, their career opportunities were quite limited, and they were still not allowed to vote in national or local elections.

_____ 5. Most progressives worked hard to end racial discrimination and prejudice against African Americans.

■ PRACTICING SKILLS *(5 points each)* Study the graph below and answer the questions that follow.

1. About how many Americans were in labor unions in 1905?

   _____

2. During which years did union membership most sharply rise?

   _____

■ COMPOSING AN ESSAY *(20 points)* Write a brief essay on *one* of the following subjects. Remember to use examples to support your answer.

1. Describe one or more concerns that led the Supreme Court to rule in favor of business and against some progressive legislation.

2. Describe some of the issues that muckraking writers raised and how the public and reformers responded to their writing.

Name _____ Class _____ Date _____

CHAPTER 18: The Age of Reform

CHAPTER TEST • FORM B

■ SHORT ANSWER *(10 points each)* Provide brief answers for each of the following. Remember to use examples to support your answer.

1. How did industrialization have both positive and negative effects on society and the U.S. economy in the Gilded Age?
2. Why did women become active in reform movement issues?
3. What organization, aside from the American Federation of Labor, represented workers and fought for their rights? What was their political position regarding capitalism?
4. What changes did progressives hope to promote with the well-planned cities, beautiful streets, and imposing architecture of the City Beautiful movement?
5. What were some of the organizations that African Americans formed to improve their position in society, and what were some of their goals?

■ PRIMARY SOURCE *(10 points each)* As a well-educated African American, W. E. B. Du Bois struggled to reconcile his identity as a man of African descent with his identity as an American citizen. He wrote eloquently about some of the subtle but powerful conflicts of cultural influences on African Americans. To explain his thinking, read the following passage and answer the questions that follow.

One feels his two-ness—an American, a Negro, two souls, two thoughts, two unreconciled strivings, two warring ideals. . . . The history of the American Negro is the history of this strife. . . . He would not Africanize America. . . . He would not bleach the Negro soul in a flood of white Americanism. . . . He simply wishes to make it possible for a man to be both a Negro and an American, without being cursed and spit upon by his fellows, without having the doors of Opportunity closed roughly in his face.

1. What does Du Bois mean when he says the African American "would not Africanize America"?
2. How could an African American attempt to "bleach the Negro soul in a flood of white Americanism"?

■ COMPOSING AN ESSAY *(30 points)* Write a brief essay on *one* of the following subjects. Remember to use examples to support your answer.

1. Explain how industrialization created problems that encouraged a variety of reformers, labor organizations, and minority associations to try to improve the lot of those at the economic bottom of society.
2. Compare the American Federation of Labor (AFL) with the Industrial Workers of the World (IWW) in terms of tactics, goals, and membership. How did they work to improve working conditions for their members?

Progressive Politicians

CHAPTER TEST • FORM A

REVIEWING FACTS *(3 points each)* In the space provided, write the name of the person or the historical term identified by each description. Choose your answers from the list below. There are two extra names or terms on the list.

Carrie Chapman Catt	initiative	Alice Paul
recall	reclamation	arbitration
Robert M. La Follette	Theodore Roosevelt	William Howard Taft
Eugene Debs	Woodrow Wilson	Upton Sinclair

_____ 1. developed a reform program in Wisconsin that became a model for other states

_____ 2. gives voters the power to introduce legislation

_____ 3. assumed the presidency after the death of President McKinley

_____ 4. wrote a novel depicting the wretched conditions at a meatpacking plant

_____ 5. enables voters to remove an elected official from office by calling for a special election

_____ 6. process by which two opposing sides allow a third party to settle a dispute

_____ 7. Socialist Party candidate for president in 1912

_____ 8. militant Quaker suffragist

_____ 9. became the president of NAWSA in 1900

_____ 10. the process of making damaged land productive again

Chapter 19, Test Form A, Continued

UNDERSTANDING IDEAS *(3 points each)* For each of the following, place the letter of the *best* choice in the space provided.

_____ 1. Which amendment gives voters the power to elect their senators directly?
   a. Sixteenth
   b. Twentieth
   c. Nineteenth
   d. Seventeenth

_____ 2. Which amendment allows Congress to levy taxes based on an individual's income?
   a. Sixteenth
   b. Twentieth
   c. Nineteenth
   d. Seventeenth

_____ 3. In 1904 the Square Deal became the campaign slogan of
   a. William Jennings Bryan.
   b. Theodore Roosevelt.
   c. William McKinley.
   d. William Howard Taft.

_____ 4. Samuel M. Jones and Tom Johnson fought for reforms in
   a. city government.
   b. the railroad industry.
   c. the meatpacking industry.
   d. the banking industry.

_____ 5. A devastating hurricane in Galveston indirectly helped bring about the establishment of
   a. city commissions.
   b. environmental laws.
   c. new banking laws.
   d. city councils.

_____ 6. The Mann-Elkins Act was passed to regulate
   a. banks.
   b. the meatpacking industry.
   c. political parties.
   d. telephone and telegraph companies.

_____ 7. The Federal Reserve Act of 1913 particularly aided
   a. large companies.
   b. small banks.
   c. farmers.
   d. conservative business groups.

_____ 8. Which amendment granted full voting rights to women?
   a. Seventeenth
   b. Twentieth
   c. Nineteenth
   d. Sixteenth

_____ 9. The use of the office of president as a "bully pulpit" was popularized by
   a. William McKinley.
   b. Theodore Roosevelt.
   c. William Howard Taft.
   d. Woodrow Wilson.

_____ 10. Progressives viewed the Ballinger-Pinchot affair as a sign that President Taft
   a. was not committed to conservation.
   b. wanted higher tariffs.
   c. wanted to reduce the powers of the Interstate Commerce Commission.
   d. was against labor.

Chapter 19, Test Form A, Continued

■ TRUE/FALSE *(2 points each)* Read each of the following statements, and then decide whether it is true or false. If the answer is true, place a *T* in the space provided; if the answer is false, place an *F* in the space.

_____ 1. The Socialist Party wanted all major industries to be publicly owned.

_____ 2. By 1901 about half of the states had given women full voting rights.

_____ 3. Presidents Taft and Wilson both supported racial segregation.

_____ 4. *The Octopus* depicted the conditions at a meatpacking plant.

_____ 5. The term *conservation* refers to the need to protect the environment.

■ PRACTICING SKILLS *(5 points each)* Study the map below and answer the questions that follow.

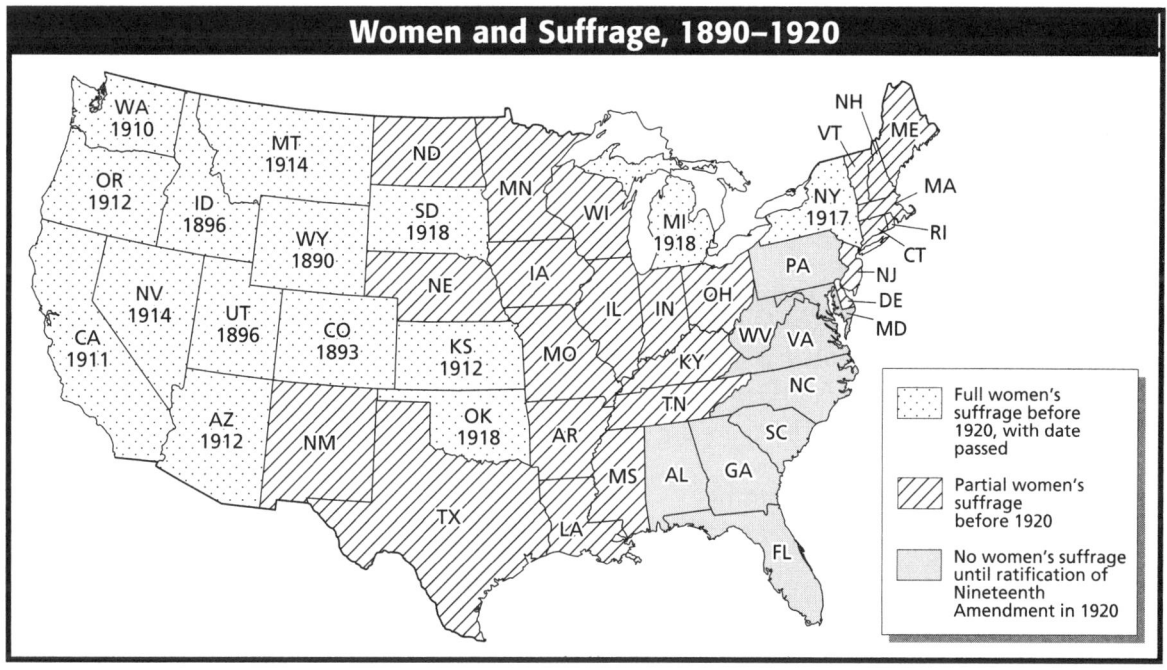

1. Which region of the United States was most supportive of women's suffrage?

_____

2. Which states gave women full suffrage during the 1800s?

_____

■ COMPOSING AN ESSAY *(20 points)* Write a brief essay on *one* of the following subjects. Remember to use examples to support your answer.

1. Describe some of the goals of progressive state leaders in the early 1900s.
2. Discuss President Roosevelt's efforts in the conservation movement.

Name _____ Class _____ Date _____

Progressive Politicians

CHAPTER TEST • FORM B

■ **SHORT ANSWER** *(10 points each)* Provide brief answers for each of the following. Remember to use examples to support your answer.

1. What is the graduated income tax?
2. Why did liquor producers and distributors oppose suffrage for women?
3. What were some of the shortcomings of progressivism?
4. How did President Theodore Roosevelt's approach to government differ from the approach of presidents during the Gilded Age?
5. What did Roosevelt's Square Deal philosphy attempt to do?

■ **PRIMARY SOURCE** *(10 points each)* The campaign for women's suffrage was an important part of the progressive agenda. But the movement faced strong opposition from various sectors of the population, including government officials. A state senator, for example, said he was against women's suffrage because he believed that the vote would cause women to lose their beauty and charm. In the excerpt below, a suffragist reacted to the senator's comment. Read the excerpt and then answer the questions that follow.

> *We have women working in the foundries.... Women in the laundries ... stand for 13 or 14 hours in the terrible steam and heat with their hands in hot starch. Surely these women won't lose any more of their beauty and charm by putting a ballot in a ballot box once a year than they are likely to lose standing in foundries or laundries all year.*

1. How would you describe the comments of the senator?
2. How would you describe the suffragist's reply?
3. What did the senator's comment suggest about men's attitudes toward women at the time?

■ **COMPOSING AN ESSAY** *(20 points)* Write a brief essay on one of the following subjects. Remember to use examples to support your answer.

1. Describe the progressive reforms enacted during President Taft's administration.
2. Explain why the Democratic Party was practically assured of a victory in the presidential election of 1912.

Name _____ Class _____ Date _____

America and the World

CHAPTER 20

CHAPTER TEST • FORM A

■ REVIEWING FACTS *(3 points each)* In the space provided, write the name of the person or the historical term that completes each sentence. Choose your answers from the list below. There are two extra names or terms on the list.

Boxer Rebellion	Russo-Japanese War	Spanish-American War
John Hay	Matthew Perry	John Dewey
Emilio Aguinaldo	William Randolph Hearst	Roosevelt Corollary
Emiliano Zapata	Platt Amendment	Foraker Act

1. _____ called for an Open Door Policy to open up trade with China.

2. During the _____ the Fists of Righteous Harmony attacked Western missionaries.

3. _____ published the *New York Journal*.

4. The _____ began shortly after the destruction of the USS *Maine*.

5. _____ was the leader of the Filipino patriots.

6. In effect, the _____ made Cuba a U.S. protectorate.

7. The _____ made it clear that the Monroe Doctrine would be enforced.

8. _____ led a rebel army against the forces of Mexico's dictator.

9. In 1854 _____ sailed to Japan to try to persuade Japan's rulers to open trade with the West.

10. Theodore Roosevelt was awarded the Nobel Peace Prize for settling the _____.

Chapter and Unit Tests   Chapter 20   97

Chapter 20, Test Form A, Continued

UNDERSTANDING IDEAS (3 points each) For each of the following, place the letter of the best choice in the space provided.

_____ 1. U.S. citizenship was granted to Puerto Ricans by the
   a. Jones Act of 1917.
   b. Hay–Bunau-Varilla Treaty.
   c. Roosevelt Corollary.
   d. Teller Amendment.

_____ 2. Which two Spanish colonies in the Americas did Spain lose as a result of the Spanish-American War?
   a. the Philippines and Japan
   b. Samoa and Hawaii
   c. Cuba and Puerto Rico
   d. Panama and Colombia

_____ 3. Who was the president who favored dollar diplomacy in Latin America?
   a. Woodrow Wilson
   b. William H. Taft
   c. William McKinley
   d. Theodore Roosevelt

_____ 4. Which of the following was NOT TRUE of Mexico's 1917 constitution?
   a. It put an end to child labor.
   b. It gave private businesses rights to minerals, oil, and water.
   c. It provided workers an eight-hour workday.
   d. It placed the interests of common welfare above individual rights.

_____ 5. The building a canal through the Isthmus of Panama was first attempted by
   a. the French.
   b. John Hay.
   c. Theodore Roosevelt.
   d. the British.

TRUE/FALSE (2 points each) Read each of the following statements, and then decide whether it is true or false. If the answer is true, place a T in the space provided; if the answer is false, place an F in the space.

_____ 1. The Panama Canal was built at sea level.

_____ 2. Liliuokalani was a champion of Hawaiian nationalism.

_____ 3. Many Americans were sympathetic to Cubans who revolted against Spain in 1895.

_____ 4. José Martí wanted Cuba to remain a Spanish colony.

_____ 5. The Anti-Imperialist League wanted the United States to annex the Philippines.

_____ 6. President Wilson favored the establishment of democratic governments in Latin America.

_____ 7. Porfirio Díaz did much to improve Mexico's economy during his rule.

_____ 8. Francisco Madero established a stable democratic government in Mexico.

Chapter 20, Test Form A, Continued

_____ 9. Western Samoa became a U.S. territory.

_____ 10. College athletes were among the U.S. cavalry that stormed San Juan Hill.

■ **PRACTICING SKILLS** *(5 points each)* **Study the graph below and answer the questions that follow.**

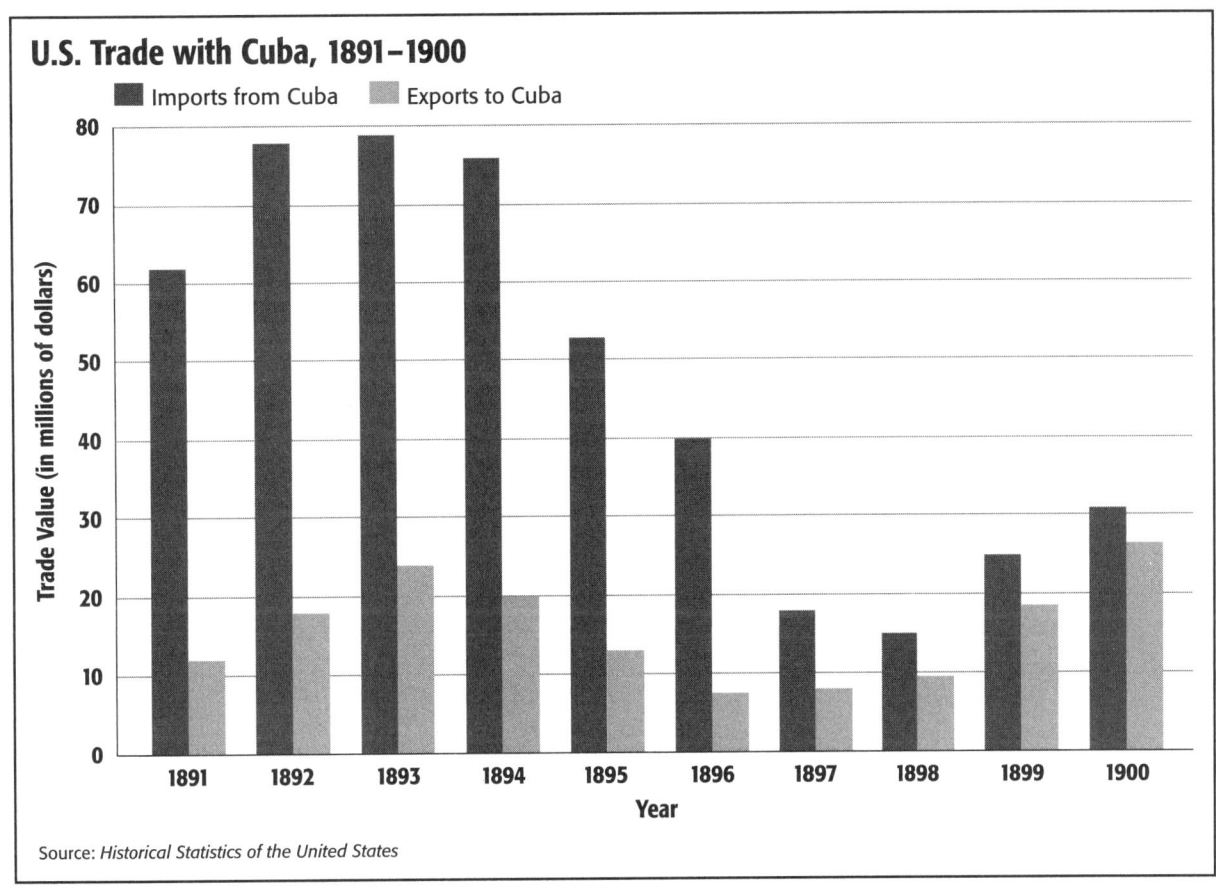

1. Which nation consistently sold more goods than it bought?

_____

2. What was the dollar value of U.S. imports from Cuba in 1896?

_____

3. What happened to trade between the two nations between 1893 and 1896?

_____

■ **COMPOSING AN ESSAY** *(20 points)* **Write a brief essay on *one* of the following subjects. Remember to use examples to support your answer.**

1. Define imperialism and explain why countries engaged in it.
2. Describe the events that led up to the Spanish-American War.

Name _____ Class _____ Date _____

America and the World

CHAPTER TEST • FORM B

■ **SHORT ANSWER** *(10 points each)* Provide brief answers for each of the following. Remember to use examples to support your answer.

1. Why did President Roosevelt issue the Roosevelt Corollary to the Monroe Doctrine?
2. How did the United States acquire the right to build a fortified naval base at Pearl Harbor?
3. Which two military actions hastened the defeat of the Spanish in Cuba?
4. What was Spain's response to the revolt in Cuba in 1895?
5. How did Japan become a world power?

■ **PRIMARY SOURCE** *(10 points each)* Imperialistic sentiments were in the minds and hearts of many Americans as the 1900s approached. In the first excerpt below, from an editorial written for the *Washington Post* in 1896, the writer sums up the nation's feelings about imperialism. In the second excerpt, Alfred Thayer Mahan, the author of *The Influence of Sea Power upon History,* recommends a course of action for the United States. Read each of the excerpts and then answer the questions that follow.

A new consciousness seems to have come upon us—the consciousness of strength—and with it a new appetite, the yearning to show our strength. . . . Ambition, interest, land hunger, pride, the mere joy of fighting, whatever it may be, we are animated by a new sensation. We are face to face with a strange destiny. The taste of Empire is in the mouth of the people even as the taste of blood in the jungle. It means an Imperial policy, the Republic, renascent [reawakened], taking her place with the armed nations.

Having . . . no foreign establishments, either colonial or military, the ships of war of the United States, in war, will be like land birds, unable to fly far from their own shores. To provide resting-places for them, where they can coal and repair, would be one of the first duties of a government proposing to itself the development of the power of the nation at sea.

1. What did the *Washington Post* writer mean by the statement, "The taste of Empire is in the mouth of the people . . ."?
2. What did Mahan propose that the United States do?
3. What might someone opposed to imperialism say to these writers?

■ **COMPOSING AN ESSAY** *(20 points)* Write a brief essay on *one* of the following subjects. Remember to use examples to support your answer.

1. Explain why the United States supported Mexican revolutionaries and yet opposed Filipino revolutionaries.
2. Describe how President Taft's and President Wilson's Latin American policies differed.

Name _____ Class _____ Date _____

CHAPTER 21: World War I

CHAPTER TEST • FORM A

REVIEWING FACTS *(3 points each)* For each of the following descriptions, place the letter of the *best* choice in the space provided.

_____ 1. Which nation was *NOT* a member of the Big Four?
   a. United States
   b. France
   c. Italy
   d. Germany

_____ 2. Whose assassination triggered the start of the Great War?
   a. Gavrilo Princip
   b. Archduke Franz Ferdinand
   c. Wilhelm II
   d. Vladimir Lenin

_____ 3. Who was the most successful German ace?
   a. Manfred von Richthofen
   b. Baron von Schwarzenstein
   c. Edward Rickenbacker
   d. Arthur Zimmermann

_____ 4. Who commanded the American Expeditionary Force?
   a. Edward F. Graham
   b. Edward Rickenbacker
   c. Sir Robert Baden-Powell
   d. John J. Pershing

_____ 5. Who headed the Food Administration's Speakers' Bureau?
   a. Carrie Chapman Catt
   b. Juliette Gordon Low
   c. Harriot Stanton Blatch
   d. Jane Addams

_____ 6. Which act increased the number of soldiers in the regular army?
   a. Sedition Act
   b. Espionage Act
   c. National Defense Act
   d. Selective Service Act

_____ 7. Who was the Wall Street investor who directed the War Industries Board?
   a. Bernard Baruch
   b. Herbert Hoover
   c. Harry Garfield
   d. Harriot Stanton Blatch

_____ 8. Which country remained neutral until it joined the Allies in 1915?
   a. France
   b. Bulgaria
   c. Ottoman Empire
   d. Italy

_____ 9. What four-month battle claimed more than a million casualties?
   a. the Somme
   b. Marne
   c. Argonne Forest
   d. Verdun

_____ 10. Nine of Wilson's Fourteen Points dealt with this issue.
   a. self-determination
   b. the League of Nations
   c. the arms race
   d. secret diplomacy

Chapter and Unit Tests   Chapter 21 **101**

Chapter 21, Test Form A, Continued

UNDERSTANDING IDEAS (3 points each) Read each of the following statements and then decide whether you agree with it or disagree with it. If you agree, place an *A* in the space provided; if you disagree, place a *D* in the space.

_____ 1. Nationalism was particularly strong in the Balkans.

_____ 2. Germany and Austria were longtime enemies.

_____ 3. Early in the war, Germany's military strategy focused on quickly defeating Russia.

_____ 4. During its policy of neutrality, the United States was untouched by the war.

_____ 5. World War I marked the first time white and black U.S. soldiers were integrated in the same units.

_____ 6. The U.S. convoy system proved to be effective in protecting U.S. soldiers.

_____ 7. Union membership grew rapidly during the war.

_____ 8. Women's war efforts helped produce the passage of the Nineteenth Amendment.

_____ 9. The United States used propaganda to gain support for the war effort.

_____ 10. The Supreme Court ruled that the Espionage and Sedition Acts violated the First Amendment.

TRUE/FALSE (2 points each) Read each of the following statements, and then decide whether it is true or false. If the answer is true, place a *T* in the space provided; if the answer is false, place an *F* in the space.

_____ 1. "Big Bertha" was the name of a famous U.S. tank.

_____ 2. Morale in the German army rose after the Battle of the Argonne Forest.

_____ 3. The fourteenth point in Wilson's Fourteen Points dealt with the League of Nations.

_____ 4. The American people warmly received the Fourteen Points.

_____ 5. Congress unanimously voted to declare war in April 1917.

Chapter 21, Test Form A, Continued

PRACTICING SKILLS *(5 points each)* Study the graph below and answer the questions that follow.

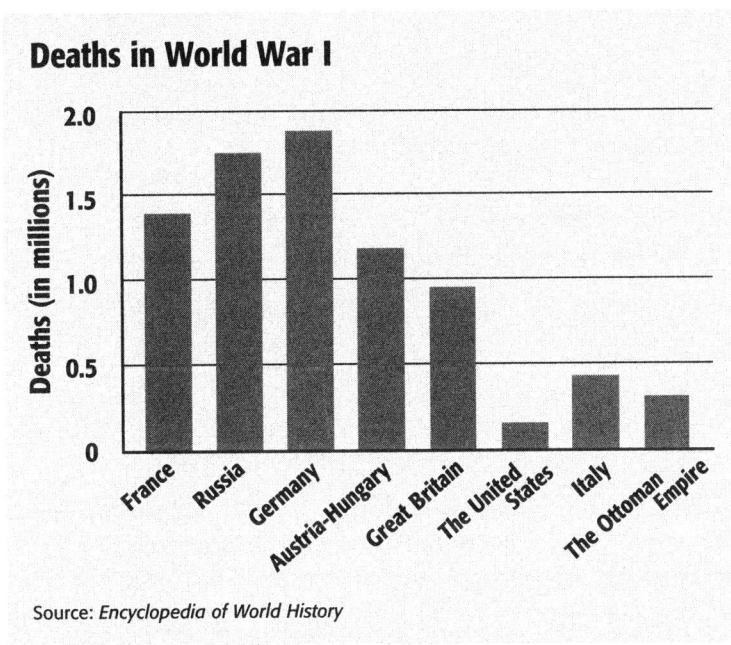

Source: *Encyclopedia of World History*

1. About how many deaths did the three Central Powers—Germany, Austria-Hungary, and the Ottoman Empire—suffer during the war?

   _____

2. Which of the Allied Powers suffered the most deaths?

   _____

COMPOSING AN ESSAY *(20 points)* Write a brief essay on *one* of the following subjects. Remember to use examples to support your answer.

1. Describe how Americans on the home front helped contribute to the war effort.
2. Explain how the population of the United States changed during the war.

Name _____ Class _____ Date _____

CHAPTER 21
World War I

CHAPTER TEST • FORM B

■ **SHORT ANSWER** *(10 points each)* Provide brief answers for each of the following. Remember to use examples to support your answer.

1. Why did so many battles on the western front lead to stalemates?
2. Why did Russia withdraw from the war in 1918?
3. How did the U.S. government attempt to limit opposition to the war?
4. What were the findings in the landmark case *Schenck* v. *United States*?
5. How was Germany punished for its role in the war?

■ **PRIMARY SOURCE** *(10 points each)* After the sinking of the British passenger liner *Lusitania* by a German U-boat in 1915, Baron von Schwarzenstein, a German citizen, offered his opinion on the incident. Read this excerpt from the piece and then answer the questions that follow.

> It was only after England declared the whole North Sea a war zone . . . that Germany with precisely the same right declared the waters around England a war zone and announced her purpose of sinking all hostile commercial vessels found therein . . . In the case of the *Lusitania* the German Ambassador even further warned Americans through the great American newspapers against taking passage thereon. Does a pirate act thus? Does he take pains to save human lives? . . . Nobody regrets more sincerely than we Germans the hard necessity of sending to their deaths hundreds of men. Yet the sinking was a justifiable act of war. . . . The scene of war is no golf links [course], the ships of belligerent powers no pleasure places. . . . We have sympathy with the victims and their relatives, of course, but did we hear anything about sympathy . . . when England adopted her diabolical [evil] plan of starving a great nation?

1. According to the author, was Germany justified in its sinking of the *Lusitania*? Why?
2. What evidence suggests that von Schwarzenstein is a moral man?
3. What did the author mean when he spoke of England's "diabolical plan of starving a great nation"?

■ **COMPOSING AN ESSAY** *(20 points)* Write a brief essay on *one* of the following subjects. Remember to use examples to support your answer.

1. Why did a local conflict between Austria-Hungary and Serbia result in a global war?
2. Discuss some of the events that led the United States to enter the war.

Name _____ Class _____ Date _____

A World Power

UNIT TEST • FORM A

UNDERSTANDING IDEAS *(3 points each)* For each of the following, place the letter of the best choice in the space provided.

_____ 1. Who was the author of the "History of the Standard Oil Company," which exposed that company's unfair business practices?
  a. W. E. B. Du Bois
  b. Samuel Gompers
  c. Ida Tarbell
  d. Daniel Burnham

_____ 2. Which amendment made alcoholic beverages illegal?
  a. First Amendment
  b. Eighteenth Amendment
  c. Nineteenth Amendment
  d. Twenty-first Amendment

_____ 3. Ray Stannard Baker's book, which told how racist attitudes and voter indifference allowed a lynching to go unpunished in Springfield, Ohio, was called
  a. *The Crisis.*
  b. *The Souls of Black Folk.*
  c. *Following the Color Line.*
  d. *The Shame of the Cities.*

_____ 4. Who assumed the presidency after the death of President McKinley?
  a. Woodrow Wilson
  b. Theodore Roosevelt
  c. James Madison
  d. Harry S Truman

_____ 5. The Mann-Elkins Act was passed to regulate
  a. banks.
  b. the meatpacking industry.
  c. political parties.
  d. telephone and telegraph companies.

_____ 6. Which political party wanted all major industries to be publicly owned?
  a. Republican Party
  b. Democratic Party
  c. Independent Party
  d. Socialist Party

_____ 7. Which war began shortly after the destruction of the USS *Maine*?
  a. World War I
  b. World War II
  c. the Spanish-American War
  d. the Russo-Japanese War

_____ 8. Who was awarded the Nobel Peace Prize for settling the Russo-Japanese War?
  a. Theodore Roosevelt
  b. James Monroe
  c. Harry S Truman
  d. William McKinley

_____ 9. The assassination of Archduke Franz Ferdinand triggered the start of
  a. World War I.
  b. World War II.
  c. the Spanish-American War.
  d. the Russo-Japanese War.

_____ 10. Which country remained neutral until it joined the Allies in 1915?
  a. France
  b. Bulgaria
  c. Italy
  d. Ottoman Empire

Chapter and Unit Tests   Unit 6   105

Unit 6, Test Form A, Continued

TRUE/FALSE *(2 points each)* Read each of the following statements, and then decide whether it is true or false. If the answer is true, place a *T* in the space provided; if the answer is false place an *F* in the space.

_____ 1. Investigative journalists and writers who exposed corruption and social problems were called muckrakers.

_____ 2. The AFL, or American Federation of Labor, was a federal government program created to help workers organize.

_____ 3. In 1904 the Square Deal became the campaign slogan of Theodore Roosevelt.

_____ 4. By 1901 about half of the states had given women full voting rights.

_____ 5. Mexico's 1917 constitution gave private businesses rights to minerals, oil, and water.

PRACTICING SKILLS *(5 points each)* Study the chart below and answer the questions that follow.

The Election of 1912

Candidate	Party	Electoral Vote	Popular Vote	% of Popular Vote
Woodrow Wilson	Democratic	435	6,296,547	41.9
Theodore Roosevelt	Progressive	88	4,118,571	27.4
William Howard Taft	Republican	8	3,486,720	23.2
Eugene Debs	Socialist		900,672	6.0
Other parties			235,025	1.6

1. Who was the Republican candidate for the 1912 presidential election?

_____

2. Which party received six percent of the popular vote?

_____

Unit 6, Test Form A, Continued

■ REVIEWING FACTS *(3 points each)* Choose from the following list to complete each of the statements below.

Seventeenth Amendment   progressivism   reclamation
Nineteenth Amendment   conservation   open shop
President Wilson   populism   initiative
President Taft

1. _____ was a largely urban reform movement that improved living and working conditions and fought corrupt political machines in the cities.

2. _____ was a largely rural reform movement that protested unfair and corrupt business practices and called for greater voter control of government.

3. _____ refers to a factory or business that does not allow its workers to belong to a union.

4. Voters can introduce legislation through the use of a(n) _____.

5. The process of making damaged land productive again is called _____.

6. The _____ gave voters the power to elect their senators directly.

7. The _____ gave full voting rights to women.

8. Theodore Roosevelt used the term _____ to describe the need to protect the environment.

9. _____ favored dollar diplomacy in Latin America.

10. _____ favored the establishment of democratic governments in Latin America.

■ COMPOSING AN ESSAY *(20 points)* Write a brief essay on *one* of the following subjects. Remember to use examples to support your answers.

1. Explain how the NAACP was formed, and discuss its work and accomplishments.
2. Explain the major causes of the Spanish-American War.

Name _____ Class _____ Date _____

UNIT 6: A World Power

UNIT TEST • FORM B

■ **SHORT ANSWER** *(10 points each)* Provide brief answers for each of the following. Remember to use examples to support your answers.

1. Describe the backgrounds of the people who were called progressives.
2. Explain the significance of the Sixteenth Amendment.
3. Explain how Progressives responded to the Ballinger-Pinchot affair.
4. Describe some of the provisions of Mexico's 1917 constitution.
5. Briefly describe the Battle of the Somme and the effects it had on World War I.

■ **PRIMARY SOURCE** *(10 points each)* The popularity of the newly invented motion picture grew rapidly during the early 1900s. Read William Dean Howell's thoughts on the industry, and answer the questions that follow.

The pictures thrown upon the luminous [lighted] curtain of the stage have been declared extremely corrupting to the idle young people lurking in the darkness before it. The darkness itself has been held a condition of inexpressible depravity [immorality] and a means of allurement [attraction] to evil.

1. According to Howell, what kind of influence did motion pictures have on those who enjoyed that entertainment?
2. According to this passage, what group of Americans generally went to see motion pictures?

■ **COMPOSING AN ESSAY** *(30 points)* Write an essay on *one* of the following subjects. Remember to use examples to support your answer.

1. What changes did progressives hope to promote by their work on well-planned cities and protection of workers? What were some of the shortcomings of progressivism?
2. Explain how the population of the United States changed during World War I and how Americans at home in the United States contributed to the war effort.

Name _____ Class _____ Date _____

CHAPTER 22: A Turbulent Decade

CHAPTER TEST • FORM A

REVIEWING FACTS *(3 points each)* In the space provided, write the name of the person or the historical term identified by each description. Choose your answers from the list below. There are two extra names or terms on the list.

Mary Anderson
Boston police strike
Marcus Garvey
United Mine Workers strike
Albert Fall
A. Philip Randolph
Alfred E. Smith
Calvin Coolidge
Seattle general strike
steel strike of 1919
Warren G. Harding
John L. Lewis

_____ 1. well-organized strike of "muddle-headed foreigners" that helped turn public opinion against organized labor

_____ 2. presidential candidate who called for a return to "normalcy" in 1920

_____ 3. organized the United Mine Workers strike

_____ 4. was convicted of receiving bribes during the Teapot Dome Scandal

_____ 5. participants in this strike threatened the "public safety," according to Calvin Coolidge

_____ 6. many Americans opposed him during the election of 1928 because of his Catholic faith

_____ 7. native of Jamaica who supported black nationalism

_____ 8. armed thugs intimidated participants in this strike that threatened to shut down a major industry

_____ 9. founded the Brotherhood of Sleeping Car Porters

_____ 10. resulted in wage increases for its participants

Chapter 22, Test Form A, Continued

■ **UNDERSTANDING IDEAS** *(3 points each)* For each of the following, place the letter of the *best* choice in the space provided.

_____ 1. Demobilization caused all of the following EXCEPT
   a. higher unemployment.
   b. lower wages.
   c. higher prices.
   d. lower consumer spending.

_____ 2. The Socialist Party believed in
   a. collective ownership of industry.
   b. the violent overthrow of the government.
   c. revolutionary Marxism.
   d. expanded capitalism.

_____ 3. The Harding administration
   a. raised taxes on wealthy Americans.
   b. increased the national debt.
   c. favored business.
   d. enforced antitrust laws.

_____ 4. The Equal Rights Amendment
   a. was irrelevant to most women.
   b. was opposed by many reformers.
   c. passed by a small margin.
   d. was opposed by the National Woman's Party.

_____ 5. Which of the following statements about the Ku Klux Klan is NOT TRUE?
   a. was officially dissolved during Reconstruction
   b. used violence to accomplish goals
   c. lost many members during the Red Scare
   d. was established by a preacher

■ **TRUE/FALSE** *(2 points each)* Read each of the following statements, and then decide whether it is true or false. If the answer is true, place a *T* in the space provided; if the answer is false, place an *F* in the space.

_____ 1. Mexicans were not affected by a 1921 law that limited immigration to the United States.

_____ 2. The Bursum Bill would have increased the power of tribal governments.

_____ 3. The revolution in Russia in 1917 established a democratic government.

_____ 4. Labor leader Eugene Debs formed the Socialist Party.

_____ 5. Most of those arrested during the Palmer raids were poor immigrants.

_____ 6. A jury found Sacco and Vanzetti not guilty of murder.

_____ 7. Organized labor had many gains during the 1920s.

_____ 8. President Coolidge favored legislation to aid farmers.

_____ 9. Farmers and workers supported the Progressive platform during the presidential election of 1924.

_____ 10. In 1924 Congress granted citizenship to all American Indians.

Chapter 22, Test Form A, Continued

■ **PRACTICING SKILLS** *(5 points each)* **Study the graphs below and answer the questions that follow.**

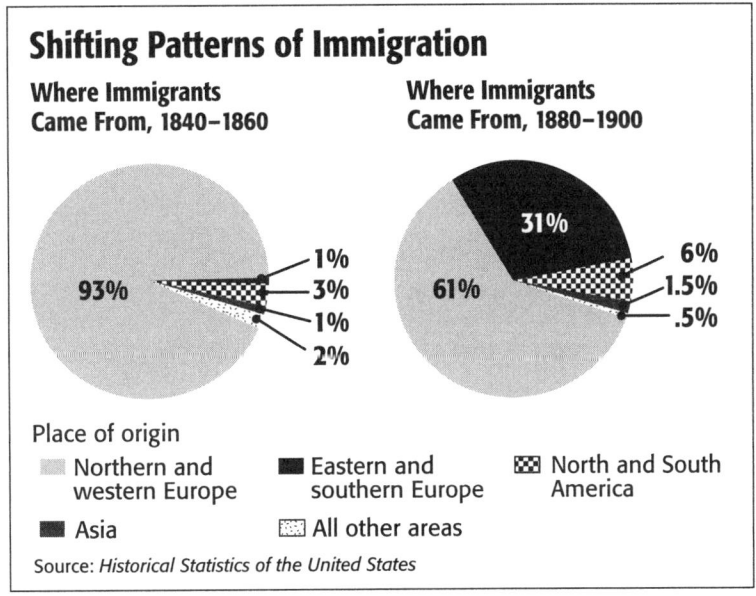

1. Where did a vast majority of immigrants come from between 1840 and 1860?

   _____

2. Between 1880 and 1900, what percentage of immigrants came from Europe?

   _____

■ **COMPOSING AN ESSAY** *(25 points)* **Write a brief essay on *one* of the following subjects. Remember to use examples to support your answer.**

1. Define the Red Scare and describe how it affected the lives of immigrants in the United States.

2. Explain why Secretary of the Treasury Andrew Mellon thought lowering taxes for the rich would spur economic growth. Did the plan work?

Name _____ Class _____ Date _____

CHAPTER 22

A Turbulent Decade

CHAPTER TEST • FORM B

■ **SHORT ANSWER** *(10 points each)* **Provide brief answers for each of the following. Remember to use examples to support your answer.**

1. How did demobilization affect the nation's economy?
2. What were the main causes of the strikes of 1919?
3. How did most Americans react to the strikes of 1919?
4. Why did the verdict in the Sacco and Vanzetti case outrage defenders of civil liberties?
5. What was President Coolidge's position on business?

■ **PRIMARY SOURCE** *(10 points each)* **Sacco and Vanzetti were Italian immigrants convicted of murder and sentenced to death. The first excerpt below is a news story from the *Atlanta Constitution* that described the execution of the two men in 1927. The second excerpt consists of remarks made by Judge Webster Thayer shortly after sentencing the two to death. Read the two excerpts and then answer the questions that follow.**

> *State Prison, Charleston, Mass.*—Nicola Sacco and Bartolomeo Vanzetti were put to death today.
>
> *They went to the embrace of the electric chair unswerving in the avowal of their innocence. They paid with their lives for the murder of a paymaster and his guard at South Braintree seven years ago.*
>
> *As the heavy voltage of electricity was shot through their bodies, bayoneted guards surrounded the ancient prison for blocks.*
>
> *In cities on three continents millions awaited word of their death, many of them convinced that the two were executed for their political beliefs, not for the South Braintree murders.*

> *This man [Vanzetti], although he may not actually have committed the crime attributed to him, is nevertheless morally culpable [guilty], because he is an enemy of our existing institutions. . . . The defendant's ideas are cognate [associated] with crime.*

1. What phrase in the first excerpt reveals the case received worldwide attention?
2. In the second excerpt, what words indicate that the judge was not a believer in the First Amendment?
3. Do you think the judge had some doubts about the guilt of Vanzetti? Why?

■ **COMPOSING AN ESSAY** *(20 points)* **Write a brief essay on *one* of the following subjects. Remember to use examples to support your answer.**

1. Explain why the movement to pass the Equal Rights Amendment failed.
2. Compare the beliefs of W. E. B. Du Bois and Marcus Garvey. How did their methods to combat discrimination and acts of violence toward African Americans differ?

Name _____ Class _____ Date _____

CHAPTER 23: The Jazz Age

CHAPTER TEST • FORM A

REVIEWING FACTS *(3 points each)* In the space provided, write the name of the person that completes each sentence. Choose your answers from the list below. There are two extra names on the list.

Eliot Ness	Al Capone	Langston Hughes
Cecil B. DeMille	Amelia Earhart	Charles Lindbergh
Frederick W. Taylor	F. Scott Fitzgerald	Henry Ford
Babe Ruth	Clarence Darrow	Paul Robeson

1. _____ was an early proponent of scientific management.

2. By implementing the assembly line, _____ revolutionized automobile production.

3. _____ organized an elite squad of detectives to go after gangsters.

4. Gangster _____ controlled Chicago's underworld.

5. Movie director _____ created biblical epics such as *The Ten Commandments.*

6. Legendary baseball players such as Lou Gehrig, Ty Cobb, and _____ had great seasons during the 1920s.

7. Defense attorney _____ represented John Scopes.

8. _____ became the first pilot to fly nonstop from New York to Paris.

9. _____ was one of the most critically acclaimed actors of the 1920s.

10. Harlem Renaissance poet _____ dealt with issues of African American cultural heritage.

Chapter and Unit Tests — Chapter 23 113

Chapter 23, Test Form A, Continued

UNDERSTANDING IDEAS *(3 points each)* For each of the following, place the letter of the *best* choice in the space provided.

_____ 1. Which of the following statements about assembly lines is NOT true?
  a. They increased productivity.
  b. They made work more tedious.
  c. They provided better advancement opportunities.
  d. They led to increased employee turnover.

_____ 2. Most advertisements during the 1920s targeted
  a. children.
  b. men.
  c. women.
  d. senior citizens.

_____ 3. Jazz emerged during the early 1900s in the city of
  a. New York.
  b. Chicago.
  c. New Orleans.
  d. Los Angeles.

_____ 4. The American writers whose work reflected their disillusionment with society became known as
  a. Untouchables.
  b. revivalists.
  c. the Lost Generation.
  d. "the big three."

_____ 5. Which amendment dealt with the prohibition of alcohol?
  a. Eighteenth
  b. Nineteenth
  c. Twentieth
  d. Sixteenth

TRUE/FALSE *(2 points each)* Read each of the following statements, and then decide whether it is true or false. If the answer is true, place a *T* in the space provided; if the answer is false, place an *F* in the space.

_____ 1. The Volstead Act was passed to enforce the Eighteenth Amendment.

_____ 2. Most women during the 1920s pursued traditionally female careers.

_____ 3. The era of silent films began in the mid-1920s.

_____ 4. Athlete Jim Thorpe became known as the Sultan of Swat.

_____ 5. The prosecuting attorney in the Scopes trial was Charles Darwin.

_____ 6. Fundamentalism declined in popularity during the 1920s.

_____ 7. Henry L. Mencken was a critic of the new writers of the Jazz Age.

Chapter 23, Test Form A, Continued

_____ 8. Henry Ford was known for underpaying his workers.

_____ 9. Most consumers in the 1920s used credit to pay for their cars.

_____ 10. Prohibition led to a rise in organized crime.

■ **PRACTICING SKILLS** *(5 points each)* **Study the map below and answer the questions that follow.**

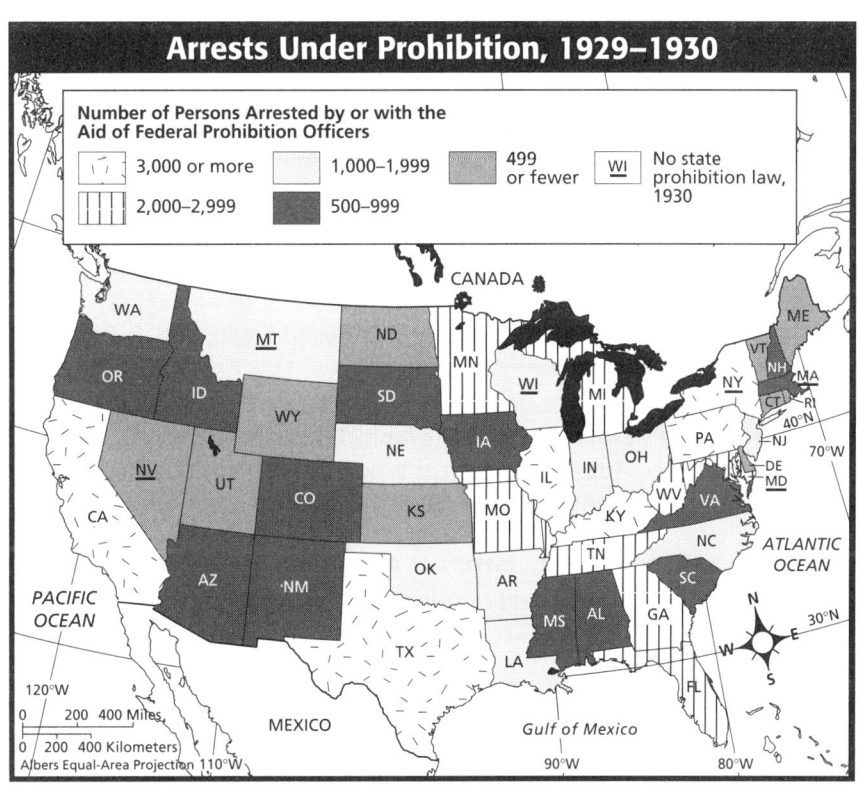

1. Which state along the Pacific coast had the most arrests?

_____

2. How many arrests were made in Nevada in 1929?

_____

3. Which two states bordering Mexico had 3,000 or more arrests in 1929?

_____

■ **COMPOSING AN ESSAY** *(20 points)* **Write a brief essay on *one* of the following subjects. Remember to use examples to support your answer.**

1. Explain why entertainment, like movies and sports, became so popular in the 1920s.
2. Explain how the assembly line changed the nature of work during the 1920s.

Name _____ Class _____ Date _____

CHAPTER 23: The Jazz Age

CHAPTER TEST • FORM B

SHORT ANSWER *(10 points each)* Provide brief answers for each of the following. Remember to use examples to support your answer.

1. What is the practice of planned obsolescence?
2. How did the writers and artists of the Harlem Renaissance affect American culture?
3. What is jazz? Where did it originate?
4. Why was the Lost Generation so named?
5. What were some of the positive and negative consequences of prohibition?

PRIMARY SOURCE *(10 points each)* The automobile drastically changed the nation. Some of these changes were positive and some not so positive. The following are excerpts from the 1920s dealing with the impact of the first cars. The first excerpt is from a letter sent to Henry Ford by the wife of an autoworker. The second excerpt is from the 1929 book *Middleton*, which chronicled life in Muncie, Indiana. The third excerpt is a report by Charles Merz about the reception the Model A received when it was unveiled to the public in 1927. Read the excerpts and then answer the questions that follow.

> *The chain system [assembly line] you have is a slave driver! My God! Mr. Ford. My husband has come home & thrown himself down & won't eat his supper—so done out! Can't it be remedied? . . . That $5 a day is a blessing—a bigger one than you know but oh they earn it.*

> *The extensive use of this new tool [the automobile] by the young has enormously extended their mobility and the range of alternatives before them; joining a crowd motoring over to a dance . . . twenty miles away may be a matter of a moment's decision, with no one's permission asked.*

> *One hundred thousand people flocked into the showrooms of the Ford Company in Detroit; mounted police were called out to patrol the crowds in Cleveland; in Kansas City so great a mob stormed Convention Hall that platforms had to be built to lift the new car high enough for everyone to see it.*

1. How do you think Mr. Ford would have replied to the letter writer in the first excerpt? Why?
2. How did the automobile affect young people in the late 1920s?
3. Why do you think so many people were interested in seeing the Model A?

COMPOSING AN ESSAY *(20 points)* Write a brief essay on *one* of the following subjects. Remember to use examples to support your answer.

1. Discuss some of the negatives brought about by the widespread use of the automobile.
2. Describe how consumer practices changed during the 1920s.

Name _____ Class _____ Date _____

The Great Depression

CHAPTER 24

CHAPTER TEST • FORM A

REVIEWING FACTS *(3 points each)* In the space provided, write the name of the person identified by each description. Choose your answers from the list below. There are two extra names on the list.

Rexford Tugwell	James Hilton	Andrew Mellon
Herbert Hoover	Nathanael West	Franklin D. Roosevelt
Josefina Fierro de Bright	William Faulkner	Eleanor Roosevelt
James T. Farrell	Ella Baker	A. J. Muste

_____ 1. helped organize resistance to discrimination in the Southwest

_____ 2. wrote about a prosperous utopia in the mountains of Tibet

_____ 3. received much of the blame for the development of shantytowns

_____ 4. wrote *The Sound and the Fury*

_____ 5. presented the American dream as a nightmare in *Miss Lonelyhearts*

_____ 6. believed businesses should deal with the depression without government help

_____ 7. organized Unemployed Leagues to demand work

_____ 8. social reformer and great political asset to her husband

_____ 9. promised a "new deal" during his election campaign

_____ 10. wrote the *Studs Lonigan* trilogy

Chapter 24, Test Form A, Continued

■ **UNDERSTANDING IDEAS** *(3 points each)* For each of the following, place the letter of the *best* choice in the space provided.

_____ 1. All of the terms below could describe the U.S. economy before the depression EXCEPT
   a. bear market.
   b. easy credit.
   c. low interest.
   d. margin buying.

_____ 2. The worst economic crisis for banks came as a result of
   a. an extended bull market.
   b. appreciating assets.
   c. borrowers defaulting on loans.
   d. increasing stock values.

_____ 3. The Great Depression was caused by all of the following EXCEPT
   a. economic troubles in Europe.
   b. a decline in world trade.
   c. the rising stock market.
   d. buying stocks on margin.

_____ 4. During the Great Depression Midwest farmers faced all of the following EXCEPT
   a. an overabundance of food.
   b. foreclosures.
   c. falling crop prices.
   d. a high demand for their products.

_____ 5. Which of the following groups believed capitalism was to blame for the Great Depression?
   a. Democrats
   b. Republicans
   c. Socialists and Communists
   d. progressives

■ **TRUE/FALSE** *(2 points each)* Read each of the following statements, and then decide whether it is true or false. If the answer is true, place a *T* in the space provided; if the answer is false, place an *F* in the space.

_____ 1. In 1932 Congress passed a bonus bill that aided World War I veterans.

_____ 2. FDR came from a wealthy and prestigious family.

_____ 3. Republicans won decisive majorities in both houses of Congress in 1932.

_____ 4. Hoover's popularity increased dramatically as the election of 1932 neared.

_____ 5. The "Scottsboro Boys" were aided by the Communist Party.

_____ 6. Some economists believe depressions are a normal part of the business cycle.

_____ 7. Immigration to the United States greatly increased during the depression.

_____ 8. The percentage of women in the workforce increased in the 1930s.

_____ 9. Southern cotton farmers faced food shortages during the depression.

_____ 10. The number of radios greatly increased during the 1930s.

Chapter 24, Test Form A, Continued

■ PRACTICING SKILLS *(5 points each)* Study the graph below and answer the questions that follow.

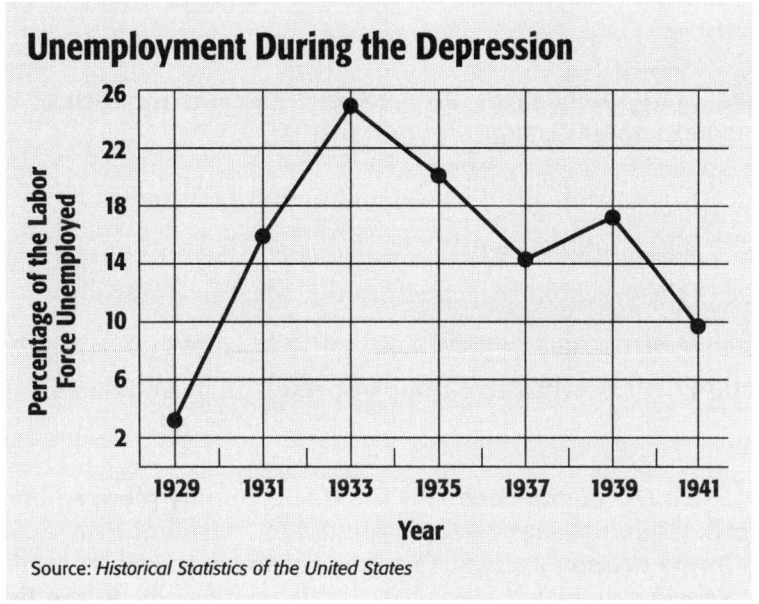

1. What percentage of people were unemployed in 1931?
   _____

2. During which year did the unemployment rate begin to drop from its peak?
   _____

3. The unemployment rate was about 20 percent in which years?
   _____

■ COMPOSING AN ESSAY *(20 points)* Write a brief essay on *one* of the following subjects. Remember to use examples to support your answer.

1. Describe how unemployment changed the lives of Americans during the Great Depression.

2. What were some of the ways in which the Great Depression affected Americans even years after it ended?

Name _____ Class _____ Date _____

The Great Depression

CHAPTER TEST • FORM B

■ SHORT ANSWER *(10 points each)* Provide brief answers for each of the following. Remember to use examples to support your answer.

1. How did the Great Depression affect tenant and migrant farmers?
2. What role did city organizations play during the Great Depression?
3. What were some of the psychological effects of the Great Depression?
4. What was the Bonus Army, and why did it gather in Washington, D.C., in 1932?
5. Why was Franklin D. Roosevelt such a popular presidential candidate in 1932?

■ PRIMARY SOURCE *(10 points each)* As the U.S. economy plunged and unemployment spiraled out of control, many people looked to President Hoover for leadership and a solution to the economic crisis. Did they get these things from him? In the following excerpts, Hoover provides the answers in his own words. In the first excerpt, he provides a solution for the widespread suffering inflicted by the depression. In the second excerpt, he talks about the idea of direct government aid. Read the excerpts and then answer the questions that follow.

> *What the country needs is a good big laugh. There seems to be a condition of hysteria. If someone could get off a good joke every ten days I think our troubles would be over.*

> *I do not believe that the power and duty of the [federal] Government ought to be extended to the relief of individual suffering. . . . The lesson should be constantly enforced that though the people support the Government the Government should not support the people.*

1. What did President Hoover recommend as a cure for the condition of hysteria?
2. How did the president feel about the government providing direct aid to suffering people?
3. If you had been alive during the depression, do you think you would have voted to re-elect Hoover in 1932? Why or why not?

■ COMPOSING AN ESSAY *(20 points)* Write a brief essay on *one* of the following subjects. Remember to use examples to support your answer.

1. Describe how popular culture and entertainment helped people of the 1930s cope with the depression.
2. Explain why President Hoover was perhaps the most hated man in America by 1932.

Name _____ Class _____ Date _____

The New Deal

CHAPTER 25

CHAPTER TEST • FORM A

■ **REVIEWING FACTS** *(3 points each)* For each of the following, place the letter of the *best* choice in the space provided.

_____ 1. Many of the New Deal recovery programs were based on his economic theories.
   a. Robert C. Weaver
   b. John Maynard Keynes
   c. John Collier
   d. Charles E. Coughlin

_____ 2. Who advised the Department of the Interior on racial matters?
   a. Huey Long
   b. Francis E. Townsend
   c. Charles E. Coughlin
   d. Robert C. Weaver

_____ 3. Which region of the nation became the Dust Bowl in the mid-1930s?
   a. West Coast
   b. Great Plains
   c. Rocky Mountains
   d. East Coast

_____ 4. Who was appointed director of the Division of Negro Affairs in the National Youth Administration?
   a. Harry Hopkins
   b. Frances Perkins
   c. Langston Hughes
   d. Mary McLeod Bethune

_____ 5. Margaret Mitchell wrote this novel about the Old South.
   a. *Gone With the Wind*
   b. *The Grapes of Wrath*
   c. *Native Son*
   d. *Their Eyes Were Watching God*

_____ 6. Which film director is recognized for *Mr. Smith Goes to Washington*?
   a. Frank Capra
   b. Thornton Wilder
   c. Robert Sherwood
   d. William Saroyan

_____ 7. Which artist is known for painting haunting images of the southwestern desert landscape?
   a. Anna "Grandma" Moses
   b. Grant Wood
   c. Georgia O'Keeffe
   d. Jacob Lawrence

_____ 8. Who founded the American Indian Defense Association?
   a. Harry L. Hopkins
   b. Frances Perkins
   c. Robert C. Weaver
   d. John Collier

_____ 9. Which critic of the New Deal proposed the Share-Our-Wealth program?
   a. Huey Long
   b. Dr. Francis E. Townsend
   c. Charles E. Coughlin
   d. Al Smith

_____ 10. Who was the depression-era photographer known for the photograph *Migrant Mother*?
   a. Gordon Parks
   b. Roy E. Stryker
   c. Dorothea Lange
   d. Margaret Bourke-White

Chapter and Unit Tests

Chapter 25, Test Form A, Continued

UNDERSTANDING IDEAS *(3 points each)* In the space provided, write the name of the New Deal act or program identified by each description. Choose your answers from the list below.

Civilian Conservation Corps
Tennessee Valley Authority
Federal Deposit Insurance Corporation
Social Security Act
National Youth Administration
Wagner-Connery Act
National Industrial Recovery Act
Works Progress Administration
Agricultural Adjustment Administration
Congress of Industrial Organizations

_____ 1. employed 8.5 million blue- and white-collar workers

_____ 2. provided high-school-and college-age people with part-time jobs

_____ 3. among other things, provided unemployment insurance

_____ 4. protected bank deposits up to a certain amount

_____ 5. the people in this program planted trees and created park trails

_____ 6. sought to increase business activity by limiting workers' hours, providing jobs, raising wages, and stabilizing prices

_____ 7. paid farmers to reduce their output of certain commodities

_____ 8. transformed economic and social life in a large region of the nation

_____ 9. guaranteed labor's right to organize unions and to bargain collectively

_____ 10. organized by labor leaders to unite workers in various industries

TRUE/FALSE *(2 points each)* Read each of the following statements, and then decide whether it is true or false. If the answer is true, place a *T* in the space provided; if the answer is false, place an *F* in the space.

_____ 1. Many of the "Okies" headed toward the East Coast after they lost their land during the drought.

_____ 2. Federal Project Number One provided work to artists.

_____ 3. John Steinbeck authored *The Grapes of Wrath*.

_____ 4. Artist Grant Wood is best known for his *American Gothic*.

_____ 5. FDR's "fireside chats" were televised from the White House.

Chapter 25, Test Form A, Continued

■ **PRACTICING SKILLS** *(5 points each)* Study the map below and answer the questions that follow.

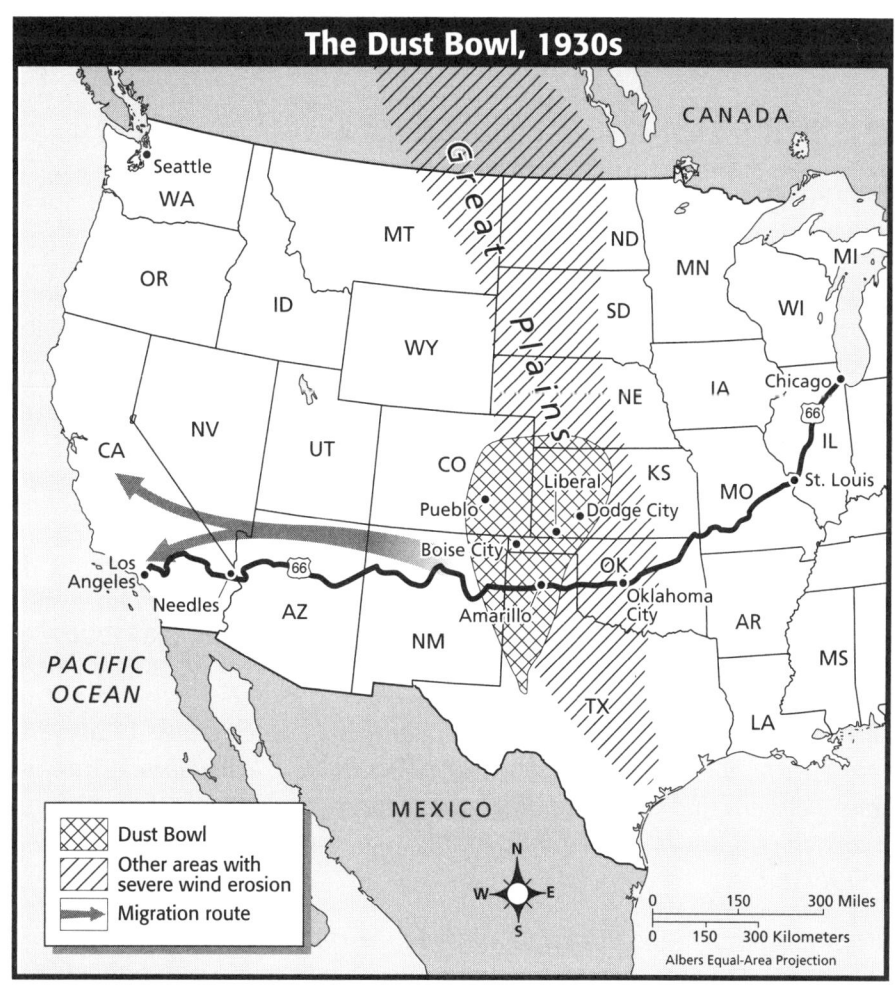

1. Which states had parts of their land within the Dust Bowl?

2. Which state became the destination of many people who moved from the Dust Bowl?

■ **COMPOSING AN ESSAY** *(20 points)* Write a brief essay on *one* of the following subjects. Remember to use examples to support your answer.

1. Critics of the New Deal thought more could be done to pull the nation out of the Great Depression. What were some of their suggestions? How were these suggestions addressed by the Roosevelt administration in the Second New Deal?

2. Describe how the introduction of electricity and indoor plumbing changed life in rural America.

Name _____ Class _____ Date _____

CHAPTER 25: The New Deal

CHAPTER TEST • FORM B

■ SHORT ANSWER *(10 points each)* Provide brief answers for each of the following. Remember to use examples to support your answer.

1. How did President Roosevelt try to "reform" the Supreme Court?
2. Describe some of the effects of the Dust Bowl.
3. Why did many federal agencies hire photographers during the Great Depression?
4. What was Federal Project Number One?
5. What were some of the advances made by African Americans during the Roosevelt administration?

■ PRIMARY SOURCE *(10 points each)* President Franklin D. Roosevelt set the tone for his administration with his inaugural address in 1933. Below is an excerpt from that address. Read the excerpt and then answer the questions that follow.

First of all, let me assert my firm belief that the only thing we have to fear is fear itself—nameless, unreasoning, unjustified terror which paralyzes needed efforts to convert retreat into advance. In every dark hour of our national life a leadership of frankness and vigor has met with that understanding and support of the people themselves which is essential to victory. I am convinced that you will again give that support to leadership in these critical days. . . .

The people of the United States have not failed. In their need they have registered a mandate that they want direct, vigorous action. They have asked for discipline and direction under leadership. They have made me the present instrument of their wishes. In the spirit of the gift I take it.

1. What did President Roosevelt believe was the only thing that the American public had to fear?
2. What promises did Roosevelt make in his speech?
3. What did Roosevelt ask in return for his leadership?

■ COMPOSING AN ESSAY *(20 points)* Write a brief essay on *one* of the following subjects. Remember to use examples to support your answer.

1. Discuss the common themes that appeared in films, novels, and plays of the New Deal Era.
2. Tell about the accomplishments of the Tennessee Valley Authority. Why did some people criticize it?

Prosperity and Crisis

UNIT TEST • FORM A

TRUE/FALSE *(2 points each)* Read each of the following statements, and then decide whether it is true or false. If the answer is true, place a *T* in the space provided; if the answer is false, place an *F* in the space.

_____ 1. Warren G. Harding was a 1920 presidential candidate who called for a return to "normalcy."

_____ 2. Calvin Coolidge supported the Boston Police Strike.

_____ 3. During the election of 1928, many Americans opposed Alfred E. Smith because he was African American.

_____ 4. The United Mine Workers Strike resulted in wage increases for its participants.

_____ 5. The Socialist Party believed in expanded capitalism.

_____ 6. The Harding administration raised taxes on wealthy Americans.

_____ 7. Organized labor made many gains during the 1920s.

_____ 8. Langston Hughes was a Harlem Renaissance poet who dealt with issues of Native American cultural heritage.

_____ 9. Most advertisements during the 1920s targeted women.

_____ 10. Prohibition led to a rise in organized crime.

_____ 11. Herbert Hoover received much of the blame for the development of shantytowns.

_____ 12. Socialists and Communists believed capitalism was to blame for the depression.

_____ 13. The popularity of sports increased in the 1920s.

_____ 14. The West Coast was referred to as the Dust Bowl in the mid-1930s.

_____ 15. The National Youth Administration provided high school and college-age people with part-time jobs.

Unit 7, Test Form A, Continued

REVIEWING FACTS *(3 points each)* In the space provided write the name of the person identified by each description. Choose your answers from the list below. There are two extra names on the list.

Franklin D. Roosevelt   Eliot Ness   Andrew Mellon
Mary McLeod Bethune   Margaret Mitchell   Eleanor Roosevelt
Huey Long   Al Capone   John L. Lewis
Charles Lindbergh   Dorothea Lange   Eugene Debs

_____ 1. proposed the Share-Our-Wealth program

_____ 2. wrote *Gone With the Wind*

_____ 3. a depression-era photographer known for her photograph *Migrant Mother*

_____ 4. organized the United Mine Workers strike

_____ 5. formed the Socialist Party

_____ 6. organized an elite squad of detectives to go after gangsters

_____ 7. the first pilot to fly nonstop from New York to Paris

_____ 8. believed businesses should deal with the depression without government help

_____ 9. promised a "new deal" during his election campaign

_____ 10. was appointed director of the Division of Negro Affairs in the National Youth Association

Unit 7, Test Form A, Continued

■ **PRACTICING SKILLS** *(5 points each)* Study the graph below and answer the questions that follow.

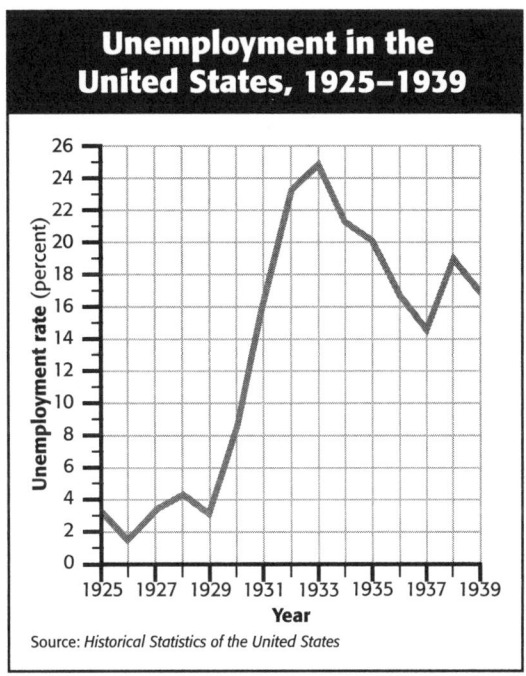

1. During what year was the unemployment rate the highest?

   _____

2. During what year was the unemployment rate the lowest?

   _____

3. During what years did the unemployment rate rise from 3 percent to 25 percent?

   _____

4. What was the unemployment rate in 1935?

   _____

■ **COMPOSING AN ESSAY** *(20 points)* Write a brief essay on *one* of the following subjects. Remember to use examples to support your answers.

1. Explain the rise and fall of support for the Ku Klux Klan during the 1920s.
2. Explain the pros and cons of assembly lines during the 1920s.

Prosperity and Crisis

UNIT TEST • FORM B

■ **SHORT ANSWER** *(10 points each)* Provide brief answers for each of the following. Remember to use examples to support your answers.

1. Describe the effects of demobilization on the nation's economy.
2. Who did advertisers target in the 1920s and why?
3. Discuss some of the effects of the Great Depression.
4. Why was Franklin D. Roosevelt such a popular presidential candidate in 1932?
5. What was Federal Project Number One?

■ **PRIMARY SOURCE** *(10 points each)* Woody Guthrie described the experiences of the common people in his music. Read his song "Talkin' Dust Bowl Blues" and answer the questions below.

Back in nineteen twenty-seven

Had a little farm and I called that heaven,

Prices up, the rain come down

Hauled my crops all in to town . . .

But the rain quit and th' wind got high,

Black old dust storm filled the sky,

I traded my farm for a Ford-machine

Poured it full of this gasoline . . .

Got to California so dadgum broke,

So dadgum hungry I thought I'd choke,

I bummed up a spud or two,

Wife fixed up some tater stew.

1. What period in our nation's history is this song describing?
2. What event does "Black old dust storm fills the sky" refer to?

■ **COMPOSING AN ESSAY** *(30 points)* Write an essay on *one* of the following subjects. Remember to use examples to support your answer.

1. What were the main causes of the strikes of 1919, and how did most Americans react to them?
2. Discuss the good and the bad effects brought about by the widespread use of the automobile.

Name _____ Class _____ Date _____

CHAPTER 26

The Road to War

CHAPTER TEST • FORM A

■ **REVIEWING FACTS** *(3 points each)* In the space provided, write the name of the person or the historical term that completes each sentence. Choose your answers from the list below. There are two extra names or terms on the list.

Anastasio Somoza	Brownshirts	Joseph Stalin
Winston Churchill	Charles Evans Hughes	Adolf Hitler
Fascist Party	Emiliano Chamorro	Benito Mussolini
Nazi Party	Blackshirts	Henry Stimson

1. In 1925 _____ overthrew the Nicaraguan government, sparking a civil war.

2. _____ proposed that the United States, Great Britain, and Japan destroy some of their warships to limit their naval strength.

3. After the assassination of Augusto César Sandino, _____ soon took over his nation's presidency.

4. The _____ believed that a military government should control all aspects of society.

5. Nazi storm troopers, known as _____, helped their leader crush all political opposition.

6. _____ feared that appeasement would only encourage Adolf Hitler.

7. The _____ was also known as the National Socialist Party.

8. _____ was the author of *Mein Kampf*.

9. _____ used underhanded tactics to take over power after Lenin's death.

10. In 1922 Italy's dictator led the _____ in a march on Rome.

Chapter and Unit Tests   Chapter 26   129

Chapter 26, Test Form A, Continued

UNDERSTANDING IDEAS *(3 points each)* For each of the following, place the letter of the *best* choice in the space provided.

_____ 1. In August 1939 Joseph Stalin signed a nonagression pact with
   a. Benito Mussolini.
   b. Adolf Hitler.
   c. Franklin D. Roosevelt.
   d. Winston Churchill.

_____ 2. The Republican candidate who faced Roosevelt in the 1940 election was
   a. Wendell Willkie.
   b. Herbert Hoover.
   c. Charles Evans Hughes.
   d. Barton K. Wheeler.

_____ 3. The attack of which country prompted Britain and France to declare war against Germany?
   a. Albania
   b. Czechoslovakia
   c. Poland
   d. Finland

_____ 4. In the Atlantic Charter, the United States and Britain agreed
   a. not to pursue territorial expansion.
   b. to appease Hitler.
   c. to remain neutral.
   d. to invade Germany.

_____ 5. Which date did Roosevelt describe as "a date which will live in infamy"?
   a. August 23, 1939
   b. September 1, 1939
   c. April 7, 1940
   d. December 7, 1941

_____ 6. In the 1920s and 1930s the United States followed a policy of
   a. imperialism.
   b. militarism.
   c. isolationism.
   d. alliance building.

_____ 7. The Kellogg-Briand Pact was violated by which nation in 1931?
   a. Japan
   b. Germany
   c. China
   d. Italy

_____ 8. In the 1930s caudillos seized power in all of the nations below *except*
   a. Cuba.
   b. Mexico.
   c. Honduras.
   d. Guatemala.

_____ 9. Hitler's government was known as the
   a. Popular Front.
   b. *Kristallnacht*.
   c. Blitzkrieg.
   d. Third Reich.

_____ 10. The Resistance was a secret organization operated by
   a. Germany.
   b. the United States.
   c. France.
   d. Norway.

TRUE/FALSE *(2 points each)* Read each of the following statements, and then decide whether it is true or false. If the answer is true, place a *T* in the space provided; if the answer is false, place an *F* in the space.

_____ 1. Stalin thought that communism and fascism were incompatible.

_____ 2. The Loyalists were victorious in the Spanish Civil War.

Chapter 26, Test Form A, Continued

_____ 3. The leaders at the Munich Conference signed a pact giving Germany control of the Sudetenland.

_____ 4. The war in Europe was a major issue in the 1940 presidential election.

_____ 5. Most U.S. citizens did not want their country to join the World Court.

■ **PRACTICING SKILLS** *(5 points each)* Study the tables below and answer the questions that follow.

Presidential Election Results, Major Candidates, 1932–1940

THE ELECTION OF 1932			
Candidate	Party	Popular Vote	Electoral Vote
Franklin D. Roosevelt	Democratic	22,809,638	472
Herbert C. Hoover	Republican	15,758,901	59

THE ELECTION OF 1936			
Candidate	Party	Popular Vote	Electoral Vote
Franklin D. Roosevelt	Democratic	27,752,869	523
Alfred M. Landon	Republican	16,674,665	8

THE ELECTION OF 1940			
Candidate	Party	Popular Vote	Electoral Vote
Franklin D. Roosevelt	Democratic	27,263,448	449
Wendell Willkie	Republican	22,336,260	82

1. In which election did Roosevelt enjoy his greatest popularity?

   _____

2. Which presidential candidate provided the biggest challenge to Roosevelt?

   _____

■ **COMPOSING AN ESSAY** *(20 points)* Write a brief essay on *one* of the following subjects. Remember to use examples to support your answer.

1. Discuss U.S. foreign policy after World War I.
2. Describe the role the United States played in Nicaragua in the 1920s and 1930s.

Name _____ Class _____ Date _____

CHAPTER 26
The Road to War

CHAPTER TEST • FORM B

■ **SHORT ANSWER** *(10 points each)* Provide brief answers for each of the following. Remember to use examples to support your answer.

1. How did Adolf Hitler gain power in Germany?
2. What military actions did Japan take in the 1930s?
3. Why did the four European leaders at the Munich Conference adopt a policy of appeasement toward Hitler?
4. What did both of the candidates in the 1940 presidential election promise?
5. Why did Japan decide to bomb Pearl Harbor?

■ **PRIMARY SOURCE** *(10 points each)* In 1916 Charles Evans Hughes almost became president of the United States. He lost to Woodrow Wilson by only 23 electoral votes. After this defeat, he turned his attentions to the issue of world peace. After World War I, Hughes provided a vision of the future. The following is an excerpt of that vision. Read the excerpt and then answer the questions that follow.

> *We emerge from the war with a new national consciousness; with a consciousness of power stimulated by extraordinary effort; with a consciousness of the possibility and potency [power] of cooperation. . . . We are unworthy of our victory, if we look forward with timidity. This is the hour and power of light, not of darkness. . . . We have made the world safe for democracy, but democracy is not a phrase or a form, but a life, and what shall that life be? . . . We have fought this War to substitute reason for force. We love our Republic because it represents to us the promise of the rule of reason. . . . If we are to establish peace within our own borders, we must cooperate to destroy the . . . spirit of tyranny whenever we find it.*

1. What did Hughes mean when he said, "We have fought this War to substitute reason for force"?
2. What do you think Hughes meant by "the spirit of tyranny"?
3. Based on his statements above, do you think Hughes campaigned for or against the United States joining the League of Nations?

■ **COMPOSING AN ESSAY** *(20 points)* Write a brief essay on *one* of the following subjects. Remember to use examples to support your answer.

1. Discuss the effects that the Great Depression had on Latin American governments.
2. Describe some of the actions taken by Joseph Stalin to turn the Soviet Union into a totalitarian state.

Name _____ Class _____ Date _____

Americans in World War II

CHAPTER 27

CHAPTER TEST • FORM A

REVIEWING FACTS *(3 points each)* For each of the following, place the letter of the *best* choice in the space provided.

_____ 1. The promise "I shall return" is linked to which of these places?
   a. Midway
   b. Bataan
   c. Coral Sea
   d. Okinawa

_____ 2. Who was given command of all U.S. Army units in the Pacific?
   a. George S. Patton
   b. Bernard Montgomery
   c. Douglas MacArthur
   d. Dwight D. Eisenhower

_____ 3. The important Allied victory that stopped the Japanese advance on Australia was the
   a. Battle of the Coral Sea.
   b. Battle of the Atlantic.
   c. Battle of Leyte Gulf.
   d. Battle of Okinawa.

_____ 4. Who was the commander of the Afrika Korps known as the Desert Fox?
   a. Chester Nimitz
   b. Erwin Rommel
   c. Douglas MacArthur
   d. Irving Berlin

_____ 5. Thanks partly to the refinement of sonar, the Allies were able to win the Battle of
   a. the Atlantic.
   b. the Coral Sea.
   c. Iwo Jima.
   d. the Bulge.

_____ 6. On D-Day, the Allies landed at
   a. Calais.
   b. Belle Isle.
   c. Normandy.
   d. Anzio.

_____ 7. What was the Germans' final counterattack?
   a. D-Day
   b. Battle of the Atlantic
   c. Battle of Midway
   d. Battle of the Bulge

_____ 8. Who led British forces to victory in North Africa?
   a. Bernard Montgomery
   b. Erwin Rommel
   c. Dwight D. Eisenhower
   d. Douglas MacArthur

_____ 9. Who was commander of the U.S. Pacific Fleet?
   a. Chester Nimitz
   b. Dwight D. Eisenhower
   c. George S. Patton
   d. Bernard Montgomery

_____ 10. What was perhaps the bloodiest battle of the Pacific war?
   a. Okinawa
   b. Midway
   c. Iwo Jima
   d. Coral Sea

Chapter and Unit Tests   Chapter 27   133

Chapter 27, Test Form A, Continued

UNDERSTANDING IDEAS (3 points each)
In the space provided, write the name of the person or the historical term identified by each description. Choose your answers from the list below. There are two extra names or terms on the list.

Carlos E. Castañeda
Holocaust
Yalta Conference
A. Philip Randolph
Harry S Truman
genocide
internment
Office of War Mobilization
Franklin D. Roosevelt
Elie Wiesel
Manhattan Project
Selective Training and Service Act

_____ 1. had to decide whether to use the atomic bomb against Japan

_____ 2. writer who was a survivor of the death camps

_____ 3. associated with Enrico Fermi and Leslie R. Groves

_____ 4. postwar peace was on the agenda

_____ 5. systematic slaughter of European Jews

_____ 6. deliberate annihilation of an entire people

_____ 7. led a march on Washington, D.C., to protest discrimination against African Americans

_____ 8. forced relocation of Japanese Americans

_____ 9. provided for the first peacetime draft in U.S. history

_____ 10. tried to improve the working conditions for Mexican Americans in Texas

TRUE/FALSE (2 points each)
Read each of the following statements, and then decide whether it is true or false. If the answer is true, place a *T* in the space provided; if the answer is false, place an *F* in the space.

_____ 1. The first atomic bomb exploded at Nagasaki.

_____ 2. Island-hopping was an effective policy adopted by the Japanese.

_____ 3. In the 1944 presidential election, Roosevelt narrowly defeated Dewey.

_____ 4. George S. Patton led the U.S. invasion of Sicily.

_____ 5. The number of women in the workforce increased greatly during the war.

Chapter 27, Test Form A, Continued

**PRACTICING SKILLS** *(5 points each)* Study the map below and answer the questions that follow.

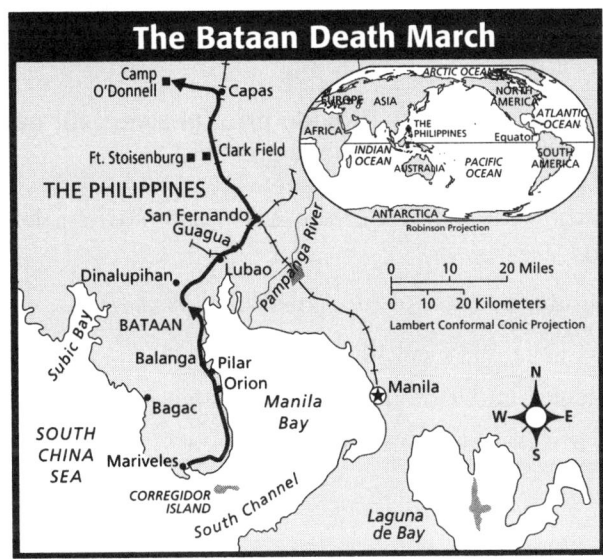

1. Where is the Bataan Peninsula in relation to the capital of the Philippines?

   _____

2. About how far did the U.S. prisoners have to march from Mariveles to San Fernando?

   _____

COMPOSING AN ESSAY *(20 points)* Write a brief essay on *one* of the following subjects. Remember to use examples to support your answer.

1. Explain the advantages the Axis Powers had over the Allies when the United States entered the war.
2. Describe women's contributions to the U.S. war effort.

Name _____ Class _____ Date _____

Americans in World War II

CHAPTER TEST • FORM B

■ **SHORT ANSWER** *(10 points each)* Provide brief answers for each of the following. Remember to use examples to support your answer.

1. What advantages did the Allies have over the Axis Powers when the United States entered World War II?
2. How did the United States prepare to fight in World War II?
3. Why were the Nazis able to carry out the Holocaust?
4. What events led to the surrender of Germany in 1945?
5. What major decision did President Truman have to make after the death of President Roosevelt?

■ **PRIMARY SOURCE** *(10 points each)* The U.S. advance across the Pacific was met with ferocious resistance from the Japanese. In the excerpt below, Eugene B. Sledge, a U.S. Marine, provides a glimpse of what it was like to engage in battle with the Japanese. Read the excerpt and then answer the questions that follow.

The Japanese fought by a code they thought was right: bushido. *The code of the warrior: no surrender. You really don't comprehend it until you get out there and fight people who are faced with an absolutely hopeless situation and will not give up. If you tried to help one of the Japanese, he'd usually detonate a grenade and kill himself as well as you. To be captured was a disgrace. . . . You developed an attitude of no mercy because they had no mercy on us. It was a no-quarter, savage kind of thing. . . . If you're reduced to savagery by a situation, anything's possible. When [Charles] Lindbergh made a trip to the Philippines, he was horrified at the way American GIs talked about the Japanese. It was so savage. We were savages.*

1. What was *bushido*?
2. Why did Sledge develop an attitude of no mercy?
3. Why do you think the GIs in the Philippines talked so savagely about the Japanese?

■ **COMPOSING AN ESSAY** *(20 points)* Write a brief essay on *one* of the following subjects. Remember to use examples to support your answer.

1. Tell how Japanese Americans were affected by the war.
2. Describe how the Allies achieved victory at Normandy.

Name _____ Class _____ Date _____

The Cold War

CHAPTER TEST • FORM A

REVIEWING THE FACTS *(3 points each)* In the space provided, write the name of the person or historical term identified by each description. Choose your answer from the list below. There are two extra names or terms on the list below.

Douglas MacArthur
Eleanor Roosevelt
containment
George Marshall
Joseph McCarthy
Mao Zedong
Potsdam Conference
United Nations
zaibatsu
Dwight D. Eisenhower
brinkmanship
blacklisted

_____ 1. meeting of allied powers to discuss details of the joint occupation of Germany after World War II

_____ 2. huge family run corporations that monopolized Japan's economy

_____ 3. postwar international organization aimed at working together for world peace

_____ 4. one of the first U.S. delegates to the United Nations, and social activist

_____ 5. Secretary of state who promoted European recovery by helping to secure economic aid for Western Europe

_____ 6. U.S. policy to stop the spread of Soviet communism

_____ 7. general who commanded troops in the Korean War and opposed President Truman's war strategy

_____ 8. president who made good on his promise to end the Korean War, and used a covert approach to international affairs

_____ 9. U.S. senator who waged war on alleged communist sympathizers

_____ 10. revolutionary communist leader of China

Chapter 28, Test Form A, Continued

TRUE/FALSE (2 points each) Read each of the following statements, and then decide whether it is true or false. If the answer is true, place a *T* in the space provided; if the answer is false, place an *F* in the space.

_____ 1. In 1947 Japan adopted a new constitution that established a democratic system of government.

_____ 2. The Baruch Plan succeeded in controlling the use of atomic energy.

_____ 3. Joseph Stalin ordered the Berlin Airlift.

_____ 4. Joseph McCarthy provided hard evidence to support his accusations against communist sympathizers.

_____ 5. The phrase "One Nation Under God" was added to the Pledge of Allegiance as a stand against the atheistic Soviet Union.

_____ 6. The Berlin Airlift attempted to remove people out of West Berlin.

_____ 7. The Marshall Plan was executed to rebuild Eastern Europe.

_____ 8. President Truman had the support of all Americans when he fired Joseph McCarthy over differences concerning the Korean War.

_____ 9. In the Korean War, American and Soviet troops fought each other in battle.

_____ 10. The U-2 incident helped to improve diplomatic relations between the United States and the Soviet Union.

MATCHING (3 points each) Match the term with its correct definition.

_____ 1. As a member of this organization, Western countries pledged to defend the other members in the event of an outside attack.

_____ 2. members advise the president on strategic matters

_____ 3. members gather strategic political and military information overseas

_____ 4. the Soviet Union's military alliance formed with other communist countries

_____ 5. an anticommunist measure that required Communist Party members and organizations to register with the federal government

a. Central Intelligence Agency
b. Internal Security Act
c. NATO
d. National Security Council
e. Warsaw Pact

Chapter 28, Test Form A, Continued

■ **PRACTICING SKILLS** *(5 points each)* Study the map below and answer the questions that follow.

1. Which nations were members of NATO in 1955?

   _____

2. Who had more members—NATO or the Warsaw Pact?

   _____

■ **COMPOSING AN ESSAY** *(25 points each)* Write a brief essay on *one* of the following subjects. Remember to use examples to support your answer.

1. How did the fear of communism affect the lives of the American people and the country as a whole?
2. Describe some of the ways in which the United States and its allies worked to contain Soviet expansion after World War II.

Name _____ Class _____ Date _____

The Cold War

CHAPTER TEST • FORM B

■ **SHORT ANSWER** *(10 points each)* Provide brief answers for each of the following. Remember to use examples to support your answers.

1. How did the Korean War help to get Dwight D. Eisenhower elected president?
2. How did the Truman Doctrine and Marshall Plan help resist the spread of communism?
3. What caused the Arab-Israeli War?
4. What were satellite nations?
5. How did Americans respond to the launch of *Sputnik*?

■ **PRIMARY SOURCE** *(10 points each)* Anne O'Hare McCormick was a journalist who commented on the impact of the Potsdam Conference. Read the following passage and answer the questions that follow.

> *There are moments when the drama of our times seems to focus on a single scene. The meeting at Potsdam [Germany] is one of those moments. We can hardly take in the sense of what happened until it is spelled out in a picture like this. The picture of three men walking in a graveyard. They are the men who hold in their hands most of the power in the world.*

1. Who are the "three men walking in a graveyard" Anne O'Hare McCormick refers to in this passage?
2. What does she mean by men "walking in a graveyard"?
3. What event are the three men attending?

■ **COMPOSING AN ESSAY** *(20 points each)* Write a brief essay on *one* of the following subjects. Remember to use examples to support your answer.

1. Compare the political, economic, and philosophical differences between the Soviet Union and the United States during the Cold War.
2. Describe some of the actions the U.S. government took during the Red Scare.

Name _____ Class _____ Date _____

Society After World War II

CHAPTER TEST • FORM A

REVIEWING FACTS *(3 points each)* In the space provided, write the name of the person, legislation, or historical term identified by each description. Choose your answers from the list below. There are two extra items on the list.

Thomas Dewey
baby boom
Rosa Parks
automation

GI Bill of Rights
Landrum-Griffin Act
Brown v. *Board of Education*
Taft-Hartley Act

George Meany
Martin Luther King Jr.
Little Rock Nine
beats

_____ 1. Supreme Court ruling that made segregation in public schools illegal

_____ 2. African American arrested for refusing to give a bus seat to a white passenger

_____ 3. Republican candidate for president in 1948

_____ 4. legislation providing financial help to World War II veterans

_____ 5. first president of AFL–CIO labor union

_____ 6. African American students admitted to an all-white high school in 1957

_____ 7. bill passed in 1947 to lessen power of organized labor

_____ 8. introduction of machinery to do work people had done previously

_____ 9. high birthrate accompanying peacetime prosperity

_____ 10. writers who protested and challenged middle-class way of life

Chapter 29, Test Form A, Continued

UNDERSTANDING IDEAS *(3 points each)* For each of the following, place the letter of the *best* choice in the space provided.

_____ 1. After World War II, many women lost their jobs because
   a. men could do a better job.
   b. priority was given to returning veterans.
   c. they had children.
   d. inflation lowered wages.

_____ 2. Adoption of the civil rights plank by the 1948 Democratic Convention led to
   a. a race riot at the convention.
   b. northern delegates leaving.
   c. fierce arguing among all the different factions of Democrats.
   d. formation of the States' Rights Party.

_____ 3. For the majority of American workers, the 1950s were a time of
   a. greater prosperity than they had ever known.
   b. plentiful jobs but little advancement.
   c. corporate mergers.
   d. hardship and struggle.

_____ 4. Changes in the workforce, income, and mobility, plus a rapidly expanding population, resulted in
   a. the development of suburbs.
   b. great strains on America's highway system.
   c. conflict between lower- and middle-class citizens.
   d. reforms of consumer law.

_____ 5. Advertisers invested heavily in television because
   a. print advertising no longer appealed to the public.
   b. they liked the variety of programming television offered.
   c. it was a good way to reach and influence a lot of consumers.
   d. it was free.

_____ 6. Many teenagers sought release from the conformity of their suburban families through
   a. drugs and alcohol.
   b. rock 'n' roll music.
   c. shopping.
   d. filmmaking.

_____ 7. Teenage discontent and rebellion were featured in the works of
   a. Charles Van Doren.
   b. Elvis Presley.
   c. J. D. Salinger.
   d. James Dean.

_____ 8. To enforce desegregation law at a school in Little Rock, Arkansas,
   a. Governor Orval Faubus sent the Arkansas National Guard.
   b. FBI agents and state police stood guard.
   c. the Little Rock Nine protested.
   d. President Eisenhower sent 1,000 federal troops.

_____ 9. The NAACP and the Montgomery Improvement Association challenged racial segregation of public transportation by
   a. organizing a boycott of the bus system by African Americans.
   b. organizing protest demonstrations and marches in the city.
   c. winning a major court battle on behalf of Rosa Parks.
   d. taking their case to the Supreme Court.

_____ 10. In the 1950s urban areas increasingly became characterized by
   a. dazzling homes of the wealthy.
   b. loss of population.
   c. slums and many displaced rural and ethnic workers.
   d. solid housing for the poor.

Chapter 29, Test Form A, Continued

■ TRUE/FALSE *(2 points each)* Read each of the following statements, and then decide whether it is true or false. If the answer is true, place a *T* in the space provided; if the answer is false, place an *F* in the space.

_____ 1. The dominant mood of the American people following World War II was fearful and anxious.

_____ 2. In the 1950s teenagers chose entertainment that criticized their parents' suburban values.

_____ 3. The Relocation Act of 1956 encouraged American Indians to move into urban areas.

_____ 4. Farming productivity increased dramatically in the 1950s, but many farmers remained poor.

_____ 5. Hispanics fared the best of all ethnic minorities in the United States in the 1950s.

■ PRACTICING SKILLS *(5 points each)* Study the chart and graph below and answer the questions that follow.

1. Which increased more, the number of colleges or the number of students?

   _____

2. What happened to the percentage of female college students?

   _____

   _____

Higher Education

	THEN	NOW
Number of Institutions of Higher Education	1,863	3,706
Annual Student Body Enrollment	2,281,000	14,715,000
Annual Number of Bachelor's Degrees Conferred	496,874	1,191,000

Student Body: Then — Female 32%, Male 68%; Now — Female 54%, Male 46%

Sources: *Historical Statistics of the United States: Colonial Times to 1970; Statistical Abstract of the United States: 1998.* Data reflects 1950 and 1995.

■ COMPOSING AN ESSAY *(20 points)* Write a brief essay on *one* of the following subjects. Remember to use examples to support your answer.

1. Summarize the progress made in civil rights for minorities from 1945 to 1960.
2. Explain the weaknesses of American society as pointed out by social critics of the 1950s.

Name _____ Class _____ Date _____

Society After World War II

CHAPTER TEST • FORM B

■ **SHORT ANSWER** *(10 points each)* Provide brief answers for each of the following. Remember to use examples to support your answer.

1. What factors led to the growth of the suburbs in the 1950s?
2. Compare and contrast the reasons for and the effects of the Taft-Hartley Act and the Landrum-Griffin Act.
3. Why did Harry S Truman win the presidential election in 1948, despite the press prediction that Thomas Dewey would win?
4. How were wages and the workplace different for laborers in the 1950s?
5. Why did so many suburban dwellers feel pressured to conform to the "ideal family image" portrayed by the media in the 1950s?
6. What methods were used in the successful Montgomery bus boycott?

■ **PRIMARY SOURCE** *(10 points each)* The United States passed the GI Bill of Rights in 1944, preparing for the return of veterans. It provided pensions and loans, as well as money for college, to allow soldiers to reenter society successfully. Its impact had even more far-reaching effects, as described by government worker Nelson Poynter. Read the excerpt and answer the questions that follow.

> *The GI . . . Bill had more to do with thrusting us into a new era than anything else. Millions of people whose parents or grandparents had never dreamed of going to college saw that they could go. . . . Essentially I think it made us a far more democratic people.*

1. How did the GI Bill of Rights directly affect the size of America's middle class? Explain the steps in this process.
2. How might the GI Bill of Rights have helped accelerate the change to an economy based on automation and white-collar employment in big businesses?

■ **COMPOSING AN ESSAY** *(20 points)* Write a brief essay on *one* of the following subjects. Remember to use examples to support your answer.

1. Summarize the progress made by minorities in civil rights from 1945 to 1960.
2. Explain the weaknesses of American society as pointed out by social critics of the 1950s.

World Conflicts

UNIT TEST • FORM A

MATCHING *(3 points each)* Match each person with the correct description. Write the names on the lines below. There are two extra names on the list.

Dwight D. Eisenhower   Douglas MacArthur   Adolf Hitler
Emiliano Chamorro   Bernard Montgomery   Francisco Franco
Charles Evans Hughes   Joseph Stalin   Erwin Rommel
George S. Patton   Harry S Truman   Clement Atlee

_____ 1. overthrew the Nicaraguan government in 1925, sparking a civil war

_____ 2. the author of *Mein Kampf*

_____ 3. signed a nonaggression pact with Adolf Hitler in 1939

_____ 4. the fascist leader of Spain

_____ 5. commander of all U.S. Army units in the Pacific

_____ 6. the commander of the Afrika Korps known as the Desert Fox

_____ 7. led British forces to victory in North Africa

_____ 8. had to decide whether to use the atomic bomb against Japan

_____ 9. leader of the Washington Conference who pushed for naval disarmament

_____ 10. made good on his promise to end the Korean War, and used a covert approach to international affairs

Unit 8, Test Form A, Continued

TRUE/FALSE *(2 points each)* Read each of the following statements, and then decide whether it is true or false. If the answer is true, place a *T* in the space provided; if the answer is false, place an *F* in the space.

_____ 1. After World War II, many working women left the workplace because they had better educational opportunities.

_____ 2. For the majority of American workers, the 1950s were a time of greater prosperity than they had ever known.

_____ 3. To enforce desegregation laws at a school in Little Rock, Arkansas, President Eisenhower sent 1,000 federal troops.

_____ 4. Hispanics fared the best of all ethnic minorities in the United States in the 1950s.

_____ 5. Many teenagers sought release from the conformity of their suburban families through rock 'n' roll music.

REVIEWING FACTS *(3 points each)* Choose from the following list to complete each of the statements below. There are two extra terms on the list.

Taft-Hartley Act	Battle of the Bulge	isolationism
GI Bill of Rights	Nazi Party	Brownshirts
Blackshirts	Fascist Party	automation
Yalta Conference	Third Reich	Resistance

1. The _____ believed that a military government should control all aspects of society.

2. Nazi storm troopers, known as _____, helped their leader crush all political opposition.

3. The _____ was also known as the National Socialist Party.

4. In 1922 Italy's dictator led the _____ in a march on Rome.

5. In the 1920s and 1930s the United States followed a policy of _____.

6. Hitler's government was known as the _____.

7. The _____ was a secret organization operated by France.

8. The _____ was the German army's final counterattack.

9. Postwar peace was on the agenda at the _____.

10. The _____ was passed in 1947 to lessen the power of organized labor.

Unit 8, Test Form A, Continued

■ **PRACTICING SKILLS** *(5 points each)* Study the graph below to answer the questions about Americans' thoughts on World War II.

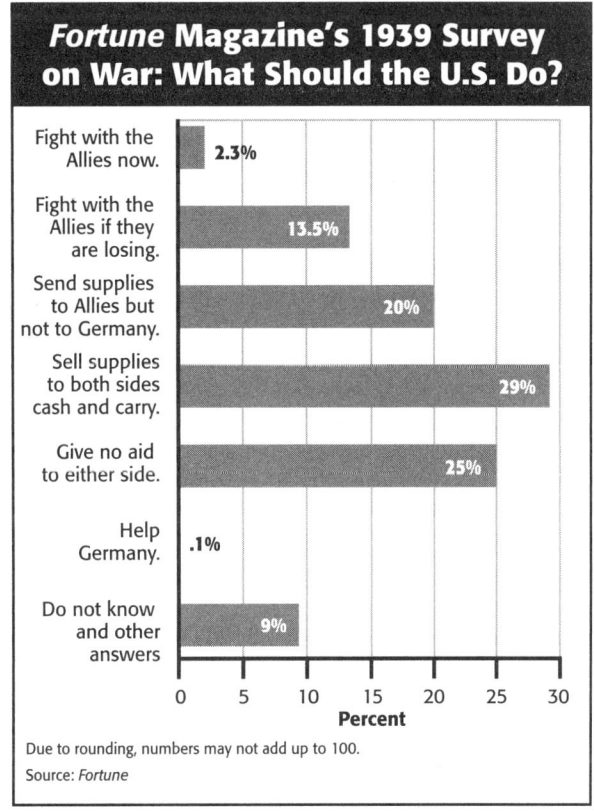

1. According to the graph, what did the largest group of Americans feel the United States should do concerning the war?

   _____

2. What percent of the population felt the United States should fight with the Allies only if they were losing?

   _____

■ **COMPOSING AN ESSAY** *(20 points)* Write a brief essay on *one* of the following subjects. Remember to use examples to support your answer.

1. Explain what caused the Montgomery bus boycott and what made it successful.
2. Explain what was decided at the Potsdam Conference.

Chapter and Unit Tests   Unit 8   **147**

Name _____ Class _____ Date _____

World Conflicts

UNIT TEST • FORM B

■ SHORT ANSWER (10 points each) Provide brief answers for each of the following. Remember to use examples to support your answers.

1. What prompted Britain and France to declare war against Germany?
2. What did the Kellogg-Briand Pact do?
3. Why did the leaders at the Munich Conference adopt a policy of appeasement toward Hitler?
4. What was the significance of the Battle of the Coral Sea?
5. What factors led to the development of suburbs?

■ PRIMARY SOURCE (10 points each) The attack on Pearl Harbor greatly influenced many Americans' views of the war. Read this young sailor's recollection of the time, and answer the questions that follow.

I was sixteen years old, employed . . . at Pearl Harbor Navy Yard. On December 7, 1941, oh, around 8:00 A.M., my grandmother awoke me. She informed me that the Japanese were bombing Pearl Harbor . . . I was asked . . . to go into the water and get sailors out that had been blown off the ships. Some were unconscious, some were dead. I brought out I don't know how many bodies . . . I tried to get into the military, but they refused . . . Finally, I wrote a letter to President Roosevelt. I told him I was angry at the Japanese bombing and had lost some friends. He okayed that I be accepted.

1. Why did this young man have to write a letter to the president before he could be accepted into the military?
2. Why do you think he was so eager to fight in the war?

■ COMPOSING AN ESSAY (30 points) Write an essay on *one* of the following subjects. Remember to use examples to support your answer.

1. How did the United States prepare to fight in World War II, and what advantages did the Allies have over the Axis Powers when the United States did enter the war?
2. Discuss what historians see as the pros and cons of President Truman's decision to use the atomic bomb.

Name _____ Class _____ Date _____

CHAPTER 30: The New Frontier and the Great Society

CHAPTER TEST • FORM A

REVIEWING FACTS *(3 points each)* In the space provided, write the name of the person, place, or historical term identified by each description. Choose your answers from the list below. There are two extra items on the list.

Fidel Castro   Peace Corps   Bay of Pigs
flexible response   Great Society   John F. Kennedy
Lee Harvey Oswald   Medicare   Medicaid
Lyndon B. Johnson   Barry Goldwater   Rachel Carson

_____ 1. President Johnson's plan for advancing social reforms and improved quality of life

_____ 2. failed invasion and overthrow of Cuba by the United States

_____ 3. charismatic Democratic president calling for sacrifices to protect freedoms

_____ 4. federal program providing free health care to the poor

_____ 5. communist leader of Cuba

_____ 6. environmentalist author of *Silent Spring*

_____ 7. conservative Republican candidate for president in 1964

_____ 8. arrested for assassination of President Kennedy

_____ 9. various ways to handle international crises

_____ 10. used his political gift to push through Kennedy's programs

UNDERSTANDING IDEAS *(3 points each)* For each of the following, place the letter of the *best* choice in the space provided.

_____ 1. A pivotal reason why Kennedy defeated Nixon in 1960 was
   a. Kennedy was younger.
   b. Kennedy fared better than Nixon in televised debates.
   c. voters liked Kennedy's policies and ideas better.
   d. Nixon lacked the experience to inspire confidence.

_____ 2. An international incident that brought the United States and the Soviet Union to the brink of nuclear war was
   a. the Bay of Pigs.
   b. the Limited Nuclear Test Ban Treaty.
   c. the Cuban missile crisis.
   d. establishment of the Berlin Wall.

Chapter and Unit Tests   Chapter 30 **149**

Chapter 30, Test Form A, Continued

_____ 3. Jacqueline Kennedy contributed most to the Kennedy administration by
   a. introducing programs to beautify America.
   b. mothering two young children.
   c. stimulating appreciation for the fine arts and culture.
   d. speaking out about her husband's heroism and idealism.

_____ 4. To help curtail rising unemployment and inflation and stimulate economic growth, Kennedy
   a. supported stronger unions and asked retailers to lower prices.
   b. reduced government spending and increased taxes.
   c. shut down inefficient government offices and combined others.
   d. asked businesses to limit prices and workers to accept fewer pay raises.

_____ 5. Kennedy's presidency was dominated by
   a. concern with international crises and the threat of nuclear war.
   b. a close and productive working relationship with Congress.
   c. problems with the military and the banking sector.
   d. struggles to establish an effective cabinet.

_____ 6. A Kennedy program aimed at improving poor Americans' standard of living was
   a. the Peace Corps.
   b. the War on Poverty.
   c. the Area Redevelopment Act.
   d. the Warren Commission.

_____ 7. In the first year of Lyndon B. Johnson's presidency, he showed that
   a. he was effective in getting Kennedy's programs passed into law.
   b. he had no intention of following Kennedy's agenda for social progress.
   c. Congress refused to consider antipoverty programs.
   d. he disapproved of U.S. military involvement overseas.

_____ 8. Which Johnson program was aimed at urban renewal?
   a. National Endowment for the Humanities
   b. Omnibus Housing Act
   c. Water Pollution Act
   d. Elementary and Secondary Education Act

_____ 9. Rachel Carson's book *Silent Spring* showed how Americans were poisoning their environment with
   a. nuclear wastes.
   b. factory wastes.
   c. raw sewage.
   d. pesticides.

_____ 10. Under Chief Justice Earl Warren, the Supreme Court made many decisions
   a. favoring civil rights for minorities.
   b. strengthening individual rights.
   c. aiding law enforcement and justice officials.
   d. establishing ethical banking practices.

Chapter 30, Test Form A, Continued

■ TRUE/FALSE *(2 points each)* Read each of the following statements, and then decide whether it is true or false. If the answer is true, place a *T* in the space provided; if the answer is false, place an *F* in the space.

_____ 1. The failure of the Bay of Pigs operation was largely due to strong support from Soviet troops.

_____ 2. Kennedy planned to stop communism's advance through strong military force, nuclear weapons, and aid to developing countries.

_____ 3. Many of Kennedy's programs failed to pass Congress because Republicans outnumbered Democrats.

_____ 4. Johnson fulfilled Kennedy's legislative goals without pursuing his own agenda.

_____ 5. Johnson's Great Society programs lost influence late in the 1960s as the Vietnam War preoccupied the nation.

■ PRACTICING SKILLS *(5 points each)* Study the map below and answer the questions that follow.

1. What states gave all or part of their electoral votes to Harry Byrd?

   _____
   _____
   _____
   _____

2. By which count was the election closer: electoral vote or popular vote?

   _____
   _____
   _____
   _____

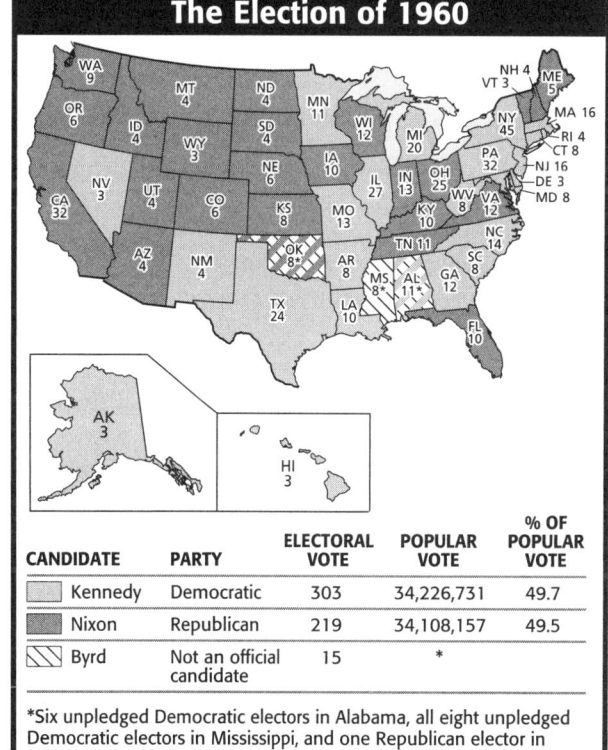

■ COMPOSING AN ESSAY *(20 points each)* Write a brief essay on *one* of the following subjects. Remember to use examples to support your answer.

1. Discuss Kennedy's public image, his influence on America, and how his assassination affected the country.

2. In what ways did Johnson propose to improve life for Americans through his Great Society agenda?

Name _____ Class _____ Date _____

CHAPTER 30: The New Frontier and the Great Society

CHAPTER TEST • FORM B

■ **SHORT ANSWER** *(10 points each)* Provide brief answers for each of the following. Remember to use examples to support your answer.

1. List factors that added to John F. Kennedy's appeal as a candidate and those that hurt his popularity.
2. What role did nuclear weapons play in President Kennedy's foreign policy?
3. Explain why Kennedy's administration was compared to Camelot.
4. How did President Johnson put Kennedy's social programs into effect? What programs was he responsible for creating?
5. What programs did Johnson and Congress establish to improve society? What legislation did they pass?
6. Name three ways the Supreme Court of the 1960s supported and expanded individual rights.

■ **PRIMARY SOURCE** *(5 points each)* In his inaugural speech, John F. Kennedy spoke of the challenges and sacrifices ahead if America was to overcome the threat of communism and nuclear war. Read the excerpt and answer the questions that follow.

> *In the long history of the world, only a few generations have been granted the role of defending freedom in its hour of maximum danger. I do not shrink from this responsibility—I welcome it. . . . The energy, the faith, the devotion which we bring to this endeavor will light our country and all who serve it—and the glow from that fire can truly light the world.*
>
> *And so my fellow Americans: ask not what your country can do for you—ask what you can do for your country.*
>
> *My fellow citizens of the world: ask not what America will do for you, but what together we can do for the freedom of man.*

1. What is the responsibility of Americans, according to Kennedy?
2. How are Americans to carry out this task?
3. Why do you think Americans found Kennedy's words inspiring?

■ **COMPOSING AN ESSAY** *(25 points each)* Write a brief essay on *one* of the following subjects. Remember to use examples to support your answer.

1. Compare and contrast the background, political style, and accomplishments of Presidents Kennedy and Johnson.
2. Discuss three international crises of Kennedy's administration. Rank them in order from least to most threatening to U.S. security, and explain your ranking.

The Civil Rights Movement

CHAPTER TEST • FORM A

REVIEWING FACTS *(3 points each)* In the space provided, write the name of the person or the historical term identified by each description. Choose your answers from the list below. There are two extra items on the list.

Ralph Abernathy	Medgar Evers	Robert Moses
Black Panthers	quotas	Black Power
Freedom Summer	Elijah Muhammad	Malcolm X
Kerner Commission	Voting Rights Act	busing

_____ 1. group that called for black self-defense groups against racist police oppression

_____ 2. SNCC leader who suggested use of white supporters in voter registration drives

_____ 3. leading Nation of Islam minister who turned to orthodox Islam

_____ 4. movement calling for black separation and pride in African culture

_____ 5. involved many volunteers in registering Mississippi African American voters

_____ 6. stressed self-discipline, self-reliance, and refusal to serve in the military

_____ 7. NAACP field secretary who was assassinated by a white racist

_____ 8. system reserving fixed number of openings in a school to certain groups

_____ 9. placed the voter registration process under federal control

_____ 10. reported white racism a root cause of tensions leading to riots

UNDERSTANDING IDEAS *(3 points each)* For each of the following, place the letter of the *best* choice in the space provided.

_____ 1. A group whose actions and courage led to desegregation of restaurants was
   a. Freedom Riders.
   b. university students staging sit-ins.
   c. the Mississippi Freedom Democratic Party.
   d. the Nation of Islam.

_____ 2. African American voter registration increased after
   a. passage of the Voting Rights Act of 1965.
   b. the 1963 March on Washington.
   c. COFO registration drives.
   d. violence in Mississippi.

Chapter 31, Test Form A, Continued

_____ 3. Riots broke out in cities around the country in the mid-1960s because of
   a. white rage against Black Power.
   b. failure of voter registration legislation to pass.
   c. African American frustration at discrimination and white racism.
   d. the call by Nation of Islam leaders for African Americans to arm themselves.

_____ 4. Black nationalist groups weakened in the second half of the 1960s because
   a. African Americans no longer believed in this philosophy.
   b. many members were lost to the Vietnam conflict.
   c. they lost support and funding by the SCLC.
   d. of internal conflicts and crises in leadership.

_____ 5. The controversy over busing quieted somewhat after
   a. the Supreme Court limited this technique as a means to achieve integration.
   b. African Americans realized they did not want their children bused.
   c. the Supreme Court established an alternative—quotas in college entrance.
   d. a bloody riot in Boston cost 47 people's lives.

_____ 6. The Supreme Court decision that struck down the quota system was
   a. *Milliken* v. *Bradley*.
   b. *Evers* v. *Smith*.
   c. *University of California* v. *Bakke*.
   d. *Brown* v. *Board of Education*.

_____ 7. An area in which the civil rights movement progressed during the 1970s was
   a. strengthening leadership and agreement on goals.
   b. changing corporate hiring practices to include more African Americans.
   c. integrating public schools and neighborhoods in the North.
   d. electing African Americans to public office.

_____ 8. The Mississippi Freedom Democratic Party rejected the regular party offer of two seats at the convention because
   a. members felt it insulted and betrayed the suffering people they represented.
   b. they planned to stage a sit-in at the White House.
   c. they wanted to see if the Selma registration drive would enjoy better success.
   d. they felt they would receive more media attention if they refused the offer.

_____ 9. The civil rights movement began to fragment when
   a. activists saw that nonviolent protest did not work.
   b. key leaders called for violence.
   c. some activists abandoned the goal of integration and the strategy of nonviolent protest.
   d. most activists began to see Islam as a better alternative.

_____ 10. The person who took over leadership of the SCLC after Martin Luther King Jr.'s death was
   a. Stokely Carmichael.
   b. Ralph Abernathy.
   c. Elijah Muhammad.
   d. Carl Stokes.

Chapter 31, Test Form A, Continued

TRUE/FALSE (2 points each) Read each of the following statements, and then decide whether it is true or false. If the answer is true, place a T in the space provided; if the answer is false, place an F in the space.

_____ 1. The Southern Christian Leadership Conference nonviolent resistance methods were accepted peacefully by white southerners.

_____ 2. Attempts to register African American voters had limited success.

_____ 3. Black Muslims believed in integration and acceptance of all races and creeds.

_____ 4. Civil rights efforts in the North failed to draw support from white Americans.

_____ 5. Martin Luther King Jr. was slain in a race riot in Memphis.

PRACTICING SKILLS (5 points each) Study the map below and answer the questions that follow.

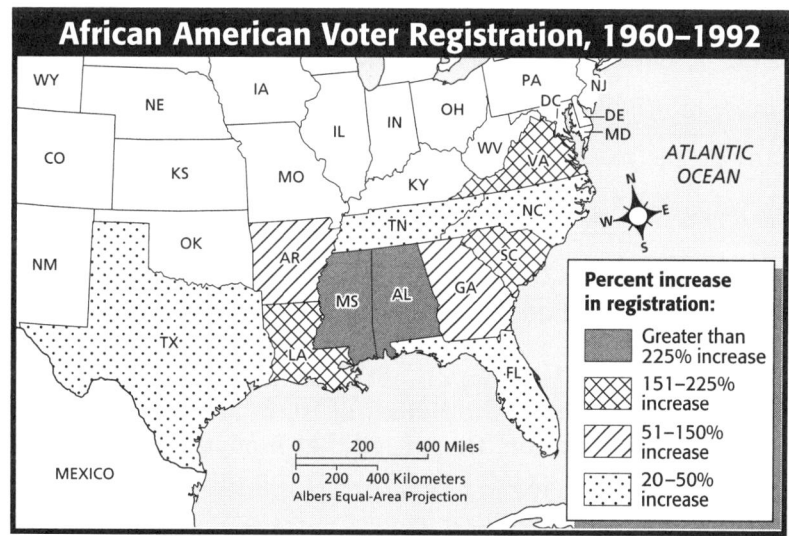

1. Which states saw the largest increase in African American voter registration?

_____

2. How much did African American voter registration in Florida increase?

_____

COMPOSING AN ESSAY (20 points) Write a brief essay on one of the following subjects. Remember to use examples to support your answer.

1. How did white violence to peaceful demonstrations by African Americans affect the progress of civil rights? How did violent response by African Americans to white injustice affect it?

2. How did busing and affirmative action programs help minorities in education and in the workplace? Why did many white Americans criticize these programs?

Name _____ Class _____ Date _____

CHAPTER 31: The Civil Rights Movement

CHAPTER TEST • FORM B

■ **SHORT ANSWER** *(6 points each)* Provide brief answers for each of the following. Remember to use examples to support your answer.

1. Describe the goals and members of the Southern Christian Leadership Conference and the Student Nonviolent Coordinating Committee. What actions did they take?
2. What protest strategies and responses by white Americans best helped civil rights progress?
3. Describe the March on Washington and the Birmingham church bombing. How did they contribute to passage of the Civil Rights Act of 1964?
4. Why did early efforts to register African American voters have such limited success?
5. What happened in Selma, Alabama, that helped pass the Voting Rights Act of 1965?
6. What did the Black Panther Party seek, and what methods did it advocate?
7. Summarize the last activities of Martin Luther King Jr. What happened to him?
8. What was the cause of urban rioting in the 1960s? What effect did the riots have?
9. Why did so many people react negatively to busing and affirmative action quotas?
10. What economic gains did African Americans make in the 1970s?

■ **PRIMARY SOURCE** *(5 points each)* Nation of Islam minister Malcolm X had wanted to become an attorney as a youngster. Seeing that this path was closed to him, he withdrew from white people, dropped out of school, and drifted into crime. While in prison, he became inspired by the Nation of Islam and proved an eloquent spokesman for this radical organization. He argued that nonviolent methods had outlived their usefulness. Read the excerpt and answer the questions that follow.

> *You're getting a new generation that has been growing right now, and they're beginning to think with their own minds and see that you can't negotiate up on freedom nowadays. If something is yours by right, then fight for it or shut up. If you can't fight for it, then forget it.*

1. What strategy does Malcolm X believe civil rights activists should employ?
2. What does he say is "yours by right"?
3. What do you think he means when he says "you can't negotiate up on freedom"?

■ **COMPOSING AN ESSAY** *(25 points)* Write a brief essay on *one* of the following subjects. Remember to use examples to support your answer.

1. How did the civil rights movement change from 1960 to 1975? Consider methods, attitudes, and achievements in your answer.
2. Violence and nonviolence both played a part in the civil rights struggle. How did each help the movement? How did each hurt it?

Struggles for Change

CHAPTER TEST • FORM A

■ REVIEWING FACTS *(3 points each)* In the space provided, write the name of the person or the historical term identified by each description. Choose your answers from the list below. There are two extra names or terms on the list.

César Chávez
Rehabilitation Act
La Huelga
American Indian Movement
James Brown
Motown

In Re Gault
Gloria Steinem
Equal Rights Amendment
Children's Defense Fund
Bob Dylan
Gray Panthers

_____ 1. Supreme Court case about the rights of minors accused of a crime

_____ 2. editor of *Ms.* Magazine who helped found the National Women's Political Caucus

_____ 3. the Delano grape strike

_____ 4. formed to help poor and minority children

_____ 5. songwriter who forged a link between folk and rock music

_____ 6. seized the trading post at Wounded Knee to protest broken treaties

_____ 7. sought to bar discrimination on the basis of sex

_____ 8. record company based in Detroit that recorded many African Americans

_____ 9. leader of the United Farm Workers

_____ 10. group that fought age discrimination

Chapter 32, Test Form A, Continued

UNDERSTANDING IDEAS (3 points each) For each of the following, place the letter of the best choice in the space provided.

_____ 1. The National Organization for Women was founded
   a. to fight against the Equal Rights Amendment.
   b. to ensure social and economic equality for women.
   c. to replace the Equal Employment Opportunity Commission.
   d. in 1956.

_____ 2. The Indians of All Tribes occupied Alcatraz
   a. to fight against the Equal Rights Amendment.
   b. to ensure social and economic equality for women.
   c. to replace the Equal Employment Opportunity Commission.
   d. to gather support for the right to self-government.

_____ 3. Woodstock was
   a. an enormous music festival.
   b. the name of a counterculture magazine of the 1960s.
   c. the location of a Rolling Stones concert.
   d. a gathering of American Indians.

_____ 4. The *Roe* v. *Wade* case
   a. set a precedent about the rights of older people.
   b. said that all Americans had a right to go to school.
   c. was concerned with abortion rights.
   d. said that women had the right to equal pay.

_____ 5. The American Association of Retired Persons
   a. supported the rights of children.
   b. worked for the rights of the disabled.
   c. lobbied for the needs of older Americans.
   d. fought against Medicaid.

_____ 6. In her book *The Feminine Mystique* Betty Friedan said that
   a. many women felt stifled by domestic life.
   b. women were very mysterious.
   c. women were very happy raising children.
   d. more women should move to the suburbs.

_____ 7. José Angel Gutiérrez helped to form
   a. many organizations to support the rights of older people.
   b. a civil rights organization in California.
   c. the Mexican American Youth Organization.
   d. the United Farm Workers Union.

_____ 8. Americans with disabilities gained support for their goals by
   a. going on strike.
   b. holding concerts.
   c. quitting their jobs.
   d. becoming very politically active.

_____ 9. Phyllis Schlafly said that
   a. women should support the ERA.
   b. women should oppose the ERA.
   c. she was disappointed when the ERA was defeated.
   d. she thought women should not be allowed to vote.

_____ 10. Andy Warhol was best known for
   a. producing Motown music.
   b. mixing folk and rock music.
   c. pop art.
   d. his abstract paintings.

Chapter 32, Test Form A, Continued

■ **TRUE/FALSE** *(2 points each)* Read each of the following statements, and then decide whether it is true or false. If the answer is true, place a *T* in the space provided; if the answer is false, place an *F* in the space.

_____ 1. The 1960s counterculture was against drug-taking.

_____ 2. César Chávez believed in and practiced nonviolence.

_____ 3. Timothy Leary urged students to stay in school.

_____ 4. In 1969, more than 70 percent of Americans said that religion was important.

_____ 5. Many Americans felt a generation gap existed between the baby boomers and their elders.

■ **PRACTICING SKILLS** *(5 points each)* Study the map below and answer the questions that follow.

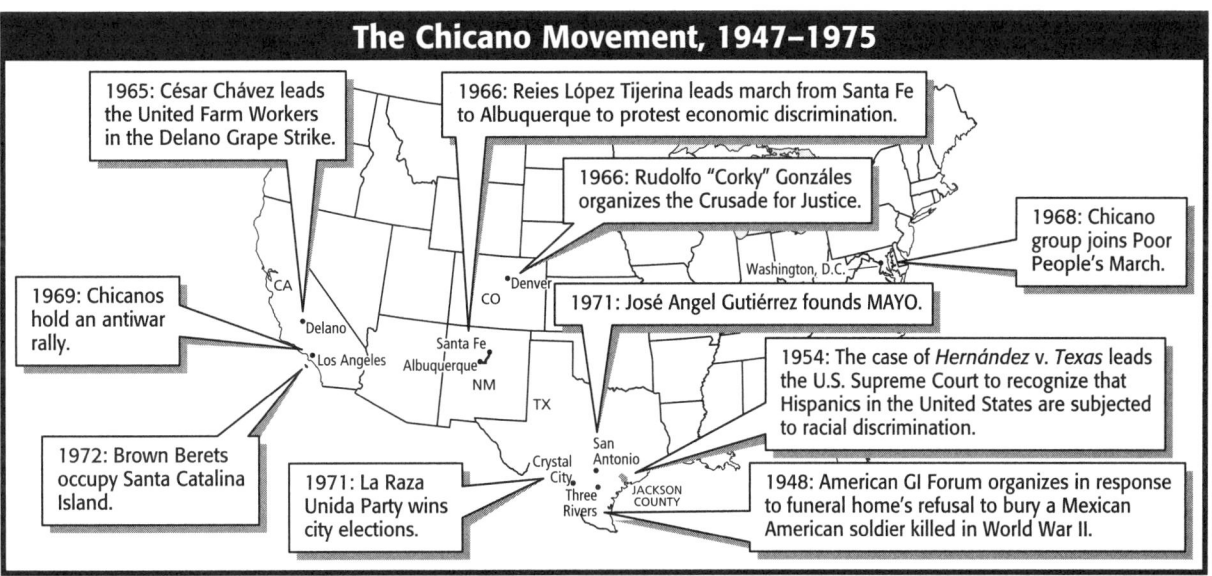

1. What Chicano protest occurred in the eastern part of the United States?

_____

2. What three events took place in California? When did they take place?

_____

■ **COMPOSING AN ESSAY** *(20 points each)* Write a brief essay on *one* of the following subjects. Remember to use examples to support your answer.

1. Explain issues that led some American Indians to embrace the Red Power movement.
2. What did Betty Friedan conclude about the women she interviewed for her book, *The Feminine Mystique*? What factors contributed to the feelings shared by these women? How did the book change some women's lives?

Name _____ Class _____ Date _____

CHAPTER 32
Struggles for Change

CHAPTER TEST • FORM B

■ **SHORT ANSWER** *(10 points each)* Provide brief answers for each of the following. Remember to use examples to support your answer.

1. What were some of the gains made by the Red Power movement during the 1960s and 1970s?
2. How did Maggie Kuhn define ageism?
3. What is "social history"?
4. What did the ERA propose? What happened to it?
5. What tactics did César Chávez employ to support the NFWA strike against grape growers? How was he successful?

■ **PRIMARY SOURCE** *(10 points each)* When American Indians occupied Alcatraz, many people wondered why. Shirley Keith was one of the people who tried to explain. Addressing a California audience in 1969, she stated the reasons for the takeover. The following is an excerpt from her speech. Read the excerpt and answer the questions that follow.

> *Let me tell you first of all that you can take credit for us being on Alcatraz because you and your government forced our backs against the wall. We're out there to create a starting point for basic changes in Indian-white relations. We reject the alternatives of the federal Indian policy. We reject either extermination of our cultures, which we refuse to have end up on museum walls for the pleasure of non-Indians. We reject the chronic and cyclical poverty of reservations and the relocation transfer of that poverty into Red Ghettoes in the cities. We reject these alternatives. . . . We're creating our own alternatives!*

1. According to Keith, who caused the American Indians' problems?
2. What does Keith say is happening to American Indian cultures?
3. What does Keith mean when she refers to the "chronic and cyclical poverty of the reservations"?

■ **COMPOSING AN ESSAY** *(20 points each)* Write a brief essay on *one* of the following subjects. Remember to use examples to support your answer.

1. What were some of the tactics used by Chicanos, American Indians, and women as each group struggled for change? How were they similar and different?
2. Describe the opposing points of view over the Equal Rights Amendment. What conclusion do you reach after reading both sides of the argument?

CHAPTER 33

War in Vietnam

CHAPTER TEST • FORM A

UNDERSTANDING FACTS *(3 points each)* For each of the following place the letter of the *best* choice in the space provided.

_____ 1. The primary use of defoliants in Vietnam was to
   a. destroy military bases of the Vietcong.
   b. destroy civilian homes and kill the Vietnamese people.
   c. expose jungle supply lines, enemy hiding places, and food supplies.
   d. poison the Vietcong people.

_____ 2. The purpose of the War Powers Act was to
   a. grant the president the right to declare war without the permission of Congress.
   b. forbid the president from ever sending troops into foreign territory.
   c. set a 60-day limit on any presidential commitment of troops to foreign land.
   d. allow the president to send troops into foreign territory for an unlimited amount of time.

_____ 3. Which of the following things did *NOT* happen at the conclusion of the war?
   a. Soldiers were welcomed home with many positive demonstrations.
   b. The Vietnam Veterans Memorial was erected in Washington, D.C.
   c. The generation gap grew between young people and their parents.
   d. The War Powers Act was passed.

_____ 4. Why did the United States refuse to support Vietnam's independence?
   a. They hoped to control Vietnam's rich rice crops.
   b. They feared Vietnam would be handed over completely to communism.
   c. They hoped to set up military bases there, to fight against communism.
   d. They hoped to gain access to Asian trade.

_____ 5. What gave the president the authority to take "all necessary measures to repel any armed attack against forces of the United States"?
   a. search and destroy missions
   b. the Tonkin Gulf Resolution
   c. Operation Rolling Thunder
   d. the Tet Offensive

Chapter 33, Test Form A, Continued

REVIEWING FACTS *(3 points each)* In the space provided, write the name of the person or the historical term identified by each description. Choose your answers from the list below. There are two extra names or terms on the list.

doves	Robert S. McNamara
hawks	Students for a Democratic Society
Henry Kissinger	Tet Offensive
Ho Chi Minh	Vietcong
Le Duc Tho	Vietminh
Ngo Dinh Diem	Vietnamization

_____ 1. a rebel group, meaning "Vietnamese Communists"

_____ 2. people who supported the war's goals

_____ 3. communist leader who organized and plotted for Vietnamese independence

_____ 4. anticommunist leader who was overthrown, in part due to repressive treatment of Buddhists

_____ 5. organization that held the first antiwar rallies and debates in the United States

_____ 6. people who opposed the war

_____ 7. month-long massive attack meant to bring down South Vietnam's government

_____ 8. a plan to turn the fighting over to the South Vietnamese and slowly pull U.S. troops out of Vietnam

_____ 9. Nixon's key foreign policy adviser

_____ 10. met with an American official in 1969 to begin negotiations aimed at ending the war

TRUE/FALSE *(2 points each)* Read each of the following statements, and then decide whether it is true or false. If the answer is true, place a *T* in the space provided; if the answer is false, place an *F*.

_____ 1. The United States' stance on communism was the primary motivation for its involvement in the Vietnam War.

_____ 2. The Democratic convention in Chicago helped boost the Democratic hopes for the 1968 election.

_____ 3. The Pentagon Papers revealed that the government frequently misled Americans about the course of the war.

Chapter 33, Test Form A, Continued

_____ 4. Many Americans opposed the antiwar movement, especially its extreme factions.

_____ 5. The Twenty-sixth Amendment raised the voting age from 18 to 21.

■ **PRACTICING SKILLS** *(5 points each)* Study the map below and answer the questions that follow.

1. What country bordered South Vietnam?

   _____

2. What two countries bordered North Vietnam?

   _____

   _____

3. What body of water is east of Vietnam?

   _____

   _____

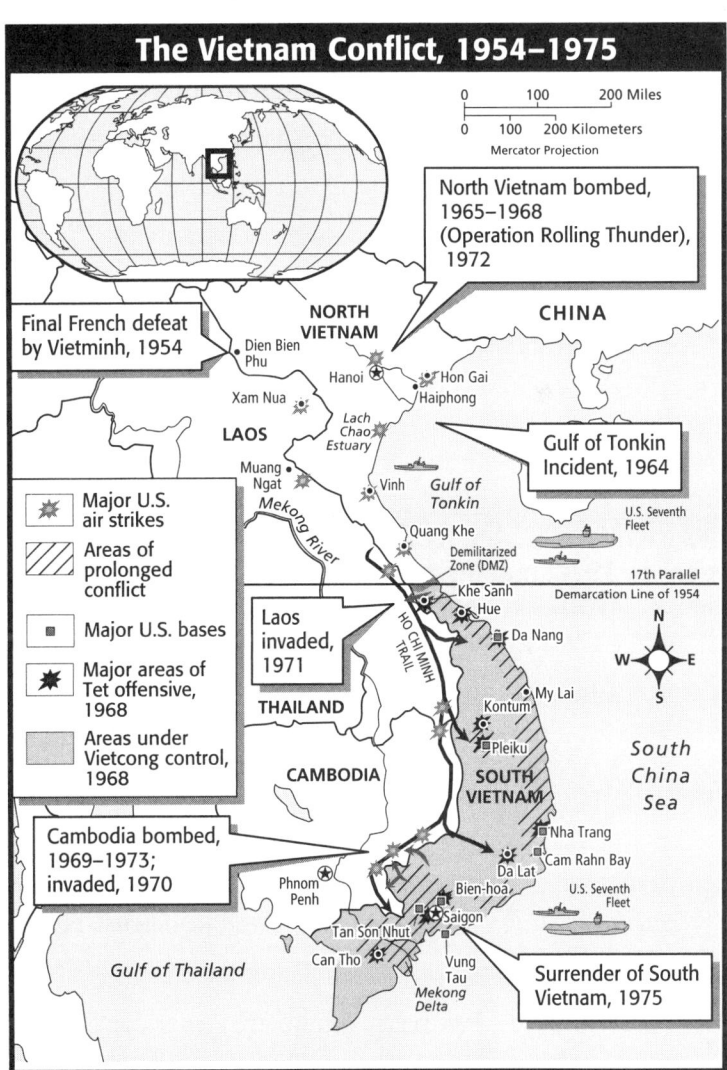

■ **COMPOSING AN ESSAY** *(30 points each)* Write a brief essay on *one* of the following subjects. Remember to use examples to support your answer.

1. Describe some of the factors that caused many Americans to have a negative view toward our involvement in the Vietnam War.
2. Describe Richard Nixon's original plan to end the Vietnam War. In addition explain what effect the bombing of Cambodia had on his plan.

Name _____ Class _____ Date _____

CHAPTER 33
War in Vietnam

CHAPTER TEST • FORM B

■ **SHORT ANSWER** *(10 points each)* Provide brief answers for each of the following. Remember to use examples to support your answer.

1. What did the Gulf of Tonkin Resolution allow the president to do?
2. What effect did the Tet Offensive have on many Americans' opinion of the war effort?
3. What were some factors that helped Richard Nixon win the 1968 presidential election?
4. How were the country's domestic programs, including those aiding the poor, affected by the Vietnam War?
5. Describe some ways the Vietnam War affected or changed our government's military policy.

■ **PRIMARY SOURCE** *(10 points each)* Senator George McGovern made this statement in 1972, making his position on the war very clear. With his eye on the presidency, McGovern hoped to cash in on the American people's frustration with the war. Read the excerpt and answer the questions that follow.

We have heard many times that Vietnam will no longer be an issue by the time the fall election approaches. . . . I don't know whether it will be or not. For the sake of the thousands of Vietnamese peasants still dying from American bombing raids, the GIs still dying of booby traps and heroin, the American POWs rotting in the jails of Hanoi, I sincerely hope it will not be an issue. But Vietnam thinking surely will be an issue, regardless of what happens in Indochina in the next four months. By 'Vietnam thinking' I mean wasting our strength on paranoiac defense policies while neglecting the needs of our own people.

1. According to McGovern, where are American POWs?
2. Describe in your own words what McGovern means by the term "Vietnam thinking."
3. What "paranoiac defense policies" is he referring to?

■ **COMPOSING AN ESSAY** *(20 points each)* Write a brief essay on *one* of the following subjects. Remember to use examples to support your answer.

1. Imagine you are the chief adviser to Richard Nixon, who you know is withholding information about the war from the American people. Write him a memorandum describing why you think this is or is not a wise decision.
2. Explain why many Vietnam War veterans were upset during and after the war.

Name _____ Class _____ Date _____

A Changing Home Front

UNIT TEST • FORM A

REVIEWING FACTS *(3 points each)* In the space provided, write the name of the person or the historical term that completes each sentence. Choose your answers from the list below. There are two extra names or terms on the list.

Tonkin Gulf Resolution
Nation of Islam
counterculture
Malcolm X
Elijah Muhammad
Great Society

American Indian Movement
Tet Offensive
Operation Rolling Thunder
John F. Kennedy
Martin Luther King Jr.
Voting Rights Act

_____ 1. gained quick Congressional approval after members witnessed the horror of the protest march in Selma, Alabama

_____ 2. supported violent resistance after spending time in prison

_____ 3. led to the confrontation at Wounded Knee and the occupation of Alcatraz prison

_____ 4. believed in the superiority of the black race

_____ 5. used by Congress to give the president the power to protect U.S. troops in danger

_____ 6. assassinated in Dallas, Texas, on November 22, 1963

_____ 7. young Americans who rejected mainstream American society

_____ 8. prominent leader whose life was cut short in Memphis, Tennessee, in 1968

_____ 9. huge North Vietnamese attack that turned American opinion against the war

_____ 10. President Lyndon Johnson's vision for solving America's domestic problems

Unit 9, Test Form A, Continued

UNDERSTANDING IDEAS (3 points each) For each of the following, place the letter of the best choice in the space provided.

_____ 1. César Chávez organized
   a. meat packers.
   b. migrant farm workers.
   c. Chicano high school students.
   d. Mexican American steelworkers.

_____ 2. Betty Friedan's *The Feminine Mystique* supported the idea that
   a. a woman's place is in the home.
   b. men should do housework.
   c. many women felt dissatisfaction in their lives.
   d. women should not gain political power.

_____ 3. The Freedom Riders rode buses in the South to
   a. protest discrimination by southern authorities.
   b. encourage voter registration.
   c. show their opposition to unfair labor practices.
   d. raise awareness of a second bus boycott.

_____ 4. President Kennedy founded the Peace Corps to
   a. solve America's inner-city problems.
   b. help underdeveloped nations.
   c. court the friendships of African countries.
   d. create jobs for unemployed young Americans.

_____ 5. The Cuban missile crisis occurred when
   a. the Soviet navy blockaded America's eastern coastline.
   b. Cuban leader Fidel Castro ordered the assassination of President Kennedy.
   c. Soviet nuclear missiles were detected in Cuba.
   d. the Bay of Pigs invasion failed.

_____ 6. The Ho Chi Minh Trail was used by
   a. the North Vietnamese as a supply route.
   b. the South Vietnamese to transfer troops.
   c. the United States to move supplies.
   d. the Vietcong to infiltrate Cambodia.

_____ 7. Kennedy's domestic agenda was called the
   a. New Frontier.
   b. Great Society.
   c. Great Frontier.
   d. New Society.

_____ 8. Operation Rolling Thunder was
   a. a North Vietnamese strike on the Vietnamese New Year.
   b. an American bombing campaign against military targets in North Vietnam.
   c. a joint French-Chinese attack on Laos to weaken North Vietnam.
   d. the Vietcong attack on Saigon.

_____ 9. In terms of getting his legislation passed through Congress, Lyndon Johnson was
   a. very unsuccessful.
   b. only occasionally successful.
   c. inconsistent.
   d. amazingly successful.

_____ 10. The domino theory stated that
   a. if one Asian nation became democratic, so would others.
   b. once a communist government was overthrown, others would follow.
   c. the United States could occupy one communist nation after another if it desired.
   d. if one nation became communist, so would others nearby.

Unit 9, Test Form A, Continued

■ TRUE/FALSE *(2 points each)* Read each of the following statements, and then decide whether it is true or false. If the answer is true, place a *T* in the space provided; if the answer is false, place an *F* in the space.

_____ 1. La Raza Unida Party was formed to get Chicanos elected to public office.

_____ 2. The Bay of Pigs invasion helped weaken Fidel Castro in Cuba.

_____ 3. Ho Chi Minh supported the French occupation of Vietnam.

_____ 4. Defoliants were used in Vietnam to cause health problems for the Vietcong.

_____ 5. *Milliken* v. *Bradley* made busing a legal means of desegregating public schools.

■ PRACTICING SKILLS *(5 points each)* Study the map below and answer the questions that follow.

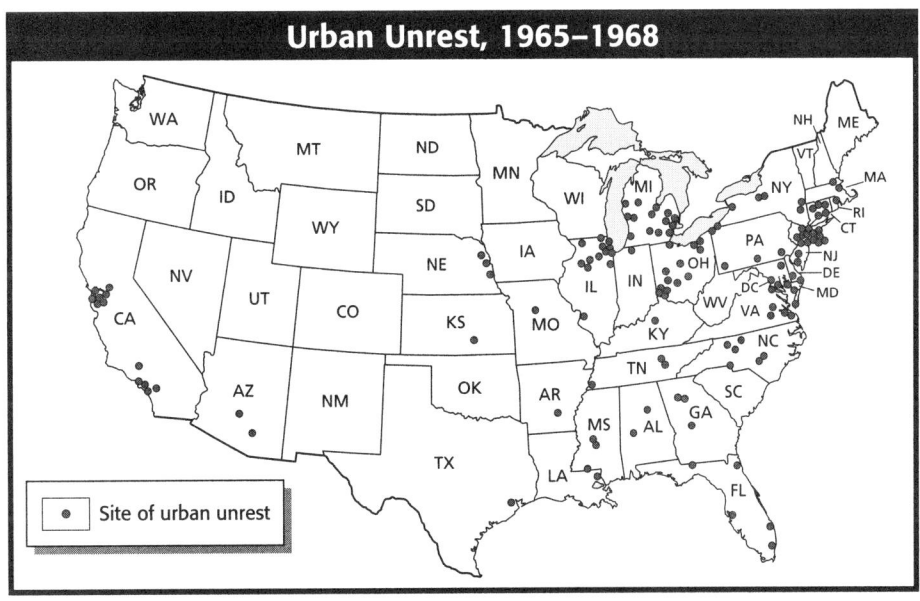

1. In what region of the United States did the highest concentration of riots occur?

   _____

2. In your opinion, why did most of the riots take place in large cities?

   _____

■ COMPOSING AN ESSAY *(20 points)* Write a brief essay on *one* of the following subjects. Remember to use examples to support your answer.

1. Describe Kennedy's public image and his influence on America. How did his assassination affect the country?
2. Describe some of the factors that changed American public opinion against the Vietnam War.

Name _____ Class _____ Date _____

UNIT 9: A Changing Home Front

UNIT TEST • FORM B

■ SHORT ANSWER *(10 points each)* Provide brief answers for each of the following. Remember to use examples to support your answer.

1. Name three ways the Supreme Court of the 1960s supported and expanded individual rights.
2. What protest strategies and white responses best helped civil rights progress?
3. Why were so many people opposed to busing and affirmative action quotas?
4. What techniques did César Chávez use to support the NFWA strike against grape growers? How successful was he?
5. Describe some ways the Vietnam War affected or changed our government's foreign policy.

■ PRIMARY SOURCE *(10 points each)* While running for president in 1960, John F. Kennedy offered his thoughts on the future of the United States in a speech to South Dakota farmers. Read the excerpt below and answer the questions that follow.

I promise you no sure solutions, no easy life. The years ahead for all of us will be as difficult as any in our history. There are new frontiers for America to conquer in education, in science, in national purpose—not frontiers on a map, but frontiers of the mind, the will, the spirit of man.

1. What does Kennedy think the coming years will be like for the United States?
2. In what areas, according to Kennedy, must America improve?

■ COMPOSING AN ESSAY *(30 points)* Write a brief essay on *one* of the following subjects. Remember to use examples to support your answer.

1. Compare and contrast the background, political style, and accomplishments of presidents Kennedy and Johnson.
2. In what ways did the civil rights movement change from 1960 to 1975? Consider methods, attitudes, and achievements in your answer.
3. How did Chicanos, American Indians, and women fight for change? How were their methods similar and how were they different?
4. How was the Vietnam War difficult for veterans, especially when they arrived back home in the United States?

Name _____ Class _____ Date _____

From Nixon to Carter

CHAPTER 34

CHAPTER TEST • FORM A

REVIEWING THE FACTS *(3 points each)* In the space provided, write the name of the person or the historical term identified by each description. Choose your answers from the list below. There are two extra names or terms on the list.

apartheid
Apollo 11
Camp David Accords
stagflation
Committee to Re-elect the President
Family Assistance Plan
Gerald Ford
Jimmy Carter
realpolitik
Silent Majority
Skylab
Strategic Arms Limitations Talks

_____ 1. the lunar module that landed on the Moon

_____ 2. the nation's first space station, placed in orbit in 1973

_____ 3. president who promised a new approach to politics that emphasized a moral vision

_____ 4. policy in which the white minority ruled and the black majority had few rights

_____ 5. combination of rising unemployment and inflation

_____ 6. agreement between Carter, Begin, and Sadat on a framework for peace in the Middle East

_____ 7. Nixon's campaign organization

_____ 8. middle-class voters who were weary of the social upheaval of the 1960s

_____ 9. guaranteed families a minimum income

_____ 10. practical politics

Chapter 34, Test Form A, Continued

TRUE/FALSE *(2 points each)* Read each of the following statements, and then decide whether it is true or false. If the answer is true, place a *T* in the space provided; if the answer is false, place an *F* in the space.

_____ 1. The Southern Strategy was Nixon's plan to pull conservative southern white voters away from the Democratic party.

_____ 2. President Nixon called for an increase in the highway speed limit in order to conserve gasoline.

_____ 3. In 1974, President Ford granted President Nixon a full pardon for his involvement in the Watergate scandal.

_____ 4. The Nixon-Kissinger approach called for "realpolitik" and emphasized national interests over moral concerns.

_____ 5. "WIN" was President Ford's plan to "Whip Inflation Now."

_____ 6. In the Three Mile Island accident, a nuclear reactor failed, nearly causing a catastrophic meltdown.

_____ 7. The Panama Canal Treaties granted Panama control over canal operations by the year 2000.

_____ 8. The divorce rate and the number of working mothers both continued to rise throughout the 1970s.

_____ 9. President Carter promised the American people he would only mislead them during times of war.

_____ 10. Democrat Barbara Jordan led the crusade to impeach Nixon after the Watergate scandal.

Chapter 34, Test Form A, Continued

■ MATCHING (3 points each) Match the correct term with its definition. There are two extra terms on the list.

_____ 1. a group founded by several oil companies to obtain higher oil prices

_____ 2. federal agency with power to enforce environmental laws

_____ 3. a bill designed to protect animals in danger of extinction

_____ 4. Carter's recommendations to solve the energy crisis, passed in 1978

_____ 5. along with Nixon, signed a treaty limiting nuclear weapons

a. Atomic Energy Commission
b. Endangered Species Act
c. Environmental Protection Agency
d. Golda Meir
e. Leonid Brezhnev
f. National Energy Act
g. Organization of Petroleum Exporting Countries

■ PRACTICING SKILLS (5 points each) Study the chart below and answer the following questions.

1. About how much did a barrel of oil cost in 1975?

   _____
   _____

2. Between what two years did the price of oil rise most?

   _____
   _____

3. About how much did a barrel of oil cost in 1981?

   _____
   _____

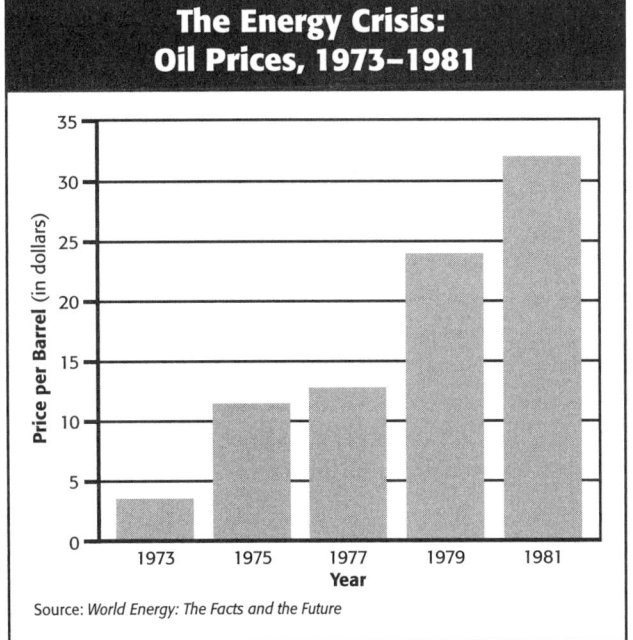

■ COMPOSING AN ESSAY (20 points each) Write a brief essay on *one* of the following subjects. Remember to use examples to support your answer.

1. Compare Nixon's and Carter's views of foreign affairs and human rights.
2. Define the term *détente*, and describe its successes and failures throughout the 1970s.

From Nixon to Carter

CHAPTER TEST • FORM B

■ **SHORT ANSWER** *(10 points each)* Provide brief answers for each of the following. Remember to use examples to support your answer.

1. Briefly describe the opposing views of the Family Assistance Plan.
2. Why did President Carter boycott the 1980 Olympics?
3. Define stagflation, and describe one way Nixon tried to remedy this economic state.
4. What did the Camp David Accords do?
5. What was the primary reason for the Watergate break-in?
6. What was the SALT treaty and why was it significant?

■ **PRIMARY SOURCE** *(5 points each)* In this statement Henry Kissinger, Nixon's chief foreign policy adviser, commented on the downfall of his friend and boss. Read the excerpt and answer the questions that follow.

Nixon had three goals: to win by the greatest electoral landslide in history; to be remembered as a peacemaker; and to be accepted by the "Establishment" as an equal. He achieved all these objectives by the end of 1972 and the beginning of 1973. And he lost them all two months later—partly because he turned a dream into an obsession.

1. When Kissinger states that Nixon wanted to be accepted by the "establishment," who is he referring to?
2. What does Kissinger say was, in part, the cause of Nixon's demise as president?
3. Did Nixon achieve his goals?

■ **COMPOSING AN ESSAY** *(25 points each)* Write a brief essay on *one* of the following subjects. Remember to give examples to support your answer.

1. Describe the major causes of the energy crisis. Include in your answer how Nixon tried to resolve these problems.
2. Describe how family structure, cultural trends, and technology changed daily life for Americans in the 1970s.

Name _____ Class _____ Date _____

CHAPTER 35
The Republican Revolution

CHAPTER TEST • FORM A

REVIEWING FACTS *(3 points each)* In the space provided, write the name of the person or the historical term identified by each description. Choose your answers from the list below. There are two extra names or terms on the list.

Lech Walesa
glasnost
Operation Desert Storm
American Indian Movement
Reaganomics
S&L crisis

Iran-Contra affair
Commonwealth of Independent States
Christa McAuliffe
Sandinistas
Sandra Day O'Connor
Ayatollah Khomeini

_____ 1. economic program that included lowering taxes for the wealthy

_____ 2. first female Supreme Court justice

_____ 3. confederation of former Soviet republics

_____ 4. Islamic leader of Iran

_____ 5. died in a space shuttle accident

_____ 6. leader of the trade union Solidarity

_____ 7. weakened many people's confidence in the economy

_____ 8. drove the Iraqis from Kuwait

_____ 9. illegal funding for weapons sent to Central America

_____ 10. rebel group that overthrew the dictator in Nicaragua

UNDERSTANDING IDEAS *(3 points each)* For each of the following, place the letter of the *best* choice in the space provided.

_____ 1. The Gramm-Rudman-Hollings Act required
   a. automatic cuts in government spending when the deficit reached a certain amount.
   b. the president to order more defense spending.
   c. Congress to balance the budget by 1986.
   d. the federal budget deficit to be increased.

_____ 2. The Contras were
   a. supported by the Soviet Union.
   b. an army recruited, financed, and armed by the CIA.
   c. strongly opposed by President Reagan.
   d. the rebels who overthrew the dictator Anastasio Somoza.

Chapter and Unit Tests

Chapter 35, Test Form A, Continued

_____ 3. William Gibson warned
   a. that technology might someday take over the world.
   b. people about the dangers of environmental poisoning.
   c. that the space shuttle would crash.
   d. the president about threats from the Soviet Union.

_____ 4. The New Right supported
   a. the Equal Rights Amendment and a strong defense.
   b. gun control and school prayer.
   c. abortion rights and gun control.
   d. school prayer and a strong defense.

_____ 5. Insider trading
   a. increased confidence in stockbrokers.
   b. was the illegal use of confidential financial information for personal gain.
   c. was the legal use of confidential financial information for personal gain.
   d. reflected the need for budget controls.

_____ 6. The Persian Gulf War was unique because
   a. women were not allowed to serve in any capacity.
   b. the war was won on the ground.
   c. television reporters were banned from reporting.
   d. it was won by using almost entirely high-tech weapons.

_____ 7. Much of the money that went to the soaring Pentagon budget between 1981 and 1985 was
   a. returned to the taxpayers.
   b. opposed by President Reagan.
   c. used to fund building nuclear weapons.
   d. used to support civil defense.

_____ 8. Glasnost was a policy of
   a. repression that sent many Soviet people to prison.
   b. openness that promised more freedom for the Soviet people.
   c. programs that boosted the Soviet military.
   d. programs that decreased foreign trade.

_____ 9. The Americans with Disabilities Act
   a. required that anyone with a disability be hired for a job.
   b. required all companies help people with disabilities.
   c. recommended that people with disabilities be allowed to use public buildings.
   d. prohibited discrimination against people with disabilities.

_____ 10. When private savings and loans failed due to risky business practices
   a. the government did nothing to help.
   b. the economy improved.
   c. the government paid billions of dollars to cover these losses.
   d. the government loosened regulations on the industry.

Chapter 35, Test Form A, Continued

■ TRUE/FALSE (2 points each) Read each of the following statements, and then decide whether it is true or false. If the answer is true, place a *T* in the space provided; if the answer is false, place an *F* in the space.

_____ 1. The War on Drugs provided money to stop drug smuggling.

_____ 2. The federal deficit increased during Ronald Reagan's presidency.

_____ 3. Women played a significant role in the Persian Gulf War.

_____ 4. Oliver North illegally funneled millions of dollars to the Sandinistas.

_____ 5. Supply-side economics argued that by taxing the rich the economy will improve.

■ PRACTICING SKILLS (5 points each) Study the map below and answer the questions that follow.

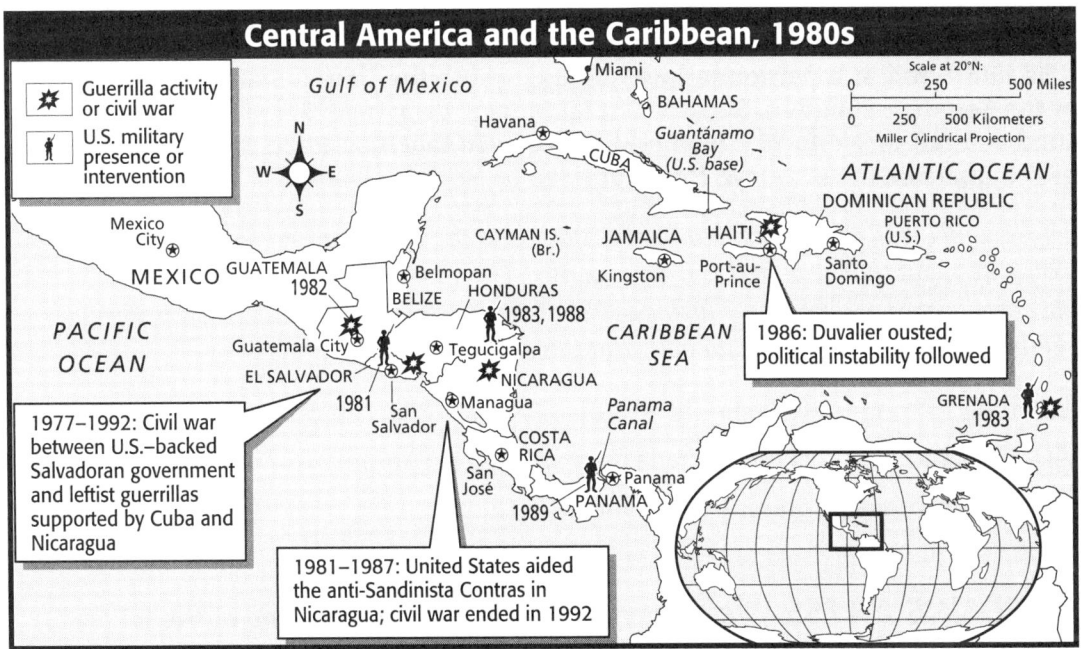

1. In which countries was there a U.S. military presence or intervention?

   _____

2. According to the map, what happened in Haiti in 1986?

   _____

■ COMPOSING AN ESSAY (20 points each) Write a brief essay on *one* of the following subjects. Remember to use examples to support your answer.

1. How did the S&L crisis affect the economy?
2. How did foreign affairs affect the 1980 presidential election?

Chapter and Unit Tests   Chapter 35 **175**

Name _____ Class _____ Date _____

The Republican Revolution

CHAPTER TEST • FORM B

■ **SHORT ANSWER** *(10 points each)* Provide brief answers for each of the following. Remember to use examples to support your answer.

1. What major change took place in Congress after the election of 1980?
2. What effect did the strikes in Poland have on U.S.–Soviet relations?
3. What happened to Chinese students who protested in Beijing in Tiananmen Square?
4. What is AIDS? When did it first emerge?
5. What did the United States do in Grenada in 1983?

■ **PRIMARY SOURCE** *(10 points each)* During the Iran-Contra scandal, Oliver North testified in Congress about his illegal activities. North insisted that by following orders he had acted as a patriot and was being loyal to the United States. The chairman of the Senate committee, Senator Daniel Inouye, disagreed. Senator Inouye was a decorated veteran of World War II who lost an arm in that war. Read the excerpt and answer the questions that follow. He responded to North's claims:

> [The] colonel was well aware that he was subject to the Uniform Code of Military Justice. . . . And that code makes it abundantly clear that orders of a superior officer must be obeyed by subordinate members—but it is lawful orders. . . . In fact, it says members of the military have an obligation to disobey unlawful orders.

1. According to Inouye, what should a soldier do when given an order?
2. What does Inouye say is the soldier's duty when given an unlawful order?
3. What is Inouye saying about Oliver North's actions?

■ **COMPOSING AN ESSAY** *(20 points)* Write a brief essay on *one* of the following subjects. Remember to use examples to support your answer.

1. How did the nuclear arms race affect the Cold War and relations between the United States and the Soviet Union?
2. What were the positive and negative effects of Ronald Reagan's presidency?

CHAPTER 36
Launching the New Millennium

CHAPTER TEST • FORM A

■ **REVIEWING FACTS** *(3 points each)* In the space provided, write the name of the person or historical term identified by each description. Choose your answers from the list below. There are two extra names or terms on the list.

World Wide Web
Los Angeles riots
Bob Dole
Madeleine Albright
Y2K bug
Hillary Rodham Clinton
Yasir Arafat
Family and Medical Leave Act
George W. Bush
Nelson Mandela
North American Free Trade Agreement
Kosovo crisis

_____ 1. elected president in 2000

_____ 2. president of South Africa

_____ 3. possible cause of widespread computer failures

_____ 4. signed a peace accord with Israeli prime minister Yitzhak Rabin

_____ 5. resulted from the Rodney King verdict

_____ 6. conflict between Serbians and Albanians

_____ 7. secretary of state for the United States

_____ 8. lowered trade barriers between the United States, Canada, and Mexico

_____ 9. linked Internet sites

_____ 10. helped draft a plan to reform the nation's health care system

■ **UNDERSTANDING IDEAS** *(3 points each)* For each of the following, place the letter of the *best* choice in the space provided.

_____ 1. Before being elected president, Bill Clinton was
   a. the governor of Kansas.
   b. the governor of Arkansas.
   c. a senator from Arkansas.
   d. vice president of the United States.

_____ 2. During the 1990s Americans experienced
   a. a severe recession.
   b. the longest and largest economic boom in history.
   c. a downturn in the economy.
   d. a huge rise in interest rates.

Chapter 36, Test Form A, Continued

_____ 3. The Chernobyl disaster
   a. was caused by a huge earthquake.
   b. reassured many people about nuclear power.
   c. created a huge cloud of radioactivity that drifted across Europe.
   d. happened in Central America.

_____ 4. Recycling
   a. is being phased out in most communities.
   b. was a passing fad.
   c. is impossible to do in large cities.
   d. reuses natural resources and reduces solid waste.

_____ 5. As president of Yugoslavia, Slobodan Milosevic
   a. moved Serbian military forces into Kosovo and provoked NATO to retaliate.
   b. moved Albanians into Kosovo.
   c. joined forces with NATO.
   d. never agreed to withdraw his troops from Kosovo.

_____ 6. Shannon Lucid was an astronaut who
   a. was unable to break the record for longest time in space.
   b. launched the Hubble space telescope.
   c. broke the record for longest number of consecutive days in space for an American.
   d. was unable to go into space because of the *Challenger* explosion.

_____ 7. At the age of 77, John Glenn
   a. became governor of Ohio.
   b. ran for Senate.
   c. served as a payload specialist on a space shuttle mission.
   d. circled Earth in the space capsule *Friendship 7*.

_____ 8. The Immigration Act of 1990
   a. decreased the number of immigrants allowed into the United States.
   b. reduced the number of skilled workers allowed into the United States.
   c. banned foreign businesses from operating in depressed areas of the country.
   d. increased the number of immigrants allowed into the United States.

_____ 9. Experts predict that the world's population
   a. will level off during the early 2000s.
   b. will decrease during the next 25 years.
   c. will grow at a very fast rate during the next 25 years.
   d. will not cause much of a problem in the future.

_____ 10. The 2000 presidential election was decided by electoral college votes from the state of
   a. Texas.
   b. Florida.
   c. New York.
   d. Utah.

Chapter 36, Test Form A, Continued

■ **TRUE/FALSE** *(2 points each)* Read each of the following statements, and then decide whether it is true or false. If the answer is true, place a *T* in the space provided; if the answer is false, place an *F* in the space.

_____ 1. Federal Reserve Chairman Alan Greenspan was responsible for an economic depression in the 1990s.

_____ 2. Israeli Prime Minister Benjamin Netanyahu was more willing to compromise with the Palestinians than his predecessor Yitzhak Rabin.

_____ 3. Republicans who signed the Contract with America asked to be thrown out of office if they broke it.

_____ 4. In the Telecommunications Act of 1996, Congress tried to regulate the Internet.

_____ 5. Rodney King was severely beaten by police in Los Angeles.

■ **PRACTICING SKILLS** *(5 points each)* Study the map below and answer the questions that follow.

1. About how much was the federal debt in 1989?

   _____

   _____

2. About how much did the federal debt increase between 1993 and 1995?

   _____

   _____

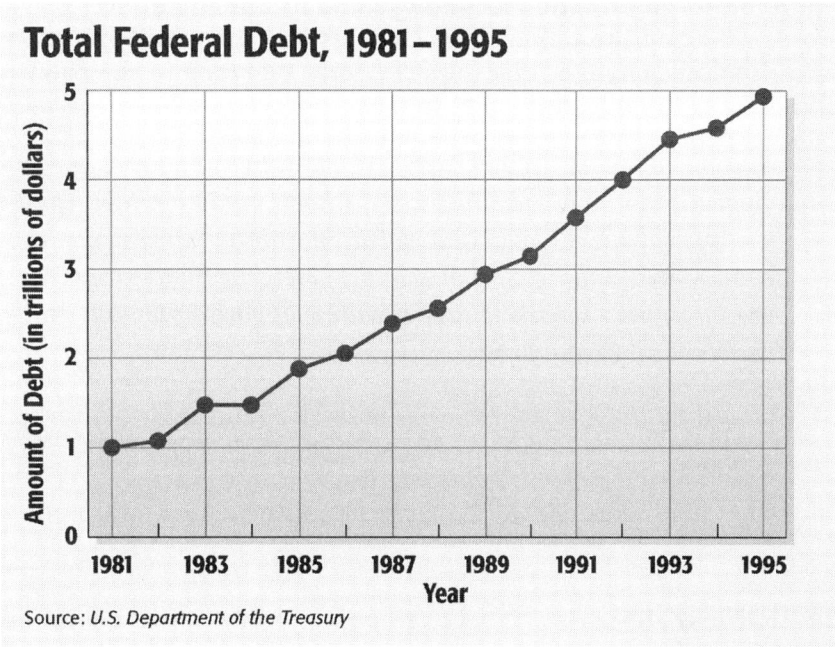

■ **COMPOSING AN ESSAY** *(20 points)* Write a brief essay on *one* of the following subjects. Remember to use examples to support your answer.

1. What were some of the causes and effects of the economic boom during the 1990s? How did economists react to what happened? Did the boom directly relate to the success or failure of companies? Why or why not?

2. How did immigration in the 1990s differ from that of a hundred years before? Describe the positive and negative responses by native-born citizens to the large numbers of immigrants coming to the United States.

Name _____ Class _____ Date _____

Life in the 1990s and Beyond

CHAPTER 36

CHAPTER TEST • FORM B

■ **SHORT ANSWER** *(10 points each)* Provide brief answers for each of the following. Remember to use examples to support your answer.

1. How did the number of married women who worked outside the home change between 1960 and 1995?
2. What did the Internet enable users to do?
3. In the election of 1992, many female voters became active in response to what congressional hearings?
4. In his first term, did President Clinton raise or lower the budget deficit?
5. Why was President Clinton impeached? Was he convicted?

■ **PRIMARY SOURCE** *(10 points each)* In 1994 Vice President Al Gore described the future of information technology and its coming effects on American life. His words reflected the tremendous changes that were and are taking place in the world of technology, changes that impact nearly everyone in the country. Read the excerpt and answer the questions that follow.

> *Multiple networks . . . will carry a broad range of services and information technology applications into homes, businesses, schools, and hospitals. These networks will form the basis of evolving national and global information infrastructures, in turn creating a seamless web uniting the world in the emergent Information Age. The result will be a new information marketplace, providing opportunities and challenges for individuals, industry and governments.*

1. According to Gore, where will the services and information technology go?
2. How does Gore say that the world will be united?
3. What does Gore say will be the result of the global information infrastructures?

■ **COMPOSING AN ESSAY** *(20 points each)* Write a brief essay on *one* of the following subjects. Remember to use examples to support your answer.

1. What are ways that population growth is affecting and will affect life in the world? What are some things that could be done to lessen these effects?
2. Bruce W. Nelan predicts that in the 2000s, economic strength will be as important or more important than military might. Why could this be true? What role do multinational corporations play in the power struggles of the global economy? How are they similar to and different from governments?

180 Chapter 36 Chapter and Unit Tests

Name _____ Class _____ Date _____

Modern Times

UNIT TEST • FORM A

■ REVIEWING FACTS *(3 points each)* In the space provided, write the name of the person or the historical term that completes each sentence. Choose your answers from the list below. There are two extra names or terms on the list.

human rights	Contract with America	Israel
Panama Canal	Gerald Ford	Camp David Accords
Soviet Union	Nicaragua	Iran hostage crisis
Watergate	China	energy crisis

_____ 1. the scandal that drove Richard Nixon from office

_____ 2. nation whose rebels were funded by the United States in an attempt to overthrow the socialist government there

_____ 3. principle emphasized by Carter's foreign policy

_____ 4. weakened the Carter presidency and helped Ronald Reagan gain the White House

_____ 5. transferred from U.S. control in the year 2000, as negotiated by Carter

_____ 6. agreements between Anwar Sadat and Menachim Begin to help stabilize the Middle East

_____ 7. the only person appointed to the position of president and vice president

_____ 8. country visited by Nixon in an attempt to divide the communist world

_____ 9. caused in part by OPEC's decision to raise prices

_____ 10. a series of vows made by the 1994 Republican-controlled House of Representatives

Chapter and Unit Tests

Unit 10, Test Form A, Continued

UNDERSTANDING IDEAS *(3 points each)* For each of the following, place the letter of the *best* choice in the space provided.

_____ 1. The Family and Medical Leave Act stated that if employees took a leave of absence for a family or medical emergency
   a. employers could fire them.
   b. employers could not fire them, but they still might lose their jobs.
   c. employers must pay them their full wages.
   d. employers must grant them unpaid time off.

_____ 2. The goal of Operation Desert Storm was to
   a. evict Kuwait from Iran.
   b. drive Iraq from Israel.
   c. force Iran out of Saudi Arabia.
   d. remove the Iraqi army from Kuwait.

_____ 3. In 1992 an independent candidate for president was
   a. Bill Clinton.
   b. Ross Perot.
   c. Michael Dukakis.
   d. Bob Dole.

_____ 4. Reaganomics was the Reagan administration's policy that used
   a. supply-side economics.
   b. bond yield practices.
   c. tax increases for the wealthy.
   d. welfare reform.

_____ 5. The 1993 L.A. riots occurred after
   a. four black police beat a white motorist.
   b. white police beat a black motorist.
   c. white police were convicted of beating a white motorist.
   d. white police were acquitted of beating a black motorist.

_____ 6. The Iran-Contra affair occurred during the presidency of
   a. Jimmy Carter.
   b. Ronald Reagan.
   c. George Bush.
   d. Richard Nixon.

_____ 7. All of the following terrorist attacks occurred in the 1990s EXCEPT
   a. the New York World Trade Center bombing.
   b. the bombing of an airliner over Lockerbie, Scotland.
   c. the truck bomb in Saudi Arabia that killed 19 U.S. soldiers.
   d. the bombing of the federal building in Oklahoma City, Oklahoma.

_____ 8. Ronald Reagan received much of his political support from the
   a. New Right.
   b. New Left.
   c. American Right.
   d. Liberal Left.

_____ 9. The Gramm-Rudman-Hollings Act was designed to
   a. decrease the federal debt.
   b. increase spending on energy.
   c. change the welfare system.
   d. regulate the telecommunications industry.

_____ 10. In the Kosovo crisis, the United States
   a. aided the Serbian army.
   b. bombed the Serbian army.
   c. used ground troops against Muslim Albanians.
   d. attempted to negotiate a peace between communist and liberal Albanians.

Unit 10, Test Form A, Continued

■ TRUE/FALSE *(2 points each)* Read each of the following statements, and then decide whether it is true or false. If the answer is true, place a *T* in the space provided; if the answer is false, place an *F* in the space.

_____ 1. Under Mikhail Gorbachev, the Soviet Union began to change dramatically.

_____ 2. Bill Clinton became the first American president to be impeached.

_____ 3. The number of Asian and Latin American immigrants increased in the 1990s.

_____ 4. Secret White House tapes helped clear Richard Nixon of wrongdoing.

_____ 5. Geraldine O'Connor was the first American female to run for vice president.

■ PRACTICING SKILLS *(5 points each)* Study the chart and graph below and answer the questions that follow.

1. What are two things considered grounds for impeachment?

   _____

   _____

2. Who holds a trial for the accused official?

   _____

   _____

The Impeachment Process

Grounds	Officials establish grounds for impeachment, which could include treason, bribery, and other offenses.
Phase 1	The House of Representatives announces articles of impeachment, thus formally accusing an official.
Phase 2	The Senate holds a trial for the accused, with a two-thirds vote needed for a conviction.
Penalty	A convicted official is removed from his or her post and cannot hold any public office in the future.

■ COMPOSING AN ESSAY *(20 points)* Write a brief essay on *one* of the following subjects. Remember to use examples to support your answer.

1. Compare Carter's and Nixon's foreign policy.
2. How did immigration in the 1990s differ from that of a hundred years before? Describe the positive and negative responses by native-born citizens to the large numbers of immigrants coming to the United States.

UNIT 10 Modern Times

UNIT TEST • FORM B

■ **SHORT ANSWER** *(10 points each)* Provide brief answers to each of the following. Remember to use examples to support your answers.

1. How did President Carter respond to the Soviet Union's invasion of Afghanistan?
2. What impeachable offenses were brought against President Clinton?
3. How did the Iran hostage crisis hurt Jimmy Carter but help Ronald Reagan?
4. Why did Richard Nixon resign the office of president?
5. What did the Camp David Accords do?

■ **PRIMARY SOURCE** *(10 points each)* In 1978, the U.S. Civil Rights Commission wrote the following passage in support of the Equal Rights Amendment (ERA). Read the statement, and then answer the questions that follow.

Measured by any standard, women continue to be disadvantaged by gender-based laws and practices, despite the enactment [passage] of equal opportunity laws. As workers, they are victims of an earnings gap that is even wider today than it was in 1956. As wives, they are still subject to laws that deny them an equal partnership in marriage. As students they are often steered away from both the education needed to break into the better paying jobs dominated by men and the sports programs that have been the traditional training grounds for leadership and the route to a college education through scholarships. . . . This reality must dispel [end] the myth that women have achieved equality under the law.

1. According to the Commission, how are women disadvantaged in the workplace?
2. How does the Commission feel women are discriminated against as students?

■ **COMPOSING AN ESSAY** *(30 points)* Write a brief essay on *one* of the following subjects. Remember to use examples to support your answer.

1. What are ways that population growth is affecting and will affect life in the world? What are some things that could be done to lessen these effects?
2. Compare the foreign policy of Carter and Nixon. Where did they stand on human rights?
3. What events led to the energy crisis? What did Nixon do to try to end it?
4. What were the positive and negative results of the Reagan presidency?

Answer Key

CHAPTER 1

TEST FORM A

REVIEWING FACTS
1. the Maya
2. Qur'an
3. feudalism
4. Crusades
5. King John
6. the Aztec
7. Agricultural Revolution
8. Renaissance
9. Isabella of Castile
10. African Diaspora

UNDERSTANDING IDEAS
1. c
2. a
3. b
4. a
5. d
6. b
7. a
8. c
9. a
10. a

TRUE/FALSE
1. T
2. F
3. T
4. T
5. F

PRACTICING SKILLS
1. Northeast, California, Southwest, Southeast
2. Great Plains

COMPOSING AN ESSAY
1. The Agricultural Revolution occurred as big game died out in the Americas. Effects include increased, more reliable food supplies; increased populations; shift toward villages and then cities; specialization of labor; development of social classes.
2. Students should communicate that the Renaissance was sparked by European traders and Crusaders who brought back classical Greek and Roman texts and new ideas. Gutenberg's printing press helped these new learnings spread throughout Europe.

TEST FORM B

SHORT ANSWER
1. They crossed a land bridge—Beringia—that connected Siberia with present-day Alaska between 12,000 and 40,000 years ago.
2. The rise of cities enabled the development of a more elaborate division of labor and specialization. Specialization, in turn, promoted the development of social classes.
3. Astronomers calculated the length of the year with great precision and observed sunspots. Scientists invented paper, a sensitive seismograph, and a system of printing with carved blocks of wood. The first printed book was also made by the Chinese.
4. It provided a foundation for the protection of individual rights and limited the powers of the monarchy.
5. European navigators learned how to use astrolabes and compasses, which were invented by the Muslims and Chinese respectively; ships became larger and better able to withstand the rough Atlantic. Other ship improvements included wider and deeper hulls and the use of rudders instead of oars.

PRIMARY SOURCE
1. It was appropriate because of the grape vines that grew there.
2. feed, freshwater, grapes, salmon for cattle
3. Grapes generally do not grow well in high latitudes.

COMPOSING AN ESSAY
1. New farm equipment increased the amount of farmable land, enabling the production of enough food to sustain large armies and a growing number of townspeople. As the military strength of the kingdoms grew, invaders were less likely to attempt to take by force what they could get by trade. Trading towns and cities gradually replaced manors as the centers of economic activity. As a result, many serfs moved from manors to towns. Trade that developed during the Crusades also prompted a shift away from feudalism.
2. The Crusades were a series of religious and military expeditions during which Christians and Muslims fought for control of Palestine. Effects on European economies: The impact of trade changed Europe's political and social order. For example, trade led to the development of a new social class, the bourgeoisie. The bourgeoisie supported monarchs, who could provide better political stability and allow trade to flourish. In return, the bourgeoisie demanded a greater degree of economic and political freedom for themselves and their cities.

CHAPTER 2

TEST FORM A

REVIEWING FACTS
1. Christopher Columbus
2. Bartolomé de Las Casas
3. Hernán Cortés
4. Francis Drake
5. John Cabot
6. Pocahontas
7. Ferdinand Magellan
8. Francisco Vásquez de Coronado
9. John Smith
10. Moctezuma II

UNDERSTANDING IDEAS
1. b
2. b
3. a
4. a
5. b

TRUE/FALSE
1. F
2. T
3. T
4. F
5. F
6. T
7. F
8. T
9. T
10. T

PRACTICING SKILLS
1. 1596–1600 and 1616–1620
2. Approximately 62 million pesos. Accept answers that are within 5 million pesos of the approximate number.
3. 1516–1520

COMPOSING AN ESSAY
1. Students should note that the *encomienda* was a system under which the Spanish colonists received the right to use American Indians as laborers in exchange for a small allowance. In reality, however, the system amounted to group enslavement, because most of the Indians were not paid for their labor. The colonists benefited because they received free labor. The Indians received no benefits.
2. Students should define the Protestant Reformation as a sweeping religious reform movement that was launched by Martin Luther in 1517. Luther and his followers protested corruption within the Roman Catholic Church and challenged many of the church's practices. Students should note that the conflict between Catholics and Protestants was not only a religious struggle but also a territorial and political one. The conflicts that ensued effectively delayed the colonization efforts of France and England until the late 1500s and early 1600s.

TEST FORM B

SHORT ANSWER

1. Columbus developed a theory about a westward route to Asia after studying charts of contemporary geographers and astronomers and reading ancient Greek and Roman texts, the Bible, and accounts of Marco Polo's travels. He theorized that Asia was only about 2,400 miles west of Portugal.
2. In practice, the system amounted to group enslavement for many Indians, because few of them were ever paid for their labors as had been intended by Queen Isabella.
3. Spain concentrated its efforts in the southwestern United States. Settlements were established in Arizona, California, New Mexico, and Texas.
4. The discovery of such a passage would have provided explorers a shorter route to the Pacific and thus to Asia.
5. It exposed many of Spain's weaknesses, thus opening the door for other European nations to begin colonization efforts in the Americas.

PRIMARY SOURCE

1. roots, herbs, acorns, walnuts, berries, and a little fish
2. the arrival of Sir Thomas Gates and his group

COMPOSING AN ESSAY

1. Women's roles were determined by ethnic or family background. Many women managed family businesses, ranchos, and haciendas. Many wealthy women learned to cook, read, sew, and write, but there were few opportunities for women to pursue higher education.
2. He was an *encomendero* who openly criticized the harsh treatment of American Indians by the Spanish colonists. He urged the Spanish government and settlers to treat the Indians with more humanity. He also asked that friars and priests convert Indians to Catholicism gradually, through "love, gentleness, and kindness."

CHAPTER 3

TEST FORM A

REVIEWING FACTS

1. a
2. c
3. d
4. b
5. a
6. a
7. c
8. b
9. c
10. d

UNDERSTANDING IDEAS

1. A
2. A
3. D
4. D
5. A
6. A
7. A
8. A
9. D
10. A

TRUE/FALSE

1. T
2. F
3. T
4. T
5. T

PRACTICING SKILLS

1. Most populous in 1680: Massachusetts; least populous in 1680: Pennsylvania; most populous in 1750: Virginia; least populous in 1750: Georgia.
2. Virginia gained 187,437 residents.

COMPOSING AN ESSAY

1. Some people left because "the towns were set so near to the others." Others left because their beliefs did not match

those of the strict Puritans. For example, Roger Williams left because he believed in strict separation of church and state, a belief not shared by Puritan authorities.

2. The fur trade altered the way of life of many Indians. Increasingly they became dependent on the fur trade for survival. The fur trade also disrupted relations among tribes. The European desire for land also adversely affected the Indians. The loss of land meant losing sources of food and sacred sites.

TEST FORM B
SHORT ANSWER
1. Problems included religious persecution, shortage of land, high land prices, crop failures, and an economic depression in the wool industry.
2. The Quakers opposed war, had no formal clergy, and ignored class privileges. They were also very tolerant of people of different nationalities and religious beliefs.
3. The colony's rules, prohibitions against slavery and rum among them, were too rigid for most people. As a result, few people wanted to settle there. Realizing this, the founders gave up their experiment, allowed slavery, and let Georgia become a royal colony.
4. People liked the emotional, inspiring messages of the preachers, as well as the emphasis on individual free will over predestination and the absolute power of God. The poor and enslaved found the Great Awakening particularly appealing because the established churches often neglected them.
5. The Treaty of Paris in 1763 gave Great Britain Canada and all French holdings east of the Mississippi except New Orleans. Britain also gained Florida from Spain, which had been an ally of the French. In anticipation of this loss, Spain had received Louisiana from the French in 1762.

PRIMARY SOURCE
1. The resolutions indicated that people have the power to improve themselves. This contradicts the idea that God predetermines people's futures.
2. The key is remembering to read over the resolutions once a week.
3. Answers will vary, but most students will probably say that he was very serious about worship and religion.

COMPOSING AN ESSAY
1. Families tended to be large. Most had six children, but families with nine or more children were common. Because of the large family sizes, there was little need to hire indentured servants or slaves. Fathers and their sons worked the fields. Women generally did not work in the fields except at harvest time. Instead, they made many of the items the family needed, including soap, candles, yarn, clothes, butter, and cheese.
2. The Iroquois League was a confederation that included the Cayuga, Mohawk, Oneida, Onondaga, and Seneca of New York and Pennsylvania. After 1712, the Tuscarora were also members. The union of these groups enabled the League to dominate the fur trade, to extend its influence over American Indians to the west, and to protect its members' independence. The Iroquois also acted as middlemen by obtaining furs from other American Indians and selling the furs to the English. They skillfully played the English and French against each other, as needed, to help the League.

UNIT 1

TEST FORM A
REVIEWING FACTS
1. Renaissance
2. Protestant Reformation
3. Crusades
4. Ferdinand Magellan

5. French and Indian War
6. New England Way
7. Northwest Passage
8. Agricultural Revolution
9. feudalism
10. Christopher Columbus

UNDERSTANDING IDEAS
1. b
2. c
3. a
4. d
5. a
6. c
7. c
8. c
9. c
10. a

TRUE/FALSE
1. T
2. T
3. F
4. T
5. F

PRACTICING SKILLS
1. 1618
2. 5 pennies per pound

COMPOSING AN ESSAY
1. The Agricultural Revolution occurred as big game died out in the Americas. Effects include increased, more reliable food supplies; increased populations; shift toward villages and then cities; specialization of labor; and development of social classes.
2. Students should define the Protestant Reformation as a sweeping religious reform movement launched by Martin Luther in 1517. Luther and his followers protested corruption within the Roman Catholic Church, challenging many of the church's practices. Students should note that the conflict between Catholics and Protestants was not only a religious struggle but a territorial and political one. The conflicts that ensued effectively delayed the colonization efforts of France and England until the late 1500s and early 1600s.

TEST FORM B

SHORT ANSWER
1. They crossed a land bridge—Beringia—that connected Siberia with present-day Alaska between 12,000 and 40,000 years ago.
2. The discovery of such a passage would have provided explorers a shorter route to the Pacific and thus to Asia.
3. People liked the preacher's emotional, inspiring messages, and the emphasis on individual free will over predestination and the absolute power of God. The poor and enslaved found the Great Awakening particularly appealing because the established churches often neglected them.
4. In the Treaty of Paris in 1763 Britain gained Canada and all French holdings east of the Mississippi except New Orleans. Britain also gained Florida from Spain, which had been an ally of the French. In 1762, in anticipation of this loss, Spain had received Louisiana from the French.
5. It exposed many of Spain's weaknesses, thus opening the door for other European nations to begin colonizing the Americas.

PRIMARY SOURCE
1. Death
2. He was beaten severely.

COMPOSING AN ESSAY
1. Students should note that the *encomienda* was a system under which the Spanish colonists received the right to use American Indians as laborers in exchange for a small allowance. In reality, however, the system amounted to group enslavement because most of the Indians were not paid for their labor. The colonists benefited because they received free labor. The American Indians received no benefits.
2. Some people left because "the towns were set so near to the others." Others left because their beliefs didn't match those of the strict Puritans. For example, Roger Williams left because he believed in strict separation of church and state, a belief not shared by Puritan authorities.

3. Students should explain that the Renaissance was a rebirth of European learning and creativity made possible in part by ideas that the Crusaders brought back to Europe. The Renaissance led to new ideas in science, art, technology, and philosophy.
4. The fur trade altered the way of life of many Indians. Increasingly they became dependent on the fur trade for survival. The fur trade also disrupted relations among tribes. The European desire for land also adversely affected the Indians. The loss of land meant losing sources of food and sacred sites.

CHAPTER 4

TEST FORM A

REVIEWING FACTS
1. a
2. c
3. d
4. a
5. c
6. c
7. a
8. b
9. b
10. a

UNDERSTANDING IDEAS
1. Olive Branch Petition
2. Quartering Act
3. Proclamation of 1763
4. Stamp Act
5. Declaration of Independence
6. Townshend Acts
7. Quebec Act
8. Treaty of Paris
9. Tea Act
10. Intolerable Acts

TRUE/FALSE
1. F
2. T
3. F
4. T
5. F

PRACTICING SKILLS
1. Spain
2. France; Britain

COMPOSING AN ESSAY
1. Women accompanied troops and worked as cooks, laundresses, and nurses; some disguised themselves as men and participated in the fighting; many other women played a variety of important roles on the homefront. American Indians fought for both sides and were important to the British and the Patriots because of their knowledge of the land. About 5,000 African American Patriots fought in the war; many received official recognition for their efforts.
2. Each of these men inspired many colonists to support the Revolution through their passionate words. Henry's "Give me liberty" speech was inspirational to many people. Paine's *Common Sense* helped transform a disorganized colonial rebellion into a focused movement for independence.

TEST FORM B

SHORT ANSWER
1. Great Britain issued the Proclamation of 1763, barring settlement west of the Appalachian Mountains. Britain hoped that separating settlers and American Indians would end fighting on the frontier.
2. The British government was deeply in debt because of the French and Indian War and needed assistance from the colonies in the form of tax revenues.
3. The First Continental Congress and its Declaration of Resolves was the last straw for George III. Acting on the king's wishes, Parliament ordered General Gage to put down the rebellion. The battles at Lexington and Concord occurred as a result.
4. Its immediate purpose was to win support for independence at home and abroad. The Declaration also weakened the public's loyalty to George III by detailing

his misdeeds, outlined the basic principles of representative government, and proclaimed basic rights of the people.
5. Women served as spies and messengers; accompanied the troops as cooks, laundresses, and nurses; distributed medical supplies; made uniforms; helped manufacture bullets; and managed businesses and farms while their husbands were off to war.

PRIMARY SOURCE
1. She wanted him to consider providing for women's rights in his "Code of Laws."
2. He did not take her very seriously and was rather condescending and patronizing.
3. She said, "Remember all Men would be tyrants if they could."

COMPOSING AN ESSAY
1. European participation gave the Americans new hope at a time when Washington's troops had been drastically reduced due to sickness and hunger. Specifically, Europeans aided the cause by providing gold, naval support, supplies, troops, and experienced military leaders.
2. By negotiating with Britain only, the United States received the land from the Atlantic coast west to the Mississippi River and from the Great Lakes south to Florida as well as fishing rights in the Gulf of St. Lawrence and off the coast of Newfoundland. Had the United States been forced to negotiate with Spain and France as well, it probably would have won its independence, but little else.

CHAPTER 5

TEST FORM A

REVIEWING FACTS
1. James Madison
2. Federalists
3. John Locke
4. checks and balances
5. Daniel Shays
6. separation of powers
7. concurrent powers
8. Judith Sargent Murray
9. Benjamin Franklin
10. reserved powers

UNDERSTANDING IDEAS
1. a
2. b
3. a
4. a
5. b
6. b
7. d
8. c
9. c
10. a

TRUE/FALSE
1. F
2. T
3. F
4. F
5. F

PRACTICING SKILLS
1. December 1787 and January 1788
2. Rhode Island

COMPOSING AN ESSAY
1. Republican Motherhood held that women could influence politics and society through their work in the home. Opportunity example: provided an outlet for women to actively challenge the traditional barriers that had limited women's education. Limitation example: by emphasizing that women's primary duties were at home, Republican Motherhood weakened women's chances of gaining greater political rights.
2. Checks and balances is a system that gives each branch of the government the means to restrain the powers of the other two. On the positive side, the system has prevented unrestricted governmental power. On the negative side, the system permits political disputes to hold up the workings of government.

TEST FORM B

SHORT ANSWER

1. Most constitutions restricted powers of governors; many reduced the influence of the church on government.
2. Weaknesses: no provisions for directly taxing people; changes to articles required the consent of all 13 states; no provisions for regulating international trade; inability to effectively deal with civil unrest.
3. It gave Congress the right to overturn state laws, tax the states, and punish the states for "failing to fulfill [their] duty."
4. The Compromise provided a bicameral legislature in which each state, regardless of size, would have an equal voice in the upper house. In the lower house, representation would be according to population.
5. First, they believed the delegates had conspired to create a new form of government, going far beyond what they had been charged to do. Second, they claimed that a strong national government would destroy states' rights. Third, they argued that the new system of government resembled a monarchy because of its concentration of power.

PRIMARY SOURCE

1. "At the working man's house hunger looks in, but dares not enter."
2. He had a strong Protestant work ethic.
3. "It is true there is much to be done . . . wears away stones."

COMPOSING AN ESSAY

1. John Locke was an English philosopher and one of the great Enlightenment thinkers. Americans were greatly influenced by Locke's theory of "natural rights." Locke believed that all people were born with the rights of life, liberty, and property and that the role of government was to protect these rights. Supporters of American republicanism embraced Locke's argument and used it to challenge older forms of political and social organization.

2. The separation of powers is upheld by a system of checks and balances that gives each branch the means to restrain the powers of the other two. Congress, for example, has a responsibility to check presidential power. The Constitution's many checks on executive power reflect the framers' bitter experience with British royal governors.

CHAPTER 6

TEST FORM A

RECALLING FACTS

1. John Jay
2. Anthony Wayne
3. Alexander Hamilton
4. Treaty of Greenville
5. Aaron Burr
6. Zebulon Pike
7. William Clark
8. Treaty of Ghent
9. Embargo Act
10. Non-Intercourse Act

UNDERSTANDING IDEAS

1. c
2. b
3. d
4. b
5. c
6. d
7. d
8. c
9. a
10. a

TRUE/FALSE

1. T
2. T
3. T
4. F
5. T

PRACTICING SKILLS

1. 1800 and 1804
2. Federalist

COMPOSING AN ESSAY

1. The Louisiana Purchase added all or part

of 13 future states to the nation. This vastly increased size made the United States more important in the eyes of other countries and had important domestic consequences as well. For example, it opened the interior of the continent to American settlement.
2. It strengthened U.S. control of the Northwest Territory; it marked the beginning of a long partnership between the two countries; and the Federalist Party, which had bitterly opposed the war, never fully recovered from the charges of disloyalty that were leveled.

TEST FORM B

SHORT ANSWER
1. It recommended 12 amendments to add protection of individual liberties to the Constitution (10 were ratified and became known as the Bill of Rights); created a federal court system; created the State, War, and Treasury Departments; and chartered the Bank of the United States.
2. Some Americans were supportive of the Revolution because they themselves had recently tasted liberty, but others were shocked at the violence.
3. Federalists wanted a strong national government and sought the development of commerce, especially with Britain. Republicans wanted to protect states' rights and individual liberties by limiting the power of the federal government. They tended to be supportive of the French rather than the British.
4. Congress wanted electors to vote for presidential and vice presidential candidates on separate ballots to avoid an electoral crisis like the one that occurred in 1880 when Jefferson and Burr, both running on the same ticket, received the same number of electoral votes.
5. Napoleon decided to sell Louisiana because he had failed to establish a base in the West Indies from which to protect it and needed money to fund his army.

PRIMARY SOURCE
1. Federalist
2. "so far as they are repugnant to the Constitution and laws of the United States"
3. the people

COMPOSING AN ESSAY
1. Hamilton was the nation's first Secretary of the Treasury and one of Washington's most trusted advisers. He believed one of the best ways to strengthen the government, both financially and politically, was to establish economic policies that helped business and industry. If businesspeople believed that the federal government had their best interests at heart, they would support its policies.
2. The Bill of Rights are the first 10 amendments to the Constitution. Examples of guarantees include freedom of religion, speech, the press; right to assemble; right to a jury trial in most civil cases; Examples of rules include requirement of grand jury indictment before persons can be tried for serious criminal charges; prohibits search and seizures without warrants; prohibits excessive fines and bail.

UNIT 2

TEST FORM A

REVIEWING FACTS
1. Sons of Liberty
2. Great Compromise
3. Olive Branch Petition
4. French Revolution
5. ratification
6. Louisiana Purchase
7. Republican Motherhood
8. concurrent powers
9. veto
10. Bill of Rights

UNDERSTANDING IDEAS
1. c
2. b
3. a

4. c
5. c
6. b
7. a
8. c
9. d
10. b

TRUE/FALSE
1. F
2. T
3. F
4. T
5. F

PRACTICING SKILLS
1. Spain
2. United States

COMPOSING AN ESSAY
1. Women: accompanied troops and worked as cooks, laundresses, and nurses; some disguised themselves as men and participated in the fighting; many played a variety of important roles on the home front. American Indians: fought for both sides; were important to the British and the Patriots because of their knowledge of the land. African Americans: about 5,000 African American Patriots fought in the war; many received official recognition for their efforts.
2. Checks and balances: a system that gives to each branch of the government the means to restrain the powers of the other two. Positive: the system has prevented any branch of government from acquiring unrestricted power. Negative: the system permits political disputes to hold up the workings of government.

TEST FORM B

SHORT ANSWER
1. Napoleon decided to sell Louisiana because he had failed to establish a base in the West Indies from which to protect it. He also needed the money to fund his army.
2. Recommended 12 amendments to include protected individual liberties to the Constitution (10 were ratified and became known as the Bill of Rights); created a federal court system; created the State, War, and Treasury departments; chartered the Bank of the United States.
3. Great Britain issued the Proclamation of 1763, barring settlement west of the Appalachian Mountains. Great Britain hoped that separating settlers and American Indians would end fighting on the frontier.
4. Weaknesses: no provisions for directly taxing people; changes to articles required the consent of all 13 states; no provisions for regulating international trade; inability to deal effectively with civil unrest.
5. The Compromise provided a bicameral legislature in which each state, regardless of size, had an equal voice in the upper house. In the lower house, representation was according to population.

PRIMARY SOURCE
1. Law
2. Paine believes the colonies should break free of England and establish their own country.

COMPOSING AN ESSAY
1. Republican Motherhood: concept that held that women could influence politics and society through their work in the home. Opportunity example: provided an outlet for women to actively challenge the traditional barriers that had limited women's education. Limitation example: by emphasizing that women's primary duties were at home, Republican Motherhood weakened women's chances of gaining greater political rights.
2. It strengthened U.S. control of the Northwest Territory; it marked the beginning of a long partnership between the two countries; the Federalist Party, which had bitterly opposed the war, never fully recovered from the charges of disloyalty that were leveled.
3. The Louisiana Purchase added all or part of 13 future states to the nation. This vastly increased size made the United States more important in the eyes of other countries and had important domestic

consequences as well. For example, it opened the interior of the continent to American settlement.
4. Checks and balances: a system that gives each branch of the government the means to restrain the powers of the other two. Positive: the system has prevented any branch of government from acquiring unrestricted power. Negative: the system permits political disputes to hold up the workings of government.

CHAPTER 7

TEST FORM A

REVIEWING FACTS
1. Henry Clay
2. Robert Fulton
3. Missouri Compromise
4. Andrew Jackson
5. Rush-Bagot Agreement
6. Samuel Slater
7. John C. Calhoun
8. James Monroe
9. Simón Bolívar
10. Eli Whitney

UNDERSTANDING IDEAS
1. a
2. a
3. b
4. a
5. a

TRUE/FALSE
1. T
2. T
3. F
4. F
5. T
6. F
7. T
8. F
9. F
10. T

PRACTICING SKILLS
1. 12 slave states
2. 12 free states
3. 1 (Missouri)

COMPOSING AN ESSAY
1. The Transportation Revolution made it easier and cheaper to move farm products, raw materials, and manufactured goods long distances. The new road, canal, and rail systems created national markets for the first time.
2. It was appropriate because the country was in the midst of great national pride resulting from the country's success in the war. It was inappropriate because the United States disputed with Spain over West Florida, and fought the Seminole War.

TEST FORM B

SHORT ANSWER
1. Many Americans were angry with the Federalist Party because of its opposition to the War of 1812.
2. The Monroe Doctrine was a foreign policy initiated by President Monroe in which the United States declared its determination to defend not only its own liberty but also the freedom of other nations.
3. The war revealed that national measures were needed to promote manufacturing within the country. In addition, the war revealed weaknesses in the nation's financial system.
4. A network of canals was built, steamboat and locomotive construction was improved, and thousands of miles of railroad track was laid.
5. Jackson believed people were capable of governing themselves, that the government was supposed to be the servant of the people, and that not just the elite were capable of serving in government.

PRIMARY SOURCE
1. Every nation has a sense of national pride.
2. Answers will vary, but most students will probably indicate a response somewhere in between respect and disdain.
3. Answers will vary, but most students will probably say "yes" because Americans can be very braggish at times.

COMPOSING AN ESSAY

1. The Industrial Revolution was a period that saw dynamic changes in manufacturing. It began in Britain in the mid-1700s with the invention of spinning machines and then spread to the United States. New machinery and the employment of interchangeable parts allowed the mass production of a wide variety of goods. As a result, large parts of the country were experiencing prosperity by 1818.
2. The war proved that the United States could stand up to a major European power. Americans began to believe that the nation could become a power in its own right, free from Europe's influence and control.

CHAPTER 8

TEST FORM A

REVIEWING FACTS

1. Francis Cabot Lowell
2. nativism
3. Know-Nothings
4. antebellum
5. yeoman farmers
6. Sarah G. Bagley
7. Nat Turner
8. Harriet Tubman
9. Cyrus McCormick
10. Denmark Vesey

UNDERSTANDING IDEAS

1. b
2. d
3. b
4. b
5. b
6. b
7. a
8. d
9. d
10. c

TRUE/FALSE

1. F
2. T
3. F
4. F
5. T

PRACTICING SKILLS

1. about 250,000 in 1800; about 6.25 million in 1860
2. Midwest

COMPOSING AN ESSAY

1. A majority of the Irish settled in city slums, worked in low-paying, dangerous jobs, and were Roman Catholic. Many actively participated in local politics. Many Germans held skilled occupations. Although there was a sizable Catholic population, they were predominantly Protestant. Many Germans settled in small towns and rural areas. Both of the groups were discriminated against.
2. One major factor was the development of the cotton gin. Other factors include the fact that farmers had grown cotton since the late 1600s, they had slave labor, and they had experience with plantation-based agriculture.

FORM B TEST

SHORT ANSWER

1. Men were expected to work outside the home and earn money to support the family. Many middle-class men worked in factories, offices, mills, and shops rather than in agriculture. Women were expected to stay home, take care of the children, do housework, and be the moral center of the family.
2. A majority of the Irish settled in city slums, worked in low-paying, dangerous jobs, and were Roman Catholic. Many actively participated in local politics. Many Germans held skilled occupations. Although there was a sizable Catholic population, they were predominantly Protestant. Many Germans settled in small towns and rural areas.
3. The majority of the planters held fewer than 20 slaves. They lived more modestly than the wealthy planters, who held 20 or more slaves. Owners' duties included assigning tasks to slaves or supervisors,

keeping records of business transactions, writing to shipowners or bankers, and contracting with brokers. Planters' wives supervised housecleaning, kept track of household finances, cared for the sick, and often taught the children.
4. To justify slavery, many white southerners interpreted the Bible to mean that white people were superior to African Americans. Some saw themselves as spiritual guardians of their slaves.
5. Many slaves told stories and folktales to relate their family histories and to teach morals.

PRIMARY SOURCE
1. Philadelphia
2. He put holes in the box and brought along a bladder of water.
3. "victory or death"; he entered the box even though the carpenter thought he would not be able to live in it for long.

COMPOSING AN ESSAY
1. As a result of the introduction of the cotton gin, farmers across the South began planting cotton. Consequently, cotton production soared. From 1815 to 1860, cotton represented more than half of all American exports. The cotton gin led to the emergence of the South as the Cotton Kingdom.
2. The Market Revolution reduced the cost of manufactured goods, therefore allowing farm families to purchase goods they had previously made at home. Farm families also bought new farm machines such as the reaper, which allowed increased crop yields and the cultivation of more land. As a result, they moved past subsistence farming and began to specialize in growing cash crops or raising livestock to sell at market.

CHAPTER 9

TEST FORM A

REVIEWING FACTS
1. William Lloyd Garrison
2. Mormons
3. Walt Whitman
4. Unitarians
5. Catharine Beecher
6. Dorothea Dix
7. Horace Mann
8. Frederick Douglass
9. Elijah Lovejoy
10. Shakers

UNDERSTANDING IDEAS
1. b
2. c
3. c
4. d
5. b
6. a
7. d
8. a
9. c
10. a

TRUE/FALSE
1. F
2. T
3. T
4. T
5. F

PRACTICING SKILLS
1. 25 percent
2. South Carolina and Mississippi

COMPOSING AN ESSAY
1. Activists succeeded in getting the Married Women's Property Act passed in New York and similar laws passed in other states. The law gave married women the right to own property; a later revision in the law allowed them to retain their earnings. Political and legal equality on the national level would be long in coming.
2. The Second Great Awakening was a renewed and passionate interest in religion that began to develop in upstate

New York and spread through much of the country. Because the movement appealed to common people, membership soared in many Protestant churches.

TEST FORM B
SHORT ANSWER
1. Women participated widely in the Second Great Awakening. In fact, female converts outnumbered males three to two. Women often led prayer groups, established and taught in Sunday schools, and supported missionary societies.
2. Transcendentalism is the belief that people can transcend material things in life to reach a higher realm of understanding.
3. The national alcohol consumption rate declined; some states and communities outlawed alcohol.
4. Many southerners were suspicious of educational reform because it was supported by northerners who also supported abolition.
5. Abolitionists were becoming increasingly frustrated with the movement's lack of progress. Consequently, they increasingly began to call for action. The publications by Garrison and Walker, which both called for immediate action, reflected this new mood.

PRIMARY SOURCE
1. institutions in Massachusetts
2. Answers will vary, but most students will probably say it is very effective, because she paints a very graphic picture of life in the institutions.
3. laws against abusive behavior; treatment or rehabilitation programs for curable people; better overall conditions

COMPOSING AN ESSAY
1. Horace Mann's reform efforts in Massachusetts established a model for free public elementary education. The public school movement argued that all children, not just those who could afford private schools, deserved the opportunity to study reading, writing, and arithmetic. The movement also helped spark the development of public high schools and reforms in colleges. During the early 1800s, opportunities for white women and African Americans to receive a college education expanded.
2. The appearance of two important publications, Walker's *Appeal*, and Garrison's *Liberator*, convinced many people to back the abolition movement. In addition, many people were reform minded because of their participation in other reform movements.

UNIT 3

TEST FORM A
REVIEWING FACTS
1. Industrial Revolution
2. American Colonization Society
3. Erie Canal
4. Dorothea Dix
5. doctrine of nullification
6. Monroe Doctrine
7. Second Great Awakening
8. Trail of Tears
9. Frederick Douglass
10. Temperance Movement

UNDERSTANDING IDEAS
1. c
2. a
3. c
4. d
5. d
6. c
7. c
8. a
9. a
10. b

TRUE/FALSE
1. F
2. F
3. T
4. F
5. T

PRACTICING SKILLS
1. slave territory
2. the South

COMPOSING AN ESSAY
1. Major factor: the development of the cotton gin. Other factors: farmers had grown cotton since the late 1600s; slave labor; experience with plantation-based agriculture.
2. The Second Great Awakening was a renewed and passionate interest in religion that began to develop in upstate New York and spread through much of the country. Because the movement appealed to common people, membership soared in many Protestant churches.

TEST FORM B

SHORT ANSWER
1. A network of canals was built, steamboat and locomotive construction was improved, and thousands of miles of railroad track was laid.
2. The majority of the planters held fewer than 20 slaves. They lived more modestly than the wealthy planters, who held 20 or more slaves. Owners' duties included assigning tasks to slaves or supervisors, keeping records of business transactions, writing to shipowners or bankers, and contracting with brokers. Planters' wives supervised housecleaning, kept track of household finances, cared for the sick, and often taught the children.
3. Jackson believed people were capable of governing themselves, that the government was supposed to be the servant of the people, and that not just the elite were capable of serving in government.
4. The national alcohol consumption rate declined; some states and communities outlawed alcohol.
5. To justify slavery, many white southerners interpreted the Bible to mean that white people were superior to African Americans. Some saw themselves as spiritual guardians of their slaves.

PRIMARY SOURCE
1. They considered the prisons to be "severe," and places of great oppression.
2. They lose their freedom when they "become wicked," i.e., commit a crime.

COMPOSING AN ESSAY
1. Activists succeeded in getting the Married Women's Property Act passed in New York and similar laws in other states. The law permitted married women the right to own property; a later revision to the law allowed them to retain their earnings. Political and legal equality on the national level would be long in coming.
2. Irish: A majority settled in city slums, worked in low-paying and dangerous jobs; most were Roman Catholic. Many actively participated in local politics. German: Many held skilled occupations. Although there was a sizable Catholic population, they were predominantly Protestant. Many Germans settled in small towns and rural areas. Both groups were discriminated against.
3. The Second Great Awakening was a renewed and passionate interest in religion that began to develop in upstate New York and spread through much of the country. Because the movement appealed to common people, membership soared in many Protestant churches.
4. Appropriate: great national pride because of the country's success in the war. Inappropriate: dispute with Spain over West Florida; Seminole War.

CHAPTER 10

TEST FORM A

REVIEWING FACTS
1. manifest destiny
2. Tejanos
3. *empresarios*
4. Bear Flag Revolt
5. Juan Cortina
6. mountain men
7. Donner party

8. Brigham Young
9. Mexican Cession
10. Oregon Trail

UNDERSTANDING IDEAS
1. d
2. b
3. b
4. c
5. a
6. b
7. d
8. a
9. c
10. a

TRUE/FALSE
1. F
2. T
3. T
4. T
5. F

PRACTICING SKILLS
1. between 1848 and 1849
2. $50 million

COMPOSING AN ESSAY
1. Students should explain that the Treaty of Guadalupe Hidalgo meant that Mexico gave up all claims to Texas and surrendered a huge region, known as the Mexican Cession, that included all or parts of a number of present-day U.S. states. They should also mention that in return for these lands, the United States agreed to pay Mexico $15 million. The United States also agreed to grant full citizenship to Mexicans who lived in the Mexican Cession.
2. Students should explain that the forty-niners were drawn to California by the lure of newly discovered gold. Students should also mention that these migrants came from as far away as Australia, China, and Europe, as well as from North America, Mexico, and South America. Students should state that people in search of gold traveled overland via the California Trail and that some sailed down the eastern seaboard of the United States to Central America, where they disembarked, crossed over by land to the Pacific Ocean, and then sailed north to San Francisco.

TEST FORM B

SHORT ANSWER
1. Some members of Congress felt that the war was an excuse to obtain more land for U.S. expansion. Abolitionist opponents felt that the real goal of the war was to acquire more slave territory.
2. By 1830 about 7,000 Americans had relocated to Texas, and the Mexican government, in addition to being concerned about the importation of African American slaves to Texas, feared a rebellion or U.S. invasion.
3. Many Americans wanted to annex Texas to fulfill their idea of the United States expanding as far westward as possible. Also, many Americans who supported annexing Texas worried that the independent republic would become an ally of Britain, which wanted Texas to supply Britain with cotton and become a market for British goods.
4. The United States acquired parts of the present-day states of New Mexico and Arizona.
5. The United States promised to make annual payments to the tribes who signed the treaty and to honor each tribe's territorial boundaries.

PRIMARY SOURCE
1. Both men and women felt the burdens of caring for their families.
2. Women had to undergo more suffering because they were with their families all of the time, especially during sickness.

COMPOSING AN ESSAY
1. Students should explain that trappers who chose to use the rendezvous system lived in the mountains year round and gathered once a year to sell their furs and buy supplies. This system, like a modern-day convention or trade show, brought

buyers and sellers together and, students should point out, helped reduce expenses and thus increased profits. Students should also discuss the fact that following each annual rendezvous, the trappers fanned out across vast mountain regions to do their trapping, and in the process they explored the mountains and pioneered trails that settlers would later use to reach the Far West.

2. Students should discuss some of the ways in which the Gold Rush led to disaster for American Indians in California, including the fact that some Indian people were forced off of gold-rich lands by white miners or forced into service in the mines. They should also mention that many American Indian villages were attacked by regular army units and volunteer militias alike and that in response to attempts by the American Indians to resist or retaliate, the U.S. Army built forts and raided villages. By 1860 such attacks, along with disease and starvation, had greatly reduced California's American Indian population (from about 300,000 to 35,000).

CHAPTER 11

TEST FORM A

REVIEWING FACTS
1. Wilmot Proviso
2. popular sovereignty
3. Fugitive Slave Act
4. Kansas-Nebraska Act
5. John Brown
6. Frederick Douglass
7. John C. Calhoun
8. Compromise of 1850
9. Confederate States of America
10. John Breckinridge

UNDERSTANDING IDEAS
1. c
2. b
3. a
4. a
5. c
6. d
7. b
8. d
9. b
10. c

TRUE/FALSE
1. T
2. F
3. T
4. T
5. T

PRACTICING SKILLS
1. 303
2. greatest number of electoral votes: Lincoln
   greatest percentage of the popular vote: Lincoln

COMPOSING AN ESSAY
1. Students should discuss the fact that the Compromise of 1850 (based on proposals made by Henry Clay) came about as an attempt to satisfy both northern and southern interests, particularly concerning the issue of slavery. To appease northern antislavery interests, California would be admitted to the Union as a free state, and the slave trade (although not slavery itself) would be abolished in the District of Columbia. To appease southern pro-slavery interests, the New Mexico Territory would be divided into two territories—New Mexico and Utah—on the basis of popular sovereignty. Students should also mention that the Compromise of 1850 included the Fugitive Slave Act, which made it a federal crime to assist runaway slaves and authorized the arrest of escaped slaves even in states where slavery was illegal.

2. Students should explain that the case involved an African American, Dred Scott, who sued for his freedom following the death of his white owner. They should indicate that the majority of the Court ruled against him, for reasons that outraged many abolitionists. These included the following: that African Americans

were "beings of an inferior order"; that no African American, slave or free, could ever enjoy the rights of a U.S. citizen; and that Scott could not, therefore, bring suit in U.S. courts. Students should also point out that under this ruling, the federal government had no authority to limit the expansion of slavery.

TEST FORM B

SHORT ANSWER
1. Northerners who opposed the Compromise of 1850 believed that any compromise on the issue of slavery, such as allowing it to exist in states that already had it, was wrong. They also objected to the inclusion of the Fugitive Slave Act. Southerners who objected to the Compromise felt that any measures that would force southern states to give up any of their rights was wrong.
2. Pro-slavery Missouri residents voted illegally in the Kansas elections, helping to elect a pro-slavery Kansas legislature. Antislavery settlers already living in Kansas refused to recognize the new government, formed the Free State Party, and elected their own legislature. Kansas thus had two territorial governments competing for control, leading pro- and antislavery groups to attack one another, often at the cost of human lives.
3. Brown hoped to give guns to slaves living nearby and establish an independent regime for liberated slaves and their supporters in the Appalachian Mountains. He also hoped that runaway slaves and free African Americans would join him in his effort to liberate slaves.
4. All but three of the southern states supported John Breckinridge, the most clearly pro-slavery candidate. Abraham Lincoln won because of his support in the mostly antislavery North.
5. Supporters of states' rights argued that since individual states had come together to form the Union, a state had the right to withdraw from the Union.

PRIMARY SOURCE
1. Very little air or light entered. The air was stifling.
2. the voices of her children

COMPOSING AN ESSAY
1. Students should explain that the idea behind popular sovereignty was to allow the citizens of each new territory to vote on whether to permit slavery in their territory. They should also point out that the Kansas-Nebraska Act used popular sovereignty as part of the plan to organize the territories of Kansas and Nebraska, especially concerning the issue of slavery. The Kansas-Nebraska Act allowed these territories to be admitted to the Union with or without slavery, depending on which system they had in place at the time of their admission.
2. Students should point out that many northerners praised Brown as a just man who had acted heroically against the evils of slavery. Students might also mention that some, such as Henry David Thoreau, offered him support while he was in prison. In contrast, students should point out that pro-slavery southerners, alarmed by the threat of slave revolts, saw Brown as a bloodthirsty fanatic who deserved to be punished. Some southerners also hoped that all the attention given to Brown might actually help persuade less wealthy white farmers to support the cause of wealthy slave owners.

CHAPTER 12

TEST FORM A

REVIEWING FACTS
1. Richmond
2. Anaconda Plan
3. Elizabeth Blackwell
4. Clara Barton
5. conscription
6. U.S. Sanitary Commission
7. Copperheads
8. Ulysses S. Grant

9. Martin Delany
10. Battle of Antietam

UNDERSTANDING IDEAS
1. b
2. b
3. c
4. a
5. c
6. c
7. c
8. d
9. b
10. d

TRUE/FALSE
1. T
2. T
3. F
4. T
5. F

PRACTICING SKILLS
1. the Union
2. non-battle causes

COMPOSING AN ESSAY
1. Students should explain that the Crittenden Compromise was proposed to preserve the Union at a time when several southern states had already seceded. They should explain that the compromise called for the old Missouri Compromise line to be drawn west through the remaining territories, meaning that north of the line slavery would be illegal and that slavery would be legal and could expand south of the line.
2. Students should discuss the fact that the large population and industrial power of the North gave the Union a much larger pool of available soldiers to fight a long and bloody war as well as more factories and material resources that could be used to replace lost or damaged military equipment. There are many examples of this superiority that students may draw from. These might include the fact that most of the nation's railroad lines were in the North and thus the Union could move troops and supplies with relative ease.

Students might also mention that the North commanded the loyalty of most of the U.S. Navy, including several southern naval officers, and that the South was forced to build its navy from scratch.

Students should also discuss how the South's superior defensive strategy and military leadership (of which General Robert E. Lee was but one example) helped it win many of the war's early battles. Students may also point out that the South had the advantage of fighting a defensive war covering an extremely large amount of land. These factors put a heavy strain on the Union's resources and leadership; the South hoped this would mean that the North might thus eventually tire of the struggle.

TEST FORM B

SHORT ANSWER
1. Confederate leaders believed that the economies of Britain and France were dependent on cotton from the American South. Therefore, southerners expected the Europeans would support the Confederacy in the war, in order to ensure access to these supplies.
2. As a naval blockade, the North's Anaconda Plan was important because it would prevent the South from selling cotton to and buying supplies from its foreign markets by sea.
3. The North's strategy depended on dividing the South geographically, while the South planned to capture Washington and invade the North.
4. Women replaced men in factories, on farms, and in arsenals and sewing rooms. Women also worked as clerks at government jobs and as bankers, morticians, saloon keepers, and steamboat captains. They also joined organizations that made bandages, bedclothes, and shirts for soldiers, educated former slaves, and established homes for injured soldiers and for children of soldiers who died in the war.

5. The Union won the battle, although it did so at great cost of human lives. The victory came after several Confederate victories and proved that the Union army could defeat the Confederacy.

PRIMARY SOURCE

1. Lincoln stated that all slaves living in areas still rebelling against the United States would be free. This meant that the proclamation applied only to slaves within the Confederate states. Therefore, slaves in border states were not free.
2. They would be received into the Union army to serve the United States.

COMPOSING AN ESSAY

1. Students should mention the unpopularity of the Confederacy's 1862 conscription law. They should also mention the tension that arose between large plantation owners and the mostly poor, nonslaveholding whites who were not exempt from the draft and who actually did most of the fighting. Students should also explain that some southerners opposed the draft because they felt it violated states' rights and freedom. They might also mention that the Confederacy's allowing soldiers to pay low prices for food and supplies, food shortages, and the fear of starvation led to food riots in many southern states.

    Students should point out that in the Union, some northerners opposed the possibility of a draft, claiming that conscription would force white working-class men to fight for the freedom of African Americans who would then come north and steal their jobs. They might also mention that some northerners sympathized with the South and preferred peace to war. Others felt that the war was too costly in terms of money and human life.
2. Students should explain that Sherman's total-war strategy, which resulted in the devastation and capture of Atlanta and Savannah, was based on the belief that in order to win the war, the North must strike at the South's economic resources and make life so terrible for the populace that they would never want to go to war again. As examples, students should choose from the following tactics: in Atlanta, after evacuating the residents, setting fire to large portions of the city; on the way to Savannah, taking whatever supplies his troops could use and destroying whatever might be of value to the Confederates; uprooting crops, burning farmhouses, slaughtering livestock, and tearing up railroad tracks.

CHAPTER 13

TEST FORM A

REVIEWING FACTS
1. Ida B. Wells
2. Compromise of 1877
3. carpetbaggers
4. amnesty
5. Civil Rights Act of 1866
6. Jim Crow
7. Black Codes
8. Fifteenth Amendment
9. Ulysses S. Grant
10. Madame C. J. Walker

UNDERSTANDING IDEAS
1. c
2. d
3. a
4. b
5. a
6. c
7. b
8. d
9. d
10. b

TRUE/FALSE
1. F
2. T
3. T
4. F
5. T

PRACTICING SKILLS
1. 1876
2. 1880

COMPOSING AN ESSAY

1. Students should note that white southerners developed the Black Codes to keep African Americans from achieving social, political, and economic equality with southern whites. These former Confederates wanted to keep African Americans tied to the land as poorly paid laborers. Students should explain that African Americans thought the codes were a thinly disguised attempt at renewing slavery but felt that they had to accept the codes to survive. Students should point out that, like African Americans, many northerners thought the Black Codes were shameful and little better than slavery.

2. Students should explain that the Fifteenth Amendment stated that U.S. citizens could not be denied the right to vote based on their race, color, or whether they had been a slave. Students should also note, however, that it did not forbid state legislatures from limiting the right to vote by passing discriminatory requirements such as literacy tests and poll taxes. In addition, the Fifteenth Amendment did not give women the right to vote.

TEST FORM B

SHORT ANSWER

1. At the end of the Civil War, many African Americans hoped to establish their own churches and schools, legalize their marriages, choose their own work, and obtain their own land.

2. Thaddeus Stevens thought that owning their own land would ensure the economic freedom of former slaves and destroy the political power held by the southern plantation owners and Civil War rebels.

3. The Freedmen's Bureau distributed food and clothing, served as an employment agency, established hospitals, operated schools, and settled contract disputes between African American workers and white planters.

4. The goals of the Ku Klux Klan were to subvert Reconstruction, destroy the Republican Party, deter African Americans from voting, and generally scare the African American population. They used murder, violence, intimidation, and theft, and they burned homes, schools, and churches to accomplish these goals.

5. Because the sharecropping system required individuals to borrow for their current everyday needs on the expectation of future earnings, it was difficult for them to get ahead. A poor crop one year would put them further in debt the following year, virtually tying them to the land.

PRIMARY SOURCE

1. The man was younger than the woman and lighter in skin color.

2. He had grown older and become more educated and ambitious.

COMPOSING AN ESSAY

1. Students should note that after the Civil War, the South's economy was in ruins. Returning Confederate soldiers were without jobs and freed slaves had little stable employment. Students should explain that after the war, sharecropping became common, a system where poor whites and former slaves worked for plantation owners in exchange for a share of the crop, a place to live, seed, farm equipment, and a mule. Merchants gave credit only to farmers who grew specific crops, usually cotton, which meant farmers did not grow other crops to feed their families and animals. Students should also point out that southern railroads were rebuilt and various factories established, promoting industrialization, which diversified the economy, making it less dependent on agriculture.

2. Students should note the following four pieces of congressional legislation:
   1. Congress extended the life of the Freedmen's Bureau, a federal agency that aided southerners, especially African Americans. Johnson vetoed it, but Congress overrode his veto.

2. Congress passed the Civil Rights Act of 1866, declaring that everyone born in the United States was a citizen with full civil rights. Again, Johnson vetoed the act and Congress overrode it.
3. Congress passed the Fourteenth Amendment to the Constitution, which required states to extend equal citizenship to African Americans and all people "born or naturalized in the United States," guaranteed due process, and promised all citizens "equal protection of the laws." The states had to ratify the amendment and did so.
4. Congress passed the Reconstruction Acts of 1867, which divided the South into five military districts and required states to ratify the Fourteenth Amendment and rewrite their constitutions to guarantee all men the vote.

UNIT 4

TEST FORM A

REVIEWING FACTS
1. Ida B. Wells
2. Jim Crow
3. John Brown
4. Frederick Douglass
5. Clara Barton
6. conscription
7. Copperheads
8. manifest destiny
9. amnesty
10. Tejanos

UNDERSTANDING IDEAS
1. c
2. c
3. d
4. b
5. a
6. b
7. d
8. c
9. b
10. b

TRUE/FALSE
1. F
2. F
3. F
4. F
5. F

PRACTICING SKILLS
1. the Union
2. non-battle causes

COMPOSING AN ESSAY
1. Students could mention that slavery was the basis of the southern economy, and that abolishing it could ruin the South economically. Also, an attack on slavery was an attack on the southern way of life and southern values. Lastly, the South believed states' rights allowed them to do as they pleased, regardless of what northerners thought.
2. Students should note that white southerners developed the Black Codes to keep African Americans from achieving social, political, and economic equality with southern whites. These former Confederates wanted to keep African Americans tied to the land as poorly paid laborers. Students should explain that African Americans thought the codes were a thinly disguised attempt at renewing slavery but felt that they had to accept the codes to survive. Students should point out that, like African Americans, many northerners thought the Black Codes were shameful and little better than slavery.

TEST FORM B

SHORT ANSWER
1. Abolitionists felt that the real goal of the war was to acquire more slave territory, so they opposed the declaration of war.
2. Brown hoped to give guns to slaves living nearby and establish an independent regime for liberated slaves and their supporters in the Appalachian Mountains. He also hoped that runaway slaves and free African Americans would join him in his effort to liberate slaves.

3. Southern supporters of states' rights argued that since individual states had come together to form the Union, a state had the right to withdraw from the Union. They also believed the north had no right to tell them how to run their states.
4. Women replaced men in factories, on farms, and in arsenals and sewing rooms. Women also worked as clerks at government jobs and as bankers, morticians, saloon keepers, and steamboat captains. They also joined organizations that made bandages, bedclothes, and shirts for soldiers, educated former slaves, and established homes for soldiers and orphanages for children of soldiers who died in the war.
5. The goals of the Ku Klux Klan were to subvert Reconstruction, destroy the Republican Party, deter African Americans from voting, and generally scare the African American population. They used murder, violence, intimidation, and theft, and they burned homes, schools, and churches to accomplish these goals.

PRIMARY SOURCE
1. Guerrilla warfare.
2. A large army and patriotism.

COMPOSING AN ESSAY
1. Students should discuss some of the ways in which the Gold Rush led to disaster for American Indians in California, including the fact that some Indian people were forced off of gold-rich lands by white miners or forced into service in the mines. They should also mention that many American Indian villages were attacked by regular army units and volunteer militias alike, and that in response to attempts by the American Indians to resist or retaliate, the U.S. Army built forts and raided villages. By 1860 such attacks, along with disease and starvation, had greatly reduced California's American Indian population (from about 300,000 to 35,000).

2. Students should explain that the idea behind popular sovereignty was to allow the citizens of each new territory to vote on whether to permit slavery in their territory. They should also point out that the Kansas-Nebraska Act used popular sovereignty as part of the plan to organize the territories of Kansas and Nebraska, especially concerning the issue of slavery. The Kansas-Nebraska Act allowed these territories to be admitted to the Union with or without slavery, depending on which system they had in place at the time of their admission.
3. Students should explain that Sherman's total-war strategy, which resulted in the devastation and capture of Atlanta and Savannah, was based on the belief that in order to win the war, the North must strike at the South's economic resources and make life so terrible for the populace that they would never want to go to war again. As examples, students should choose from the following tactics: in Atlanta, after evacuating the residents, setting fire to large portions of the city; in Savannah, taking whatever supplies his troops could use and destroying whatever might be of value to the Confederates; uprooting crops, burning farmhouses, slaughtering livestock, and tearing up railroad tracks.
4. Students should note that after the Civil War, the South's economy was in ruins. Returning Confederate soldiers were without jobs and freed slaves had little stable employment. Students should explain that after the war, sharecropping became common, a system where poor whites and former slaves worked for plantation owners in exchange for a share of the crop, a place to live, seed, farm equipment, and a mule. Merchants gave credit only to farmers who grew specific crops, usually cotton, which meant farmers did not grow other crops to feed their families and animals. Students should also point out that southern railroads were rebuilt and various factories established, promot-

ing industrialization, which diversified the economy, making it less dependent on agriculture.

CHAPTER 14

TEST FORM A

REVIEWING FACTS
1. Comstock Lode
2. Sand Creek Massacre
3. Homestead Act
4. Battle of the Little Bighorn
5. Geronimo
6. Klondike Gold Rush
7. Treaty of Medicine Lodge
8. Dawes General Allotment Act
9. Chief Joseph
10. Wovoka

UNDERSTANDING IDEAS
1. c
2. d
3. c
4. d
5. d
6. a
7. b
8. b
9. a
10. c

TRUE/FALSE
1. F
2. F
3. T
4. T
5. F

PRACTICING SKILLS
1. 30 million
2. from about 15 million to close to zero

COMPOSING AN ESSAY
1. Students should explain how mining camps were often lawless places initially composed of single men and how the advent of families changed the nature of the camps. Students should also note how the presence of men in need of basic services such as housing, food, and laundry encouraged businesses to spring up to serve those needs. Students might also mention the change in levels of lawlessness as the camps changed into towns.
2. Students should note that the U.S. Department of Agriculture publicized varieties of wheat that were better suited to growing on the Great Plains than traditional winter wheat. Department agents also taught dry farming, techniques that conserved moisture in the soil. Students should explain that new farming equipment included plows and harvesters. Students should also point out that steam-powered machines were expensive for small farmers, putting them in debt when they tried to compete with larger farmers.

TEST FORM B

SHORT ANSWER
1. Railroad companies sold excess lands to settlers who built farms near the railroad lines. This allowed them to easily ship their crops to market. Railroad companies also paid for the fares of potential land buyers, allowing them to move West cheaply, and sold them land on credit.
2. Settlers built sod houses because trees for lumber and stone for bricks were in scarce supply on the Great Plains. Made from chunks cut from heavy topsoil, the material for sod houses was easily available. Sod buildings were well insulated, windproof, and fireproof. The disadvantages to sod buildings included that they were damp, dirty, and difficult to keep clean, and sod bricks were very heavy to carry.
3. African American and white cowboys were treated much the same. Discrimination against African Americans in the post–Civil War era was much less severe in the West. However, they were more likely to be assigned unpleasant tasks by many ranch owners.

4. Three factors helped end the cattle boom. Supply exceeded demand as many ranchers ran too many cattle on the open range. This caused a glut in cattle and a downswing in prices. To control access to water and land, ranchers put up barbed wire, newly invented in 1874. This limited the availability of open land for grazing cattle. Bad weather, especially blizzards, caused the death of thousands of cattle.
5. Unions negotiated with or fought owners who tried to reduce miners' wages and assisted the families of injured or killed miners through distribution of union dues. They also tried to keep out workers who were willing to work for lower-than-standard wages.

PRIMARY SOURCE
1. Students could note that other homes might have white paint on the exterior, fences surrounding the land, carpets on the stairs, and an organ in the parlor or living room.
2. She loved the area, wishing for no better.

COMPOSING AN ESSAY
1. Students should explain that the U.S. government hoped to open more land to settlers, force American Indians onto reservations, and induce American Indians to become farmers. Students should note that the U.S. government wanted American Indians to give up their traditional ways of life and become assimilated into "white America." In addition, should valuable resources be discovered on reservation lands, the government wanted the Indians to give up even their reservations. Students should explain that in return for this, the American Indians expected the government to follow through on its promises for money, yearly supplies for thirty years, and reservation land that would be theirs forever.

   In response to whether these expectations were met, students might note that the government reduced the size of the reservation or changed its location as settlers demanded more land. When valuable resources were discovered on the Indians' promised land, the government tried first to renegotiate agreements and then used armed forces to get the American Indians off their reservations. In addition, government agents diverted supplies meant for American Indians.
2. Students should describe the three types of settlers (white Americans from the East, southern African Americans, and foreign immigrants) and the reasons they moved West. Students should also note the different problems the new environment presented: lack of water, lack of building materials, and extremes of temperature. Students might also note that these factors resulted in a tremendous amount of work for men, women, and children.

CHAPTER 15

TEST FORM A

REVIEWING FACTS
1. Bessemer process
2. patent
3. Elijah McCoy
4. social Darwinism
5. trust
6. vertical integration
7. Cornelius Vanderbilt
8. horizontal integration
9. Knights of Labor
10. Eugene V. Debs

UNDERSTANDING IDEAS
1. c
2. d
3. b
4. c
5. c
6. a
7. b
8. b
9. b
10. c

TRUE/FALSE
1. T
2. F

3. T
4. T
5. F

PRACTICING SKILLS
1. the Great Lakes and Northeast
2. the Northwest

COMPOSING AN ESSAY
1. Students should explain that the widespread availability of steel led to its increased use in the 1800s, especially as a source of strong building materials. Specifically, they should point out that steel was used to create the heavy machinery that turned out mass-produced goods; it was also used in the construction of rails and as a building material in the construction of buildings and bridges. Students may also point out other items made of rust-resistant steel, such as nails and wire.
2. Students should explain that Carnegie bought companies that provided the materials and services upon which his businesses depended. In this way, he controlled businesses at each stage of production and could sell steel at a lower price than his competitors. As an example, students should point out that he purchased iron and coal mines, which provided the raw materials for his steel mills. He also bought steamship lines and railroads to transport these materials.

TEST FORM B

SHORT ANSWER
1. Answers may be chosen from the following:
   - the rapid increase of rail lines, either in length or number
   - the completion of the transcontinental railroad
   - the development of trunk lines, or major railroads
   - the development of feeder, or branch, lines connecting trunk lines to outlying areas
   - bigger, more efficient locomotives
   - the compressed-air brake
   - communications systems between train and stations
   - improvements in track design
   - standardized track gauge, or width, between rails
2. The bourgeoisie consists of the people who own the means of production, while the proletariat consists of the workers.
3. He wanted to create a planned community that would offer his employees good homes, shops, and churches and encourage them to become healthy, educated, and virtuous workers. It also helped him control his workers.
4. It made foreign products more expensive and thus allowed American businesses to dominate the U.S. market.
5. Scrip could only be used to pay rent to the company or to buy goods—usually at high prices—at company stores.

PRIMARY SOURCE
1. Joy, happiness, the intimacy of home, and sweetness.
2. He sees how tired and unhealthy people look, and he concludes that uninterrupted labor cannot be a good thing.

COMPOSING AN ESSAY
1. Students should explain that laissez-faire capitalism calls for no government intervention in the economy. They should make clear that this means that most business leaders felt that if businesses were kept free from government control and allowed to compete in a free market, the economy would prosper. In contrast, students should point out that communism argued against the individual ownership of property. This means that in a communist state, property and the means of production are owned by everyone in the community and that the needs of all would be provided for without regard to social role. Students should infer from this that in order to succeed, a communist state would require more government involvement than would a state run according to laissez-faire capitalist principles.

2. Students should discuss various other industries that contributed to the development of railroads. For example, the need for locomotives, rails, and railcars poured money into the steel and railroad-car construction industries. Students should also mention other industries that grew with the development of the railroads, such as the meatpacking industry, which benefited from refrigerated cars, and various manufacturers, which could now sell their products nationwide.

CHAPTER 16

TEST FORM A

REVIEWING FACTS
1. steerage
2. Denis Kearney
3. Elisha Otis
4. mass transit
5. suburbs
6. conspicuous consumption
7. settlement houses
8. vaudeville
9. Jane Addams
10. ragtime

UNDERSTANDING IDEAS
1. b
2. d
3. b
4. d
5. a
6. a
7. d
8. b
9. b
10. c

TRUE/FALSE
1. T
2. F
3. F
4. F
5. T

PRACTICING SKILLS
1. northern and western Europe
2. northern and western Europe

COMPOSING AN ESSAY
1. Students should explain that many native-born white Americans saw immigration as a threat. They should cite some of these nativists' reasons for their reaction against recent immigrants, from the feeling that these newcomers were simply "too different" to fit into American society to more serious reasons, including blaming immigrants for a variety of social problems and radical political activity. Nativists also opposed immigrants for economic reasons, charging that immigrants' willingness to work cheaply robbed native-born Americans of their jobs and lowered everyone's wages.
2. Students should point out that rapid urban growth and the rise of big business increased the opportunities for young, single women to work outside the home and created many new jobs, such as salesclerks and secretaries. They might also point out that women filling these positions were paid lower wages than men. Most married middle-class women worked at home. Students should mention that smaller families, increased reliance on purchased goods, and new household technologies gave some women more time to engage in other activities, such as reading, and taking part in cultural events.

TEST FORM B

SHORT ANSWER
1. Many came to escape poverty and religious or political persecution. Many came seeking new economic opportunities, often with the intention of making enough money in the United States to return home and buy land.
2. The old immigrants were mostly Protestants from northwestern Europe. Most new immigrants were from southern or eastern Europe, as well as from Asia, French Canada, and the Middle East, and tended to be Catholic, Greek Orthodox, or Jewish.
3. The act denied U.S. citizenship to people

born in China and prohibited the immigration of Chinese workers.
4. The invention of the elevator and the development of steel frames made it possible to build bigger and taller skyscrapers.
5. Many city residents relaxed in parks, attended musicals and theater shows, read, and watched and played sports.

PRIMARY SOURCE
1. She describes them as "those things which cultivated men have come to consider reasonable and goodly."
2. because they work long hours and are underpaid

COMPOSING AN ESSAY
1. Students should describe the tendency of many members of this class to indulge in conspicuous consumption in order to impress others with their success. Many built large houses imitating European architectural styles, purchased homes abroad, and spent time at their huge country estates. Students should also indicate that many newly wealthy people staged expensive parties and other extravagances. They should also point out that many wealthy people gave money to various causes, most of them in the arts, entertainment, and higher education. Students might also mention that some critics felt this philanthropy was merely another form of conspicuous consumption.
2. Students should point out that the goal of both movements was to battle poverty and social injustice. Settlement houses sought to provide social and cultural services to people living in neighborhoods where they might otherwise not receive them. Students should point out that these services were in the form of providing education and cultural opportunities to poor people and improving their living conditions. Students might also note that a related goal was to provide settlement house volunteers, who were mostly young women, with fulfilling careers. Students should explain how the Social Gospel movement centered on churches as a vehicle for confronting social injustices and improving living conditions for workers and other poor people. Students should cite such examples of Social Gospel programs and services as free public kindergartens, gymnasiums, classes in domestic and industrial skills, meals programs, and a variety of cultural programs.

CHAPTER 17

TEST FORM A
REVIEWING FACTS
1. James Pendergast
2. graft
3. Gilded Age
4. Stalwarts
5. Half-Breeds
6. Charles Guiteau
7. mugwumps
8. cooperatives
9. graduated income tax
10. Mary Elizabeth Lease

UNDERSTANDING IDEAS
1. b
2. c
3. c
4. c
5. a
6. c
7. d
8. a
9. b
10. a

TRUE/FALSE
1. T
2. F
3. T
4. F
5. T

PRACTICING SKILLS
1. There are fewer farms on more land today.
2. fewer

COMPOSING AN ESSAY
1. Students should describe the various ways

that party workers helped immigrants get settled in their new homeland. Students should also describe how Tammany Hall helped newcomers find temporary housing and jobs and become naturalized citizens and thus be able to vote for Tammany Hall candidates. Students should point out, however, the failure of Tammany Hall to offer any extensive programs to address long-standing poverty and poor housing.

2. Students should point out that each of these major farmers' organizations tackled economic and political issues of concern to farmers, and each organized cooperatives to buy farm equipment and to market farm products. Students should point out that the Grange's main focus was on forcing states to regulate railroad freight and grain-storage rates. They should also point out that the Alliance offered farmers low-cost insurance and lobbied for tougher bank regulations, government ownership of the railroads, and a graduated income tax.

TEST FORM B

SHORT ANSWER

1. because they dominated city governments and were very successful at getting their members elected to local offices
2. In 1871 Nast published some 50 political cartoons criticizing Tweed and Tammany Hall. Based on the cartoons and a series of newspaper articles, Tweed was indicted for fraud and extortion. After escaping from jail, Tweed was arrested in Spain when officials recognized him from one of Nast's drawings.
3. Arthur abandoned his opposition to reform, responded sympathetically to calls for reform, and eventually helped along the passage of the Pendleton Civil Service Act.
4. Harrison and the Congress quickly set out to reward their supporters with jobs and money, thereby undercutting Cleveland's efforts at reform.

5. The purpose of these laws was to create state commissions to regulate railroads and other businesses that involved the public interest.

PRIMARY SOURCE

1. Because he has inside information about the plans to make a park, he can buy up land from sellers who have no idea that their property will probably increase in value.
2. He slyly calls his price "a good price" that will reward him for what he refers to as his "investment and foresight."

COMPOSING AN ESSAY

1. Students should explain that the increasing number of scandals led political opponents to challenge Grant when he came up for re-election. Students should point out that many critics saw the corruption of the day as a result of the spoils system, and many argued that civil service jobs should be granted on the basis of merit rather than patronage. Students should also discuss other reforms that citizens began pushing for and mention that in general the public became more skeptical about the ethics and behavior of politicians.
2. Students should mention the coalition of farm, labor, and reform leaders who helped organize the Populist Party. They should also discuss the fact that many of these leaders' objectives, such as a graduated income tax, bank regulation, government ownership of railroads and telegraph companies, a shorter workday, and voting reforms, would be unlikely to appeal to business leaders who valued private ownership, little or no government involvement in the running of private enterprise, or any measure that would reduce the length of an average workday.

UNIT 5

TEST FORM A

REVIEWING FACTS
1. Geronimo
2. Chief Joseph
3. patent
4. social Darwinism
5. vertical integration
6. conspicuous consumption
7. settlement houses
8. Jane Addams
9. graft
10. cooperatives

UNDERSTANDING IDEAS
1. b
2. b
3. a
4. b
5. a
6. c
7. d
8. a
9. c
10. a

TRUE/FALSE
1. T
2. T
3. F
4. T
5. F

PRACTICING SKILLS
1. in the Northeast
2. the Northwest

COMPOSING AN ESSAY
1. Students should explain how mining camps were often lawless places initially composed of single men and how the advent of families changed the nature of the camps. Students should also note how the presence of men in need of basic services such as housing, food, and laundry encouraged businesses to spring up to serve those needs. Students might also mention the change in levels of lawlessness as the camps changed into towns.

2. Students should describe the various ways that party workers helped immigrants get settled in their new homeland. Students should also describe how Tammany Hall helped newcomers find temporary housing and jobs and become naturalized citizens and thus be able to vote for Tammany Hall candidates. Students should point out, however, the failure of Tammany Hall to offer any extensive programs to address long-standing poverty and poor housing.

TEST FORM B

SHORT ANSWER
1. Railroad companies sold excess lands to settlers who built farms near the railroad lines. This allowed them to easily ship their crops to market. Railroad companies also paid for the fares of potential land buyers, allowing them to move West cheaply, and sold them land on credit.
2. It made foreign products more expensive and thus allowed American businesses to dominate the U.S. market.
3. Scrip could only be used to pay rent to the company or to buy goods—usually at high prices—at company stores.
4. The invention of the elevator and the development of steel frames made it possible to build bigger and taller skyscrapers.
5. Political machines dominated city governments and were very successful at getting their members elected to local offices.

PRIMARY SOURCE
1. Students could note that other homes might have white paint on the exterior, fences surrounding the land, carpets on the stairs, and an organ in the parlor or living room.
2. She loved the area, wishing for no better.

COMPOSING AN ESSAY
1. Students should explain that the United States government hoped to open more land to settlers, force American Indians onto reservations, and induce American

Indians to become farmers. Students should note that the U.S. government wanted American Indians to give up their traditional ways of life and become assimilated into "white America." In addition, should valuable resources be discovered on reservation lands, the government wanted the Indians to give up even their reservations. Students should explain that in return for this, the American Indians expected the government to follow through on its promises for money, yearly supplies for 30 years, and reservation land that would be theirs forever.

In response to whether these expectations were met, students might note that the government reduced the size of the reservation or changed its location as settlers demanded more land. When valuable resources were discovered on the Indians' promised land, the government tried first to renegotiate agreements and then used armed forces to get the American Indians off their reservations. In addition, government agents diverted supplies meant for American Indians.

2. Students should describe the three types of settlers (white Americans from the East, southern African Americans, and foreign immigrants) and the reasons they moved west. Students should also note the different problems the new environment presented: lack of water, lack of building materials, and extremes of temperature. Students might also note that these factors resulted in a tremendous amount of work for men, women, and children.

3. Students should explain that laissez-faire capitalism calls for no government intervention in the economy. They should make clear that this means that most business leaders felt that if businesses were kept free from government control and allowed to compete in a free market, the economy would prosper. In contrast, students should point out that communism argued against the individual ownership of property. This means that in a communist state, property and the means of production are owned by everyone in the community and that the needs of all would be provided for without regard to social role. Students should infer from this that in order to succeed, a communist state would require more government involvement than would a state run according to laissez-faire capitalist principles.

4. Students should describe the tendency of many members of this class to indulge in conspicuous consumption in order to impress others with their success. Many built large houses imitating European architectural styles, purchased homes abroad, and spent time at their huge country estates. Students should also indicate that many newly wealthy people staged expensive parties and other extravagances. They should also point out that many wealthy people gave money to various causes, most of them in the arts, entertainment, and higher education. Students might also mention that some critics felt this philanthropy was merely another form of conspicuous consumption.

CHAPTER 18

TEST FORM A

REVIEWING FACTS
1. Daniel Burnham
2. muckrakers
3. Ida Tarbell
4. Triangle Shirtwaist Fire
5. Eighteenth Amendment
6. progressivism
7. populism
8. W. E. B. Du Bois
9. National Association for the Advancement of Colored People
10. Samuel Gompers

UNDERSTANDING IDEAS
1. b
2. c
3. a
4. a
5. c

6. a
7. c
8. c
9. b
10. c

TRUE/FALSE
1. F
2. F
3. T
4. T
5. F

PRACTICING SKILLS
1. about 2 million
2. between 1915 and 1920

COMPOSING AN ESSAY
1. Students should discuss the fact that the Supreme Court struck down some progressive legislation, ruling that it was contrary to the Fourteenth Amendment, which prohibits states from depriving "any person of life, liberty, or property, without due process of law." Students may also explain that businesses used this argument to claim that regulation of their businesses unfairly deprived them of their property. Students may note that the Court also ruled that some progressive social legislation denied workers their freedom of contract, which was the freedom to negotiate the terms of their employment, even if that meant that they negotiated to work 14 to 16 hours a day. Example: in *Lochner* v. *New York*, in which the Court overturned New York law limiting bakers' workdays to 10 hours.
2. Students should explain that the public enjoyed reading about corruption, and muckrakers helped popularize some of the issues reformers wanted to address. Students should give some examples of writings and issues, such as Lincoln Steffens and Claude Wetmore's article in *McClure's*, "Tweed Days in St. Louis," in which they compared the corrupt political machine in St. Louis to Boss Tweed's control of New York City. Other examples could be Lincoln Steffens' writing about political corruption in *The Shame of the Cities*, Ray Stannard Baker on the plight of African Americans in *Following the Color Line*, or Ida Tarbell's exposé of Standard Oil business practices, "History of the Standard Oil Company."

TEST FORM B

SHORT ANSWER
1. Industrialization brought great profits for some, but the lower classes were left out of the general prosperity, working long hours for little pay in often unsafe conditions. Workers often lived in crowded, unsanitary conditions. Economic growth provided many new goods and services to an expanding middle class, but the gap widened between rich and poor.
2. Women became active in the reform movement because, for working class women, the issues of poor pay, long hours, and unsafe conditions encouraged them to try to make changes to better their own conditions. For middle class, wealthy, and college-educated women, reform movements were socially acceptable areas of activity where they could use their skills and training to influence politics and society.
3. The Industrial Workers of the World fought for workers' rights. A Communist organization, the IWW opposed capitalism and wanted to "emancipate the working class."
4. Progressives hoped to instill a stronger sense of patriotism in citizens, especially immigrants, through the building of monuments and beautification of cities.
5. The primary goal of the National Association for the Advancement of Colored People (NAACP) was to end racial discrimination. This organization worked for social reforms that would ensure equal rights for African Americans and attempted to change segregation laws by bringing cases before the Supreme Court. Similarly, the National Urban League also fought for racial equality, improved job opportunities, and housing

for urban African Americans. The National Association of Colored Women performed volunteer reform work.

PRIMARY SOURCE
1. He means that the African American does not want to change or replace American culture and way of life with African culture.
2. An African American could attempt to "bleach the Negro soul in a flood of white Americanism" by adopting white mannerisms, dress, style, and attitudes in general. This could (and often has) taken such forms as straightened (or "processed") hair, adopting white speech patterns, and rejection of African American culture by individual African Americans in favor of "white" culture.

COMPOSING AN ESSAY
1. Students should explain that industrialization relied on cheap labor to generate increased profits, goods, and services for the upper and middle classes. Students should point out that, because workers were in plentiful supply and were not protected by laws that would regulate safety, hours, and pay, they did not have a very strong bargaining position. Workers could be hired cheaply and would agree to work for long hours in poor and unsafe conditions. Industrialization also led to increased urbanization, crowding workers into cities to live in substandard housing.

    Students may also note that the increase in the middle class that came from industrialization meant that more people could afford to go to college, where many learned about these social problems for the first time, and then joined reform movements in an attempt to do something about them. Similarly, many descendants of former slaves, American Indians, and other minorities and women were able to afford more education. In this way, many learned about the legal possibilities for changing racial discrimination, segregation, and voting rights, and ways in which to organize to effect change.

2. Students should compare the goals of the American Federation of Labor, which tried to work within the system to improve the working conditions of capitalist businesses, with that of the IWW, which wanted to gain control of the businesses and liberate the workers from capitalist bondage. Students should also compare tactics and targeted membership of the two organizations. Students should point out that the AFL negotiated with management over hours, safety issues, and pay, and limited its membership to skilled workers. They should also explain that the IWW organized unskilled workers, including lumber workers, migrant farmworkers, miners and textile workers, and minority workers, and actively recruited female workers. Their methods included boycotts, general strikes, and industrial sabotage.

CHAPTER 19

TEST FORM A

REVIEWING FACTS
1. Robert M. La Follette
2. initiative
3. Theodore Roosevelt
4. Upton Sinclair
5. recall
6. arbitration
7. Eugene Debs
8. Alice Paul
9. Carrie Chapman Catt
10. reclamation

UNDERSTANDING IDEAS
1. d
2. a
3. b
4. a
5. a
6. d
7. c
8. c

9. b
10. a

TRUE/FALSE
1. T
2. F
3. T
4. F
5. T

PRACTICING SKILLS
1. the West
2. Idaho, Utah, Wyoming, and Colorado

COMPOSING AN ESSAY
1. Students should note some of the following: establishment of direct primaries; increased taxes on railroads and public utilities; creation of commissions to regulate insurance companies, public utilities, and railroads; passage of laws to curb excessive lobbying; conservation of natural resources; abolishment of convict labor; improved social services for the poor.
2. Students should mention Roosevelt withdrew from sale millions of acres of public land, setting aside 150 million acres as forest reserves; he doubled the number of national parks, created national monuments and wildlife sanctuaries, and urged Congress to pass the Newlands Reclamation Act.

TEST FORM B

SHORT ANSWER
1. The graduated income tax taxes people with high incomes at a higher rate than those with low incomes.
2. Liquor producers and distributors feared that women would vote for prohibition.
3. Many business regulations fell short of reforming the capitalist system; reforms such as the initiative, referendum, and recall had little impact at the national level; problems of African Americans were not addressed adequately or worsened.
4. Roosevelt believed the president should use the office as a "bully pulpit" to speak out on vital issues; presidents of the Gilded Age generally took a hands-off approach to government.
5. Roosevelt wanted to balance the interests of business, consumers, and labor.

PRIMARY SOURCE
1. His comments were insensitive and highly sexist.
2. She was obviously very angry with the senator's comments but instead of using angry words to rebut, she chose instead to make her point with witty sarcasm. She put the senator in his place.
3. It suggested that at least some men did not view women as equals.

COMPOSING AN ESSAY
1. Students should mention he filed many antitrust suits; urged Congress to pass Mann-Elkins Act; promoted conservation by adding vast areas to the nation's forest reserves; supported reforms to aid working people, particularly child laborers; urged Congress to create the Department of Labor and to pass mine safety laws; partly responsible for the adoption of the Sixteenth Amendment.
2. Students should explain the primary reason was a division in the Republican Party that saw Roosevelt leave the party and run on the Progressive Party ticket. Another reason was that voters were attracted to Wilson's reform program, which called for tariff reduction, banking reform, laws benefiting wage earners and farmers, and stronger antitrust legislation.

CHAPTER 20

TEST FORM A

REVIEWING FACTS
1. John Hay
2. Boxer Rebellion
3. William Randolph Hearst
4. Spanish-American War
5. Emilio Aguinaldo

6. Platt Amendment
7. Roosevelt Corollary
8. Emiliano Zapata
9. Matthew Perry
10. Russo-Japanese War

UNDERSTANDING IDEAS
1. a
2. c
3. b
4. b
5. a

TRUE/FALSE
1. F
2. T
3. T
4. F
5. F
6. T
7. T
8. F
9. F
10. T

PRACTICING SKILLS
1. Cuba
2. $40 million
3. Trade steadily declined during the period.

COMPOSING AN ESSAY
1. Imperialism: the quest for colonial empires. Factors: the need to maintain economic and military strength; desire for power and prestige; need for markets and raw materials; feelings of racial superiority; duty to spread political system and Christian religion.
2. Americans were sympathetic to the cause of Cuban rebels; the U.S. media used sensationalism and propaganda to increase public sympathy for the Cubans and to get the government to intervene; a letter that was critical of President McKinley from Spain's minister to the United States was intercepted by a spy; the United States blamed Spain for the destruction of the USS *Maine*.

TEST FORM B

SHORT ANSWER
1. He wanted to make it clear to European powers that the United States would use force to stop them from seizing territory in the Dominican Republic.
2. The Hawaiian League forced Kalakaua at gunpoint to sign a new constitution and grant the United States exclusive rights to build a naval base.
3. The Rough Riders took control of the ridge above Santiago and the U.S. Navy sank the Spanish fleet off the coast of Cuba as it attempted to escape from a naval blockade.
4. Thousands of farmers were put in concentration camps to prevent them from supplying the rebels with food. As a result, about 200,000 Cubans died from starvation and disease.
5. Its rise to power began when it agreed to begin trading with the West in the mid-1800s. From that point, it built its industries and military. Japan's defeat of Russia in several key battles during the Russo-Japanese War showed the world it was a modern world power to be reckoned with.

PRIMARY SOURCE
1. The writer wanted to convey the point that Americans were greatly in favor of expanding their territory, and that it was natural to desire such a thing.
2. Mahan proposed that the United States develop naval bases overseas by acquiring islands.
3. The anti-imperialist might bring up the negative aspects of imperialism—invading other countries, oppressing people, etc.—for the writers to think about.

COMPOSING AN ESSAY
1. Students should mention that support for Mexican revolutionaries included the fact that President Wilson wanted Victoriano Huerta's "government of butchers" ousted from power because of the murder of newly elected president Francisco Madero. To help, he lifted the arms

embargo to the revolutionary armies of Villa, Zapata, and Carranza. Opposition to Filipino revolutionaries was that the United States wanted to annex the Philippines rather than let it become independent because of its military and commercial importance.
2. Students should explain that Taft believed that dollar diplomacy—extending U.S. influence in the region through investments—was the best way to protect the region from European intervention. Wilson believed that democratic governments, not dollars, would keep European powers out of Latin America.

CHAPTER 21

TEST FORM A

REVIEWING FACTS
1. d
2. b
3. a
4. d
5. c
6. c
7. a
8. d
9. a
10. a

UNDERSTANDING IDEAS
1. A
2. D
3. D
4. D
5. D
6. A
7. A
8. A
9. A
10. D

TRUE/FALSE
1. F
2. F
3. T
4. T
5. F

PRACTICING SKILLS
1. approximately 3.4 million (Accept answers that are within 200,000 of this figure.)
2. Russia

COMPOSING AN ESSAY
1. Students should describe how Americans voluntarily conserved energy, recycled essential materials, and started victory gardens, all to make more items available for the soldiers overseas. Americans also contributed directly by purchasing Liberty bonds.
2. Students should explain that the labor shortage spurred the immigration of 150,000 Mexicans to the United States during the war. In the meantime, the lure of job opportunities and the prospects of higher wages brought about the Great Migration from the South to northern cities. Hundreds of thousands of African Americans moved northward during the war years.

TEST FORM B

SHORT ANSWER
1. The nature of trench warfare—which featured two armies holed up in trenches separated by a narrow no-man's-land—made it very difficult for one side to win decisive battles and quick victories as it had in previous wars.
2. In 1917 the Bolsheviks seized control of the government after the Russian people had overthrown the czar. Bolshevik leader Vladimir Lenin, who was opposed to the war, quickly took steps to withdraw Russia from the conflict.
3. Congress passed the Espionage and Sedition Acts, outlawing acts of treason and making it a crime to criticize the government, flag, or the military. It also became a crime to oppose the draft, war-bond drives, or the arms industry.
4. The Supreme Court found that the Espionage and Sedition Acts did not violate the First Amendment.
5. Germany lost its colonies, was disarmed, was forced to admit full responsibility for

the war, and was assessed billions of dollars in reparations. In addition, it lost the Alsace-Lorraine and had to give up the resource-rich Saar to France for 15 years.

PRIMARY SOURCE
1. The author felt Germany was justified in its actions because England had announced that it would sink all German commercial ships found within its waters.
2. He said that he has sympathy for all the victims and their families.
3. He referred to England's blockade of Germany, which was intended to stop all supplies, including food, from reaching the nation.

COMPOSING AN ESSAY
1. Students should note that the major European powers engaged in an arms race with their rivals. To protect themselves, the nations formed alliances, each promising to aid the other if attacked by a third power. The alliances held war at bay for a time, but created the risk that a minor incident could trigger a major war. This proved true when Archduke Franz Ferdinand was assassinated and nations felt compelled to honor their alliances. The alliance system soon turned a local conflict into a global war.
2. Students should mention that in 1915 a German U-boat sank the *Lusitania*, killing 128 Americans. Later in the year and in early 1916, several other American passengers lost their lives as Germany attacked British and French ships. After stopping such attacks for a while, Germany resumed full-scale U-boat warfare in 1917, prompting the United States to break off diplomatic relations with Germany. Germany then torpedoed five American merchant ships. After American newspapers intercepted the Zimmerman Note in March 1917, President Wilson concluded that the United States could no longer remain neutral.

UNIT 6

TEST FORM A

UNDERSTANDING IDEAS
1. c
2. b
3. c
4. b
5. d
6. d
7. c
8. a
9. a
10. c

TRUE/FALSE
1. T
2. F
3. T
4. F
5. F

PRACTICING SKILLS
1. Taft
2. Socialist

REVIEWING FACTS
1. progressivism
2. populism
3. open shop
4. initiative
5. reclamation
6. Seventeenth Amendment
7. Nineteenth Amendment
8. conservation
9. President Taft
10. President Wilson

COMPOSING AN ESSAY
1. The National Association for the Advancement of Colored People began when a group of African American and white progressives met in New York City to discuss the lynching of two African American men in Springfield, Illinois, the previous year. They decided to form a group dedicated to ending racial discrimination. The NAACP published a monthly magazine, which publicized cases of racial inequality. They used the court system to

fight restrictions on voting and other civil rights. *Guinn* vs. *United States* outlawed the "grandfather clause"; *Buchanan* vs. *Warley* struck down racially segregated housing in Kentucky. During World War I the NAACP convinced the army to open up more opportunities for black soldiers.

2. On February 9, 1898, the New York *Journal* published a letter written by Enrique Dupuy de Lome, in which he insulted President McKinley. America was outraged. On February 15, the battleship USS *Maine* was blown up, killing 260 sailors. Most Americans blamed Spain for the explosion. On April 25, Congress declared war on Spain.

TEST FORM B

SHORT ANSWER
1. Most progressives were native born, middle or upper class, and college educated.
2. The Sixteenth Amendment allowed Congress to levy taxes based on an individual's income. This provided a way to fund government programs.
3. Progressives viewed the Ballinger-Pinchot affair as a sign that President Taft was not committed to conservation. Theodore Roosevelt broke from Taft because of the affair.
4. Mexico's 1917 constitution put an end to child labor, provided workers an eight-hour workday, and placed the interests of common welfare above individual rights.
5. In July the Allied Powers launched an offensive near the Somme River in northern France. Their goal was to exhaust the enemy's reserves. During this battle British forces suffered some 60,000 casualties in a single day. The four-month-long battle left more than 1 million dead or wounded.

PRIMARY SOURCE
1. a negative evil influence
2. young people who had nothing better to do

COMPOSING AN ESSAY
1. Students should explain that progressives hoped to instill a stronger sense of patriotism in citizens, especially immigrants, through the building of monuments and the beautification of cities. They hoped to promote improved working conditions, shorter hours, and better pay. Many business regulations fell short of reforming the capitalist system. Reforms such as the initiative, referendum, and recall had little impact at the national level. Problems of African Americans were not addressed adequately or worsened.
2. Students should explain that the labor shortage spurred the immigration of 150,000 Mexicans to the United States during the war. In the meantime, the lure of job opportunities and the prospects of higher wages brought about the Great Migration from the South to northern cities. Hundreds of thousands of African Americans moved northward during the war years. While working to produce needed food and equipment for the troops, Americans voluntarily conserved energy, recycled essential materials, and planted victory gardens, all to make more items available for the soldiers overseas. Americans also contributed directly by purchasing Liberty Bonds.

CHAPTER 22

TEST FORM A

REVIEWING FACTS
1. Seattle general strike
2. Warren G. Harding
3. John L. Lewis
4. Albert Fall
5. Boston police strike
6. Alfred E. Smith
7. Marcus Garvey
8. steel strike of 1919
9. A. Philip Randolph
10. United Mine Workers strike

UNDERSTANDING IDEAS
1. d

2. a
3. c
4. b
5. c

TRUE/FALSE
1. T
2. F
3. F
4. T
5. T
6. F
7. F
8. F
9. T
10. T

PRACTICING SKILLS
1. northern and western Europe
2. 92 percent

COMPOSING AN ESSAY
1. Students should mention that the Red Scare was a period of anticommunist hysteria during 1919 and 1920. Immigrants, particularly those involved in unions, came under great suspicion. Antiradical fears reached such heights that several elected members of the New York State Assembly were expelled because of their membership in the Socialist Party. During the Palmer raids, thousands of suspected radicals were arrested. Hundreds of these people, mostly poor immigrants who had recently arrived in the country, were deported.
2. Students should explain that Mellon proposed to eliminate the high wartime taxes imposed on the wealthy. He reasoned that if taxes were lower, the rich would have more money to invest and the economy would grow. Mellon argued that the benefits would then trickle down to the middle and lower classes in the form of jobs and higher wages. Congress listened to Mellon and cut taxes for the wealthy. The strategy appeared to work—the postwar slump ended, unemployment was low, and most sectors of the economy had entered a period of tremendous growth.

TEST FORM B

SHORT ANSWER
1. The return of 4.5 million soldiers to the workforce caused unemployment to rise and wages to fall. Consumers made purchases they had put off during the war. Soon the demand for goods outpaced the supply, and prices soared. Demobilization was also one of the factors behind the recession of 1920–1921 and the farm crisis that developed in the 1920s.
2. As a result of demobilization, employers were able to pay their employees low wages and require them to work long hours. Workers protested these conditions by going on strike. Workers also went on strike to demand recognition for their unions.
3. Americans generally did not favor strikes because they considered such activity un-American. Many Americans saw labor unrest as proof of a coming worker's revolution, such as the one that occurred in Russia in 1917.
4. They believed that the men had been convicted not because of the evidence presented but because they were immigrants and radicals.
5. Coolidge was even more pro-business than Harding. With Coolidge's support, Congress passed the Revenue Act of 1926, which repealed the gift tax, cut estate taxes in half, and reduced surtaxes on great wealth.

PRIMARY SOURCE
1. "In cities on three continents millions awaited word. . . . "
2. The judge said that "the defendant's ideas are cognate [associated] with crime." This suggests the judge did not take much stock in the freedom of speech.
3. He probably had very strong doubts, as suggested by his own remarks: ". . . although he may not actually have committed the crime. . . ."

COMPOSING AN ESSAY
1. Students should explain that the amendment met opposition from many reform-

ers, including women. During the Progressive Era, reformers had battled for legislation regulating the hours and working conditions of female workers. Passage of the amendment, it was feared, would make such legislation unconstitutional.

2. Students should mention that Du Bois wrote articles for the NAACP's *Crisis*, detailing the atrocities committed against African Americans. He believed in racial pride and solidarity but opposed black nationalism. His message was aimed at the educated elite. Garvey also believed in racial pride and solidarity. Unlike Du Bois, however, Garvey supported the cause of black nationalism. His Universal Negro Improvement Association hoped to foster economic independence through the establishment of black-owned businesses and to create an independent black homeland in Africa. Garvey's message was aimed at working-class African Americans living in urban areas.

CHAPTER 23

TEST FORM A

REVIEWING FACTS
1. Frederick W. Taylor
2. Henry Ford
3. Eliot Ness
4. Al Capone
5. Cecil B. DeMille
6. Babe Ruth
7. Clarence Darrow
8. Charles Lindbergh
9. Paul Robeson
10. Langston Hughes

UNDERSTANDING IDEAS
1. c
2. c
3. c
4. c
5. a

TRUE/FALSE
1. T
2. T
3. F
4. F
5. F
6. F
7. F
8. F
9. T
10. T

PRACTICING SKILLS
1. California
2. 499 or fewer
3. California and Texas

COMPOSING AN ESSAY
1. Students should explain that because of the economic boom in the 1920s, more Americans had bigger paychecks and more free time than in the past. They therefore used entertainment to fill their leisure hours.
2. Students should mention that the assembly line made factory work more tedious and led to increased rates of turnover. Unskilled factory workers had little chance for advancement. Upper-level positions for clerical workers, managers, and salespeople increased, but these jobs were unavailable to most factory workers. Because most of these jobs required at least a high school education, few recent immigrants qualified for them. Discriminatory hiring practices also closed most of these jobs to African Americans.

TEST FORM B

SHORT ANSWER
1. It is the practice of making products specifically designed to go out of style and then replacing them with up-to-date models.
2. They made people better understand African cultural heritage and issues of central importance to African Americans. Through this understanding, they helped advance the cause of civil rights.
3. Jazz is a hybrid of various musical styles, incorporating West African rhythms, elements of African American spirituals,

and ragtime and European harmonies. Jazz originated among African American musicians in the South. It emerged in the early 1900s in the entertainment district of New Orleans known as Storyville.
4. The tag was one given to a new generation of young American writers by poet Gertrude Stein. It refers to the writers' scorn for middle-class consumerism and the superficiality of the postwar years and their reflections on the destructiveness of World War I.
5. Positive: Alcoholism and the number of alcohol-related deaths declined. Negative: It turned millions of otherwise law-abiding Americans into lawbreakers.

PRIMARY SOURCES
1. Mr. Ford probably wouldn't have handled the letter himself—he had created a department to handle any problems that existed in an employee's home life. The department probably would have contacted her and given her a lecture in values and behaviors that Ford thought were proper. The worker probably would have received the same treatment.
2. The automobile gave young people great mobility. It widened their choices of activities, near and far.
3. The Ford Motor Company had kept the new design secret, and public excitement had escalated in the days before its unveiling. In addition, people were aware of all the wonderful freedoms and opportunities automobile ownership provided, including the ability to travel to distant places only dreamed of before.

COMPOSING AN ESSAY
1. Students should note that accidents, parking problems, pollution, and traffic jams were some negative results. In addition, some critics claimed that the automobile reduced people's sense of neighborliness.
2. Students should mention that by 1925, about 75 percent of buyers purchased their cars on installment credit. The availability of credit enabled many families to buy two cars or to buy more expensive ones. It also enabled them to trade in their old cars for new ones more frequently. Buying on credit also applied to many other products, enabling people to trade in products simply because they were out of style or not up-to-date.

CHAPTER 24

TEST FORM A
REVIEWING FACTS
1. Josefina Fierro de Bright
2. James Hilton
3. Herbert Hoover
4. William Faulkner
5. Nathanael West
6. Andrew Mellon
7. A. J. Muste
8. Eleanor Roosevelt
9. Franklin D. Roosevelt
10. James T. Farrell

UNDERSTANDING IDEAS
1. a
2. c
3. c
4. d
5. c

TRUE/FALSE
1. F
2. T
3. F
4. F
5. T
6. T
7. F
8. T
9. T
10. T

PRACTICING SKILLS
1. 16 percent
2. 1933
3. 1932 and 1935

COMPOSING AN ESSAY
1. Students should describe how many unemployed people were forced to sell apples on the street. Many people traveled

from city to city—often hitchhiking or hopping freight trains—in search of work. African Americans found it more difficult to find work than most people because of discrimination and prejudice.

2. Students should mention that even years after the depression, memories of those lean years remained vivid. Habits of scrimping and saving, of making every penny count, would stay with members of this generation for the rest of their lives. A strong desire for financial stability and material comforts shaped the outlook of many Americans who came of age during the depression.

TEST FORM B

SHORT ANSWER

1. Conditions were particularly bleak for tenant farmers in the South. When cotton prices plummeted, many tenant farmers were ruined and forced to leave the land they had lived on all their lives. Migrant farmworkers in the Southwest also experienced difficulties. Many of these illegal aliens and recent Mexican immigrants were forced to leave the country. Those who remained often faced discrimination and poor working conditions.
2. City governments, religious groups, and charitable organizations provided direct relief. In addition, Mexican American communities formed *mutualistas* to help each other; some Chinese American communities set out open barrels of rice; Harlem residents organized rent parties.
3. More than 20,000 Americans committed suicide in 1932. Many people felt a great shame for being unemployed and suffered from depression. Many parents who could not support their families were consumed by guilt.
4. The Bonus Army was a group of 10,000 World War I veterans and their families who gathered in Washington to support a veterans' bonus bill before Congress.
5. He had a dynamic personality and had promised a "new deal" to lead the nation out of its troubles. To some Americans, just the fact that he was *not* Hoover was enough to make FDR popular.

PRIMARY SOURCE

1. He recommended a good joke every 10 days.
2. Hoover was totally against any type of direct government aid.
3. Most students will probably answer *no*. Hoover seemed to be out of touch with the realities of the grave economic situation.

COMPOSING AN ESSAY

1. Students should mention that many people looked to popular culture and entertainment as a means of escape. The movies and radio provided plenty of offerings that reinforced the theme of survival in a difficult world. New forms of popular literature such as comic books offered inexpensive forms of entertainment. In addition, many novels of the time offered tales that took readers' minds off their economic worries.
2. Students should explain that people disliked the president because his policies had failed to end the Great Depression. He had opposed direct aid to farmers as well as to jobless factory workers.

CHAPTER 25

TEST FORM A

REVIEWING FACTS

1. b
2. d
3. b
4. d
5. a
6. a
7. c
8. d
9. a
10. c

UNDERSTANDING IDEAS
1. Works Progress Administration
2. National Youth Administration
3. Social Security Act
4. Federal Deposit Insurance Corporation
5. Civilian Conservation Corps
6. National Industrial Recovery Act
7. Agricultural Adjustment Administration
8. Tennessee Valley Authority
9. Wagner-Connery Act
10. Congress of Industrial Organizations

TRUE/FALSE
1. F
2. T
3. T
4. T
5. F

PRACTICING SKILLS
1. NE, CO, NM, TX, OK, KS
2. CA

COMPOSING AN ESSAY
1. Students should mention that some liberal reformers wanted the government to grant pensions to all people over age 60. Huey Long believed the government should tax the rich and use that money to provide a guaranteed income and a home to every American. In response to these suggestions, the Second New Deal planners initiated more public works programs, a Social Security plan, and wage and hour improvements for laborers.
2. Students should describe how electricity and indoor plumbing made life easier and greatly improved people's health by providing better sanitation and safer water supplies. With the availability of electricity and other government incentives, modern practices and industry came to new regions. The South changed the most. The region finally began to diversify its economy and rely less on traditional cash crops such as cotton.

TEST FORM B

SHORT ANSWER
1. He asked Congress for the power to appoint one new justice for each of the justices who was age 70 or over—a total of six. Roosevelt wanted to create a Court that would be more likely to uphold his reform legislation.
2. Thousands of farmers were driven off their lands by a severe drought that turned a 50-million-acre region into a wasteland. Many of them chose to start new lives in California. Once there, however, they found themselves in fierce competition with other farm laborers looking for work.
3. Roosevelt believed that opponents of federal relief programs might change their minds if they could see the frightful living conditions of migrant farmworkers and city-dwellers.
4. It was a WPA project that provided work to artists in the fields of writing, theater, music, and the visual arts.
5. Roosevelt named more than 100 African Americans to posts in the federal government. One core group of these African American government officials evolved into the Federal Council on Negro Affairs, which became known as the Black Cabinet or Black Brain Trust.

PRIMARY SOURCES
1. fear itself
2. He promised leadership and direct, vigorous action.
3. He asked for understanding and support.

COMPOSING AN ESSAY
1. Students should discuss how many writers incorporated themes of the depression into their works. For example, Steinbeck wrote about a poor family that traveled from the Dust Bowl to California in *The Grapes of Wrath;* many films of the period were escapist, e.g., the Marx Brothers' *Duck Soup;* many popular plays focused on traditional American values.
2. Students should mention that the TVA built a number of new dams and several power stations that provided electricity, flood control, and recreational facilities for a rural seven-state region that had been scarred by overcut forests and frequent flooding. Other TVA projects com-

bated illiteracy, malaria, and soil erosion, and tried to improve the region's standard of living. Critics of the TVA said it was an example of the government abusing its power. Shareholders in private utility companies feared the TVA would cause them to lose money.

UNIT 7

TEST FORM A

TRUE/FALSE
1. T
2. F
3. F
4. T
5. F
6. F
7. F
8. F
9. T
10. T
11. T
12. T
13. T
14. F
15. T

REVIEWING FACTS
1. Huey Long
2. Margaret Mitchell
3. Dorothea Lange
4. John L. Lewis
5. Eugene Debs
6. Eliot Ness
7. Charles Lindbergh
8. Andrew Mellon
9. Franklin D. Roosevelt
10. Mary McLeod Bethune

PRACTICING SKILLS
1. 1933
2. 1926
3. 1929–1933
4. 20 percent

COMPOSING AN ESSAY
1. The new Klan was established in 1915 at Stone Mountain, Georgia, by a preacher named William Joseph Simmons. The Klan grew not only in the South but also in northern and midwestern towns and cities, due to the Red Scare. By the end of the 1920s, membership declined steadily due to a decrease in the hysteria surrounding the Red Scare, a booming economy, negative publicity, and scandals at the national level of the organization.
2. Assembly lines increased productivity because products could be made more quickly. However, the lines also made work more tedious, which led to increased employee turnover. Unskilled factory workers had little chance for advancement. Upper-level positions increased, but they were unavailable to most factory workers and immigrants because such positions required at least a high school diploma.

TEST FORM B

SHORT ANSWER
1. Demobilization caused higher unemployment as 4.5 million soldiers returned home. Because the supply of workers outnumbered the jobs available, wages dropped. Prices increased because consumers made more purchases than they did during the war, and goods were in short supply. These forces contributed to the recession of 1920–1921 and the farm crisis that developed during the 1920s.
2. Advertisements of the 1920s targeted women because they were the caretakers of the family. Advertisers often used their products to promote a healthy family and a strong family life.
3. During the Great Depression, farmers faced falling crop prices and foreclosures on their farms. Unemployment was high, and many people traveled from city to city in search of work. The suicide rate went up due to people's shame and guilt over not being able to provide for their families.
4. He had a dynamic personality and had promised a "new deal" to lead the nation out of its troubles. To some Americans,

just the fact that he was not Hoover was enough to make FDR popular.
5. Federal Project Number One provided work to artists in the fields of writing, theater, music, and the visual arts.

PRIMARY SOURCE
1. the Great Depression
2. The line refers to the severe "Dust Bowl" drought that struck the Great Plains in the mid-1930s.

COMPOSING AN ESSAY
1. The main causes of the strikes were a result of demobilization. Employers could pay low wages and require long hours. Workers protested these conditions by going on strike. Workers also went on strike to demand recognition of their unions. Most Americans did not favor strikes because they considered such an activity as un-American. They also felt those who had jobs should be grateful.
2. Students should mention that automobiles enabled people to do more traveling. Cars brought spread-out families closer together more often. However, the automobile also brought accidents, parking problems, pollution, and traffic jams. Some critics claimed that the automobile reduced people's sense of neighborliness.

CHAPTER 26

TEST FORM A

REVIEWING FACTS
1. Emiliano Chamorro
2. Charles Evans Hughes
3. Anastasio Somoza
4. Fascist Party
5. Brownshirts
6. Winston Churchill
7. Nazi Party
8. Adolf Hitler
9. Joseph Stalin
10. Blackshirts

UNDERSTANDING IDEAS
1. b
2. a
3. c
4. a
5. d
6. c
7. a
8. b
9. d
10. c

TRUE/FALSE
1. T
2. F
3. T
4. T
5. T

PRACTICING SKILLS
1. 1936
2. Wendell Willkie

COMPOSING AN ESSAY
1. Students should mention that the United States followed a policy of partial isolation after the war. Isolationism led the United States to shun membership in international organizations, such as the League of Nations and the World Court.
2. Students should note that the United States played a large role in Nicaraguan politics throughout the 1920s and 1930s. In 1926 President Coolidge ordered in the U.S. Marines to protect American commercial interests and to negotiate an end to a civil war; in the treaty, the sides agreed to allow the United States to train a new Nicaraguan National Guard to maintain order after the United States withdrew; Augusto César Sandino organized a revolt against the government of Adolfo Díaz and the U.S. Marines; the Marines never defeated Sandino's forces; in 1933 President Hoover withdrew the troops; a year later, U.S.-trained Anastasio Somoza ordered Sandino's assassination; Samoza took over as president in 1937 and with United States backing, ruled the country until 1979, the date of the Sandinista revolution.

TEST FORM B

SHORT ANSWER

1. Hitler's National Socialist Party won nearly 40 percent of the vote in 1932 elections. The next year he became chancellor of Germany. His Third Reich then claimed dictatorial powers.
2. In 1931 Japan invaded Manchuria. In 1934 and 1935 the Japanese began a rapid naval buildup. In 1937 Japanese and Chinese troops clashed near Beijing; a full-scale war developed. Japan then occupied northern China and began bombing Chinese cities. Japanese troops brutally assaulted and occupied Nanjing in late 1937.
3. They believed that they could avoid a larger conflict by giving in to some of Hitler's demands.
4. Both Willkie and Roosevelt promised to keep the United States out of the European conflict.
5. Japan was reacting to strengthening U.S. resistance to Japanese aggression. This resistance included freezing all Japanese assets in the United States and placing an embargo on shipments of gasoline, machine tools, scrap iron, and steel to Japan.

PRIMARY SOURCE

1. He meant that had the nation not fought the war, there would not be the opportunity to "rule with reason" because dictators would be in power.
2. The spirit of tyranny refers to the aspirations of dictators and unjust rulers of the world.
3. Hughes wanted the United States to join the League of Nations.

COMPOSING AN ESSAY

1. Students should mention that prices for Latin American crops dropped tremendously during the Great Depression. Workers lost their jobs and the gap between wealthy landowners and the landless people widened. In the 1930s caudillos seized power in Cuba, the Dominican Republic, Guatemala, and Honduras.
2. Students should describe how, in 1927, the government began taking over privately owned lands and reorganizing them into large state-run farms. Farmers who protested were sent to forced labor camps. Stalin used the Red Army to suppress all dissent. In the late 1930s Stalin began a campaign to purge all perceived enemies from the Communist Party and the Red Army. As many as 30 million people may have died as a result.

CHAPTER 27

TEST FORM A

REVIEWING FACTS

1. b
2. c
3. a
4. b
5. a
6. c
7. d
8. a
9. a
10. a

UNDERSTANDING IDEAS

1. Harry S Truman
2. Elie Wiesel
3. Manhattan Project
4. Yalta Conference
5. Holocaust
6. genocide
7. A. Philip Randolph
8. internment
9. Selective Training and Service Act
10. Carlos E. Castañeda

TRUE/FALSE

1. F
2. F
3. F
4. T
5. T

PRACTICING SKILLS
1. Bataan is west of Manila.
2. approximately 50 miles (Because of the irregular path, accept answers that are within 10 miles.)

COMPOSING AN ESSAY
1. Students should explain how the Axis Powers had two distinct advantages. First, Germany and Japan had already secured firm control of the areas they had invaded. As a result, the United States and the Allies faced a long, drawn-out fight on several fronts. Second, Germany and Japan were better prepared for war. In the 1930s both nations had rearmed and built airfields, barracks, and military training centers.
2. Students should mention that between 1940 and 1944 the number of women in the labor force increased by about 6 million. Women worked in war plants and replaced men in a host of jobs ranging from newspaper reporting to truck driving.

TEST FORM B

SHORT ANSWER
1. The Allies had two major things in their favor—the vast military of the Soviet Union and the tremendous production capacity of the United States.
2. Government and private industries cooperated to increase production, and union leaders agreed not to strike. Mobilizing required a greatly expanded federal government. Between 1940 and 1945 the number of federal employees nearly tripled. The War Production Board was created to increase military production. Taxes were increased and anti-inflationary measures such as rationing were enacted. In addition, the Selective Training and Service Act was passed in order to increase the size of the military.
3. The Nazis took advantage of a long history of anti-Semitism that stretched back to the Middle Ages. A flood of Nazi propaganda against Jews stirred up this anti-Semitism. Some non-Jews in countries occupied by the Nazis either assisted or failed to prevent the Nazis from sending Jews off to the death camps. In addition, the absence of direct action by the Allies allowed the Holocaust to happen.
4. During the early months of 1945 Allied bombers continued to blast German cities. In March, Allied troops crossed the Rhine from the west and drove into the heart of Germany. Soviet forces, in the meantime, drove into Germany from the east. Both forces advanced on Berlin. In April, Hitler committed suicide in his bunker deep under the ruins of Berlin. On May 7, Germany surrendered unconditionally.
5. Truman had to decide whether to use the atomic bomb against Japan.

PRIMARY SOURCE
1. *Bushido* was the code of the warrior, which was never to surrender under any circumstances.
2. He discovered that niceness was not returned with niceness, only violence.
3. They remembered the atrocities that had been committed against American soldiers during the Bataan Death March.

COMPOSING AN ESSAY
1. Students should explain how Japanese Americans living on the Pacific Coast were forced to live in relocation camps. Many young men in the camps volunteered for military duty. They served in segregated units. One nisei combat team, the 442nd, fought in Europe and became one of the most decorated units in the armed services. Several thousand Japanese Americans also served in the Military Intelligence Services as interpreters and translators in the Pacific.
2. Students should mention that the Allies put in place a system of dummy installations and false clues to convince the Germans that the invasion of German-occupied France would take place near Calais on the English channel. Instead, they landed at Normandy, catching the Germans unprepared.

CHAPTER 28

TEST FORM A

REVIEWING FACTS
1. Potsdam Conference
2. *zaibatsu*
3. United Nations
4. Eleanor Roosevelt
5. George Marshall
6. containment
7. Douglas MacArthur
8. Dwight D. Eisenhower
9. Joseph McCarthy
10. Mao Zedong

TRUE/FALSE
1. T
2. F
3. F
4. F
5. T
6. F
7. F
8. F
9. F
10. F

MATCHING
1. c
2. d
3. a
4. e
5. b

PRACTICING SKILLS
1. The United States, Canada, Iceland, Great Britain, Greece, Norway, Denmark, France, Belgium, Netherlands, West Germany, Portugal, Italy, Turkey
2. NATO

COMPOSING AN ESSAY
1. Answers will vary. Communism frightened many Americans because it seemed to be spreading across the globe, and was therefore a threat to the American way of life. This fear led to paranoia and the subsequent Red Scare culture of the 1950s during which many Americans grew distrustful of others. Also, communism and the Soviet Union's attempt to spread it gave rise to the nuclear threat, which affected daily life in the United States. Nuclear fallout shelters were sold and built, Americans practiced nuclear strike preparedness, and even schools staged drills to make students ready should a nuclear conflict occur.
2. Answers will vary. President Truman vowed to support free people who were under attack from outside enemies or armed minorities, in essence saying the United States would fight Soviet expansion in other lands. The Marshall Plan was instituted to keep Western European nations strong so they would not endure social, economic, or political collapse, which could make them vulnerable to Soviet takeovers. The United States and British air forces executed the Berlin Airlift to stop the Soviets from driving the western powers from Berlin. Finally, western nations joined together to form NATO to defend each other in case of any outside attack, which, if it came, would most likely be from a communist nation.

TEST FORM B

SHORT ANSWER
1. Eisenhower was a popular WWII general who had patriotic appeal. He confidently promised to end the Korean War and strongly resist communism.
2. The Truman Doctrine vowed to support people being attacked by minorities or outsiders, essentially the Soviet Union. The Marshall Plan kept Western European nations strong so they would not endure an economic, political, or social collapse and hence fall under Soviet domination.
3. After British troops withdrew from Palestine, Jewish leaders proclaimed the new state of Israel. Arab nations refused to recognize Israel as a country and organized military efforts to recapture the land for Palestine.
4. Satellite nations were Eastern European countries taken over and controlled by the Soviet Union.

5. Many Americans felt the United States was falling behind the Soviet Union in technological developments. The U.S. government quickly established NASA and the National Defense Education Act to "catch up."

PRIMARY SOURCE
1. Harry Truman, Joseph Stalin, and Winston Churchill
2. She is likely referring to Europe in the aftermath of World War II, with its destruction of property and human life.
3. the Potsdam Conference in Germany after World War II

COMPOSING AN ESSAY
1. Answers will vary. The United States was committed to a democratic government, individual freedoms, and a capitalist economy. Most Americans opposed the Soviet system, which was based on a state-run economy controlled by the government at every level; one-party rule, meaning there were no fair elections and people could not voice their choice for leadership; the full suppression of religion; and the use of force to crush all opposition. These ways differed widely from life in the United States at the time. These differences led to the distrust and dislike of each other during the Cold War.
2. Answers will vary. The government set up the Central Intelligence Agency to gather strategic political and military information overseas. The Loyalty Review Board was set up in 1947 to investigate the political leanings of all federal employees. The House Un-American Activities Committee questioned liberal political groups, peace organizations, and labor unions. HUAC's later questioning of Hollywood directors and writers led to jail terms for some in the film industry. The Internal Security Act was passed to require party members and organizations to register with the federal government. Finally, the Joseph McCarthy hearings ruthlessly questioned the patriotism of hundreds of Americans, many of whom had their reputations destroyed in the process.

CHAPTER 29

TEST FORM A

REVIEWING FACTS
1. *Brown* v. *Board of Education*
2. Rosa Parks
3. Thomas Dewey
4. GI Bill of Rights
5. George Meany
6. Little Rock Nine
7. Taft-Hartley Act
8. automation
9. baby boom
10. beats

UNDERSTANDING IDEAS
1. b
2. d
3. a
4. a
5. c
6. b
7. c
8. d
9. a
10. c

TRUE/FALSE
1. F
2. T
3. T
4. T
5. F

PRACTICING SKILLS
1. the number of students
2. it increased

COMPOSING AN ESSAY
1. Answers will vary but answers should mention Truman's ban on job discrimination in the military and government jobs, court decisions declaring segregation laws and school segregation illegal, the integration of some schools, and the desegregation of public transportation in Montgomery, Alabama.

2. Answers will vary but may include criticisms of discrimination, materialism, greed, conformity, the threat of nuclear war, and the limitations of corporate jobs.

TEST FORM B

SHORT ANSWER

1. Answers will vary, but students should include the prosperity and mobility of middle-class workers, economies of building planned communities, improved and expanded highway systems, and the pressures of a high birth rate.
2. The Taft-Hartley Act of 1947 restricted union powers in a time when inflation had aroused discontent among workers. Passed in 1959, the Landrum-Griffin Act cracked down on union corruption when the gains made by unions were compromised by exposure of links to organized crime.
3. Answers should mention the conflict over civil rights, the formation of the Progressive Party that split the Democratic Party into three factions, and the weak support Truman received from other delegates. They should describe Truman's cross-country train campaign, in which he aggressively attacked the "do-nothing Congress."
4. Students should include details of higher earnings, the emergence of automation and large corporate structures, and the shift from blue-collar to white-collar and "pink-collar" work.
5. Answers may vary but should mention the homogenized nature of suburban life and constant bombardment by books, magazines, and television advertising, which extolled the advantages of a suburban lifestyle in order to increase material consumption of goods.
6. Answers should include African Americans' use of nonviolent resistance and economic strategies such as the bus boycott to wear down opposition and inspirational, charismatic leadership to keep the community from losing heart.

PRIMARY SOURCE

1. Answers should mention the greater earning potential given to the majority of Americans. College graduates got better jobs with more income. A great many more families became prosperous and so entered the middle class, with its greater buying power.
2. College education prepared workers for the white-collar jobs that were replacing blue-collar jobs as machines took over much mechanical labor. As corporations formed, they required educated workers to fill service and management positions.

COMPOSING AN ESSAY

1. Answers will vary but should include descriptions of the findings of the Committee on Civil Rights in 1947, the civil rights plank of the Democratic Party in 1948, the *Brown* v. *Board of Education* decision in 1954, the experience of the Little Rock Nine, and the results of the Montgomery bus boycott in 1956. Students should also mention the Félix Longoria incident and the work of the GI Forum and the League of United Latin American Citizens, and the experiences of Asian Americans and American Indians.
2. Answers will vary but should explore American problems with materialism, greed, racial hostilities, and the insistence on conformity. Students should touch on the threat of nuclear war, job pressures that take away individuality and independence, and a way of life that encourages selfishness and blindness to the problems of others.

UNIT 8

TEST FORM A

MATCHING

1. Emiliano Chamorro
2. Adolf Hitler
3. Joseph Stalin
4. Francisco Franco
5. Douglas MacArthur
6. Erwin Rommel

7. Bernard Montgomery
8. Harry S Truman
9. Charles Evans Hughes
10. Dwight D. Eisenhower

TRUE/FALSE
1. F
2. T
3. T
4. F
5. T

REVIEWING FACTS
1. Fascist Party
2. Brownshirts
3. Nazi Party
4. Blackshirts
5. isolationism
6. Third Reich
7. Resistance
8. Battle of the Bulge
9. Yalta Conference
10. Taft-Hartley Act

PRACTICING SKILLS
1. sell supplies to both sides, cash and carry
2. 13.5%

COMPOSING AN ESSAY
1. After Rosa Parks was arrested for refusing to give up her bus seat to a white passenger, the NAACP and the Montgomery Improvement Association challenged racial segregation of public transportation by organizing a boycott of the bus system by African Americans. Their use of nonviolent resistance and the economic consequences for the busing industry helped wear down the opposition. In 1956 the Supreme Court declared both Montgomery's and Alabama's segregation laws unconstitutional. By the end of the year, Montgomery had a desegregated bus system.
2. The Allied leaders met at the Potsdam Conference in July 1945. The leaders divided Germany into four occupation zones. The British, the French, and the Americans each took control of a zone in the western, industrialized part of Germany. The Soviets agreed to control the poorer, more rural eastern zone. The four powers also set up occupation zones in Austria and agreed to jointly administer the city of Berlin, which lay within the Soviet-controlled zone of Germany. They pledged to crush the Nazi Party, reestablish local governments, and rebuild German industry. They also agreed to return German refugees to their homes.

TEST FORM B

SHORT ANSWER
1. Britain and France declared war against Germany when Germany attacked Poland.
2. The Kellogg-Briand Pact outlawed war "as an instrument of national policy" but allowed countries to go to war in self-defense.
3. The leaders at the Munich Conference believed that they could avoid a larger conflict by giving in to some of Hitler's demands.
4. The Allied victory at the Battle of the Coral Sea stopped the Japanese advance on Australia.
5. The development of suburbs was due to many factors including changes in the workforce, higher incomes, better mobility, and a rapidly expanding population.

PRIMARY SOURCE
1. He was only sixteen, not old enough to join the armed forces.
2. He was angry that so many people had been killed. It was more real to him than it might have been to others because he had seen the effects of the attack firsthand.

COMPOSING AN ESSAY
1. Government and private industries cooperated to increase production, and union leaders agreed not to strike during the war. The federal government hired many more people, and the War Production Board was created to increase military production. Taxes were increased, and anti-inflationary measures such as rationing were enacted. The Selective

Training and Service Act was passed in order to increase the size of the military. The Allies had two major things in their favor, the vast manpower of the Soviet Union and the tremendous production capacity of the United States.
2. Historians who agreed with President Truman's decision to use the atomic bomb state that Japan's top military leaders fiercely opposed the peace overtures made by the Allies. If the war continued, many more American lives would have been lost. Those who disagree with the use of the bomb point out that Tokyo was considering peace negotiations. They say that with the promised Soviet declaration of war by early August, victory would have been possible without using the bomb. Some argue that Truman dropped the bomb to demonstrate the U.S. might and to strengthen its postwar position.

CHAPTER 30

TEST FORM A

REVIEWING FACTS
1. Great Society
2. Bay of Pigs
3. John F. Kennedy
4. Medicaid
5. Fidel Castro
6. Rachel Carson
7. Barry Goldwater
8. Lee Harvey Oswald
9. flexible response
10. Lyndon B. Johnson

UNDERSTANDING IDEAS
1. b
2. c
3. c
4. d
5. a
6. c
7. a
8. b
9. d
10. b

TRUE/FALSE
1. F
2. T
3. F
4. F
5. T

PRACTICING SKILLS
1. Mississippi, Alabama, Oklahoma
2. popular vote

COMPOSING AN ESSAY
1. Answers will vary but may mention how Kennedy's charm, appearance, and intelligence added to his charisma; how his appeals to idealism and sacrifice inspired the young; and how his heroic war record impressed citizens. Answers should describe the shock of Americans and their feeling that political innocence ended with Kennedy's assassination.
2. Answers should mention Johnson's initiatives to provide insurance and health care for the elderly and poor, to improve education and housing for the poor, to encourage and expand the arts and educational television, and to protect and repair damage to the environment.

TEST FORM B

SHORT ANSWER
1. Students may mention Kennedy's service record, good looks, sophistication, intelligence, and inspiring appeal to rise to a challenge. Negatives included public bias against his religion, his youth, and his lesser political experience (compared to Nixon). His choice of a contrasting running mate appeared a disadvantage, but ultimately proved a help in winning southern states.
2. Fear of nuclear conflict caused Kennedy to widen his options for international response. It also complicated relations with Cuba and led the United States to the brink of war when the Soviets sent missiles to Cuba. This close call led Kennedy and Khrushchev to find ways to ease tensions between the countries: the Limited Nuclear Test Ban Treaty and

establishment of direct communications via a hot line.
3. Answers should mention the seemingly charmed lives lead by a cultured, handsome first family; the appeal of Kennedy's youth, idealism, and intelligence; the inspiration of a call to serve and sacrifice in a moral cause.
4. Johnson worked tirelessly and used his considerable political skills to push Kennedy's agenda. He secured passage of Kennedy's tax cut bill, created the Office of Economic Opportunity, the Job Corps, Head Start, and Volunteers in Service to America.
5. Students should list Medicare and Medicaid, the NEA and NEH, and the Corporation for Public Broadcasting. Legislation included the Elementary and Secondary Education Act, Water Quality Act, Air Quality Act, and Water Pollution Act.
6. The Warren Court required that population density determine number of representatives; required that those accused of crimes be provided lawyers, have a lawyer present during police investigations, and be informed of their rights when arrested.

PRIMARY SOURCE
1. Americans should defend freedom as a universal right.
2. They must focus on serving their country and improving the world climate of democracy rather than focus on selfish interests.
3. Answers will vary but may include the appeal of heroism and casting America as a force for good, saving the world from an evil force.

COMPOSING AN ESSAY
1. Answers will vary but should include details that show Kennedy's wealth and charisma, sophisticated and intellectual approach, his high-minded appeal to American heroism and unselfishness, and his preoccupation with nuclear threats and international crises. By contrast, they should point to Johnson's poor beginnings and crudeness; his physical, workaholic approach to political processes; his gifts for compromise; and his capacity for getting enormous amounts of legislation passed quickly.
2. Answers should include the Berlin Crisis, which ended in the erection of the Berlin Wall and symbolized the dilemma of the Cold War; the Bay of Pigs, which humiliated the United States and empowered Fidel Castro, as well as increasing Soviet support to Cuba; the Cuban Missile Crisis, which nearly precipitated nuclear war and finally brought the superpowers together to negotiate a test ban treaty and find ways of communicating.

CHAPTER 31

TEST FORM A

REVIEWING FACTS
1. Black Panthers
2. Robert Moses
3. Malcolm X
4. Black Power
5. Freedom Summer
6. Elijah Muhammad
7. Medgar Evers
8. quotas
9. Voting Rights Act
10. Kerner Commission

UNDERSTANDING IDEAS
1. b
2. a
3. c
4. d
5. a
6. c
7. d
8. a
9. c
10. b

TRUE/FALSE
1. F
2. T
3. F

4. T
5. F

PRACTICING SKILLS
1. Mississippi and Alabama
2. 20–50 percent

COMPOSING AN ESSAY
1. Answers will vary in wording. Students should explain that white violence against peaceful African Americans created a groundswell of outrage that accelerated passage of legislation. Black violence gained prominent attention but frightened whites and increased resistance to civil rights.
2. Students should touch on how busing and quotas immediately placed African American students in better schools and accelerated the integration process. At the same time, they struck white Americans as unfair and extreme, since bused children had to be removed from their neighborhoods to go to school, and quotas meant that some deserving white students had to be turned away to make room for the required number of minority students.

TEST FORM B

SHORT ANSWER
1. The SCLC was a church-based organization that used nonviolent resistance to protest and get its message to the public. The SNCC was an association of student activists who staged sit-ins and peaceful demonstrations to integrate restaurants.
2. Nonviolent protests and demonstrations, which triggered violent responses by white racists, were most effective in bringing about public outrage and rapid change.
3. On August 28, 1963, 200,000 gathered in Washington, D.C., drawing national attention to the struggle for civil rights and giving Martin Luther King Jr. a national stage. This success was followed by a bombing in which four African American girls were killed in a church in Birmingham. Outrage over the murders lent support for the Civil Rights Act, which passed within the year.
4. Activists who attempted to register voters faced violence and death from outraged white racists. African Americans feared to register because they faced losing jobs as well as personal violence and death threats.
5. Police attacked activists protesting against the violence used to prevent voter registration by African Americans. Public outrage against the attacks led to speedy passage of the Voting Rights Act just five months later.
6. Black Panthers wanted "land, bread, housing, education, clothing, justice, and peace" as well as the freedom "to determine [their] own destiny." They advocated self-defense against "racist police oppression" and armed themselves with guns.
7. King lived in a slum in Chicago and led marches to end housing discrimination. He organized a Poor People's Campaign and march on Washington to protest lack of government spending on the poor. When he went to Memphis to support a strike by sanitation workers, King was shot and killed by a sniper.
8. African Americans' frustration with discrimination and white racism led to more than 100 riots in two years' time. The riots caused destruction and death and left white and African Americans more polarized than ever.
9. Busing made some parents angry about their children being sent outside their neighborhoods; others did not want integrated schools. Quotas seemed unfair to some white Americans, who called them "reverse discrimination.".
10. More than 4,500 African Americans were elected to public office. They owned more businesses. More were better educated, entered professional jobs, and earned more money. The income gap in many professions narrowed.

PRIMARY SOURCE

1. They should fight for their goals.
2. freedom
3. He is likely saying that negotiation, nonviolence, and discussion are not enough to end racism.

COMPOSING AN ESSAY

1. Answers will vary. Answers should focus on gains made through nonviolent protest by Christian-led groups in the early stages of the civil rights movement, then contrast the shift toward an attitude that violence and more radical rhetoric could advance Nation of Islam–based Black Power. Students should point out how some African American leaders called for separation from white Americans whereas early activists held up integration and equality as goals. Achievements include gaining enforceable voting rights, desegregation of public places and schools, and better economic opportunities. Perhaps the most dramatic achievement of the civil rights movement has been the number of African Americans elected to public office.
2. Answers will vary in wording but should point out that white racist violence against nonviolent protesters and demonstrators outraged many Americans and hastened the political process of change. Some African Americans came to see nonviolent protest as an ineffective tool once a certain level of rights had been achieved. On the other hand, violence by African Americans in the form of urban riots and gun battles with police hurt the movement by polarizing society into pro and con camps.

CHAPTER 32

TEST FORM A

REVIEWING FACTS

1. *In Re Gault*
2. Gloria Steinem
3. La Huelga
4. Children's Defense Fund
5. Bob Dylan
6. American Indian Movement
7. Equal Rights Amendment
8. Motown
9. César Chávez
10. Gray Panthers

UNDERSTANDING IDEAS

1. b
2. d
3. a
4. c
5. c
6. a
7. c
8. d
9. b
10. c

TRUE/FALSE

1. F
2. T
3. F
4. F
5. T

PRACTICING SKILLS

1. In 1968, Chicanos joined the poor people's march in Washington, D.C.
2. 1965: César Chávez leads the United Farm Workers in the Delano Grape Strike; 1969: Chicanos hold an antiwar rally; 1972: Brown Berets occupy Santa Catalina Island.

COMPOSING AN ESSAY

1. Answers will vary. Students should name the taking of tribal lands, the reservation system, chronic poverty and unemployment for Indians, discrimination throughout the country, and a feeling of hopelessness about the possibility of changes coming from anywhere outside of Indians themselves.
2. Answers will vary. Students should state that Betty Friedan concluded women were fundamentally dissatisfied in their lives as housewives. Women were discriminated against in the workplace and were feeling that they were not leading useful and productive lives as full-time

homemakers. The book inspired many women to look closely at their lives and demand changes, such as increased opportunities and equal treatment in the workplace.

TEST FORM B
SHORT ANSWER
1. Through the Red Power movement, American Indians were able to regain some of their lands, make the nation more aware of discrimination against Indians, and instill a sense of pride in American Indians throughout the United States.
2. She defined ageism as arbitrary discrimination against people or groups on the basis of how old they were.
3. Social history is the study of ordinary people, such as workers, women, farmers, immigrants, and others who had been left out of traditional history books.
4. The ERA proposed a ban on discrimination on the basis of sex. It was passed by Congress, but fell three states short of approval and failed to become law.
5. He led a 300-mile march to Sacramento and called for a nationwide boycott of grapes. The boycott put economic pressure on growers to negotiate a settlement.

PRIMARY SOURCE
1. The U.S. government forced the American Indians' backs to the wall and gave them no choice but to protest.
2. She says that Indian cultures are being exterminated; cultural artifacts are taken from the cultures and end up in museums where mostly non-Indians look at them.
3. Keith is saying that the poverty on American Indian reservations is ongoing and continuous and works in cycles that are extremely difficult to break.

COMPOSING AN ESSAY
1. Answers will vary. Students should describe the various political activities, protests, strikes, boycotts, occupations, and other actions that the different groups used to make changes. Then they should generally characterize each group, noting that all three groups tried to use the media as much as they could; that the Chicanos relied on strikes, boycotts, marches, and political action; that American Indians were more confrontational as they had less access to the political process; and that women used political action as well as protests, books, and articles.
2. Answers will vary. Students should describe in detail each point of view. They should include arguments for the amendment regarding how women were discriminated against in the workplace (pay, promotions, position), education, sports, and other areas of life and needed the full weight of the federal government in support of needed changes. Students should explain why people opposed the amendment: the amendment was seen as a threat to traditional women's roles in the family, the ERA addressed only the needs of highly educated professional women, and it would nullify any legal distinctions between men and women.

CHAPTER 33

TEST FORM A
UNDERSTANDING FACTS
1. c
2. c
3. a
4. b
5. b

REVIEWING FACTS
1. Vietcong
2. hawks
3. Ho Chi Minh
4. Ngo Dinh Diem
5. Students for a Democratic Society
6. doves
7. Tet Offensive
8. Vietnamization
9. Henry Kissinger
10. Le Duc Tho

TRUE/FALSE
1. T
2. F
3. T
4. T
5. F

PRACTICING SKILLS
1. Cambodia
2. Laos and China
3. the South China Sea

COMPOSING AN ESSAY
1. The American public grew negative toward the war for a variety of reasons. One was that over time it seemed like the United States could not win the war. This made people wonder why the country should bother fighting it at all. Others felt that the United States was going against what the South Vietnamese people wanted, so in effect we were involved in another country's business, a country that seemed not to want us involved at all. The mounting death toll, the horrible images on television, and the fact that the U.S. government specifically misled the American people all contributed to a negative attitude about the war.
2. Nixon planned Vietnamization as one of his strategies to end the war. Vietnamization was the gradual turning over of the fighting to the South Vietnamese, phasing the American military out over time. In this way Nixon hoped to achieve "peace with honor," a way to spare the United States the humiliation of outright defeat. While Nixon supported Vietnamization in public, he privately wanted to escalate the war. When he bombed Cambodia, people realized his Vietnamization plan was just talk and a failure.

TEST FORM B

SHORT ANSWER
1. The Gulf of Tonkin Resolution allowed the president to send American troops into battle if it was necessary to other American troops who might be attacked.
2. The Tet Offensive shattered American confidence in the military. People questioned whether it was even possible to win the war. Tet made public criticism of the war rise dramatically.
3. The 1968 Democratic National Convention in Chicago hurt the Democrats' chances of defeating Nixon. Nixon and other Republicans seized the opportunity and ran on a "law and order" platform that appealed to many Americans.
4. The U.S. government spent increasingly larger percentages of the federal budget on the Vietnam War, taking money away from federal domestic programs.
5. Since the war, most American presidents have been reluctant to commit U.S. ground troops to any war or conflict. Fearing "another Vietnam," politicians and leaders seem to want only to place American troops in wars or situations that are clearly winnable.

PRIMARY SOURCE
1. "rotting in the jails of Hanoi"
2. "Vietnam thinking" probably refers to America wasting all our resources on the war alone instead of using them to solve our own country's problems.
3. He uses the word "paranoiac" because he feels the U.S. government is too fearful of the spread of communism.

COMPOSING AN ESSAY
1. Students who think this is a wise decision may state that it is not necessary for the public to know every detail of the war; that the president certainly, as the commander in chief of the armed services, has the right to run the war without dispensing all information. They also might argue that most Americans do not understand the goals or intricacies of the foreign relations at play in the war, and that it would be a breach of national security to release that information. Those in favor of telling the public might say it is a good move to build trust with the American people and bring them around

to the president's opinion of how the war should be waged.

2. Many veterans went to Vietnam to fight for their country and its way of life. They considered it an honorable act to defend the nation's freedom. Yet when they returned home they learned that many Americans did not support the war or their efforts, and that many Americans were angry at them for fighting in the unpopular war. This led to anger and disillusionment. There was no welcome-home parade as in other wars, and veterans felt like they put their lives on the line for nothing. While in Vietnam, many soldiers, under harsh conditions, wondered whether the war could even be won, and questioned the real purpose of it.

UNIT 9

TEST FORM A

REVIEWING FACTS
1. Voting Rights Act
2. Malcolm X
3. American Indian Movement
4. Nation of Islam
5. Tonkin Gulf Resolution
6. John F. Kennedy
7. counterculture
8. Martin Luther King Jr.
9. Tet Offensive
10. Great Society

UNDERSTANDING IDEAS
1. b
2. c
3. a
4. b
5. c
6. a
7. a
8. b
9. d
10. d

TRUE/FALSE
1. T
2. F
3. F
4. F
5. F

PRACTICING SKILLS
1. the East Coast
2. Many African Americans who were involved in riots lived in large cities.

COMPOSING AN ESSAY
1. Answers will vary but may mention how Kennedy's charm, appearance, and intelligence added to his charisma; how his appeals to idealism and sacrifice inspired the young; and how his heroic war record impressed citizens. Answers should describe the shock of Americans and their feeling that political innocence ended with Kennedy's assassination.
2. American public opinion grew negative toward the war for a variety of reasons. One was that over time, it became clear that the United States could not win the war easily. Also, the mounting death toll, and the fact that the U.S. government specifically misled the American people all contributed to a negative attitude toward the war.

TEST FORM B

SHORT ANSWER
1. The Warren Court required that population density determine number of representatives; required that those accused of crimes be provided lawyers, have a lawyer present during police investigations, and be informed of their rights when arrested.
2. Nonviolent protests and demonstrations that triggered violent responses by white racists were most effective in bringing about public outrage and rapid change.
3. Busing made parents angry about children being sent outside their neighborhoods; some did not want integrated schools. Quotas seemed unfair to whites, who called them "reverse discrimination."

4. He led a 300-mile march to Sacramento and called for a nationwide boycott of grapes. The boycott put economic pressure on growers to negotiate a settlement.
5. Since the war, American leaders have been reluctant to commit U.S. ground troops to any war or conflict without being certain of the consent of the American people and the nation's political allies. Also, to avoid "another Vietnam," recent presidents have committed U.S. troops only to operations that could end quickly.

PRIMARY SOURCE
1. difficult and uncertain
2. education, science, and national purpose

COMPOSING AN ESSAY
1. Answers will vary but should include details that show Kennedy's wealth and charisma, his sophisticated and intellectual approach, his high-minded appeal to American heroism and unselfishness, and his preoccupation with nuclear threats and international crises. By contrast, they should point to Johnson's poor beginnings and crudeness; his physical, workaholic approach to political processes; his gifts for compromise; and his capacity for getting enormous amounts of legislation passed quickly.
2. Answers will vary. They should focus on gains made through nonviolent protest by Christian-led groups in the early stages of the civil rights movement, then contrast the shift toward an attitude that violence and more radical rhetoric could advance Nation of Islam–based Black Power. Students should point out how some African American leaders called for separation from whites, whereas early activists held up integration and equality as goals. Achievements include gaining enforceable voting rights, desegregation of public places and schools, and better economic opportunities. Perhaps the most dramatic achievement of the civil rights movement has been the number of African Americans elected to public office.
3. Answers will vary. Students should describe the various political activities, protests, strikes, boycotts, occupations, and other actions that the different groups used to make changes. Then they should generally characterize each group, noting that all three groups tried to use the media as much as they could; that the Chicanos relied on strikes, boycotts, marches, and political action; that American Indians were more confrontational because they had less access to the political process; and that women used political action as well as protests, books, and articles.
4. Many veterans went to Vietnam to fight for their country and its way of life. They considered it an honorable act to defend the nation's freedom. Yet when they returned home they learned that many Americans did not support the war or their efforts and that many Americans were angry at them for fighting in the unpopular war. This led to anger and disillusionment. There was no welcome-home parade as in other wars, and veterans felt like they put their lives on the line for nothing. While in Vietnam, many soldiers, under harsh conditions, wondered whether the war could even be won, and questioned the real purpose of it.

CHAPTER 34

TEST FORM A

REVIEWING FACTS
1. *Apollo 11*
2. *Skylab*
3. Jimmy Carter
4. apartheid
5. stagflation
6. Camp David Accords
7. Committee to Re-elect the President
8. Silent Majority
9. Family Assistance Plan
10. realpolitik

TRUE/FALSE
1. T
2. F
3. T
4. T
5. T
6. T
7. T
8. T
9. F
10. T

MATCHING
1. g
2. c
3. b
4. f
5. e

PRACTICING SKILLS
1. about $12
2. between 1977 and 1979
3. about $32

COMPOSING AN ESSAY
1. Nixon's view of foreign affairs dealt only with what was best for the United States. Whether a policy was immoral or not did not matter; what did was whether or not the policy was good for the United States. He called this realpolitik. Carter, on the other hand, was willing to do things that were not always in America's best interest if it meant righting an international wrong. His stance was essentially the opposite of Nixon's. Carter felt human rights and human dignity were always the priority when it came to international relations.
2. Détente referred to the lessening of political tension between the United States and the Soviet Union. The two nations invariably went through periods of détente, along with periods of high tension. Détente occurred when Nixon flew to Moscow and had summit talks with Brezhnev. Détente declined during the Ford administration and into the Carter administration. It reached its low point after the Soviet invasion of Afghanistan in 1979.

TEST FORM B
SHORT ANSWER
1. Supporters of the plan believed it would help cut down on federal bureaucracy, while opponents of the plan felt it would make needy families too dependent on the U.S. government.
2. Carter was protesting the Soviet Union's invasion of Afghanistan in 1979.
3. Stagflation was the combination of rising unemployment and inflation. Nixon tried to stop it by imposing wage and price controls.
4. The accords established peace between Egypt and Israel and for a while helped stabilize the Middle East.
5. Nixon hoped to gain political information on his enemies in the Democratic National Committee.
6. The SALT treaty limited the number of missiles the United States and the Soviet Union could have. It was a small step toward reducing the threat of nuclear war.

PRIMARY SOURCE
1. The establishment referred to regular mainstream American society.
2. According to Kissinger, Nixon turned his dream into an obsession.
3. Yes, but because of the Watergate scandal he lost all that he had achieved.

COMPOSING AN ESSAY
1. Arab nations punished the United States for its support of Israel by cutting off oil sales to America. Then OPEC announced it was raising the price of oil. This triggered a rise in the price of gasoline, electricity, and heating oil. Nixon tried to help the situation by calling for energy conservation. He also lowered the speed

limit and increased support for the use of nuclear energy to replace oil as the chief energy source.

2. The 1970s saw a large increase in the number of immigrants to the United States from Asia and Latin America. This led to calls for bilingual education and changes in the voting process. More and more Americans divorced in the 1970s, and the increase in the number of single parents changed the basics of family life in much of the country. The invention of the personal computer, video games, and VCRs changed how Americans spent their work and free time.

CHAPTER 35

TEST FORM A

REVIEWING FACTS
1. Reaganomics
2. Sandra Day O'Connor
3. Commonwealth of Independent States
4. Ayatollah Khomeini
5. Christa McAuliffe
6. Lech Walesa
7. S&L crisis
8. Operation Desert Storm
9. Iran-Contra affair
10. Sandinistas

UNDERSTANDING IDEAS
1. a
2. b
3. a
4. d
5. b
6. d
7. c
8. b
9. d
10. c

TRUE/FALSE
1. T
2. T
3. T
4. F
5. F

PRACTICING SKILLS
1. Honduras, El Salvador, Panama, Grenada
2. Duvalier was ousted and political instability followed.

COMPOSING AN ESSAY
1. Answers will vary. Students should explain why the S&Ls failed and that they were insured by the federal government. They should say that through the insurance, the government had to spend billions of dollars to pay depositors back and that this increased the federal deficit, which was already very high. Students should also point out that the bank failures made everyone nervous about the state of the economy.
2. Answers will vary. Students should explain what happened in the hostage crisis in Iran and why. They should point out that Jimmy Carter's popularity sank lower and lower as the crisis wore on. Finally, they should point out how Ronald Reagan used the crisis to his advantage in the campaign by calling Carter weak and promising a new, far stronger government.

TEST FORM B

SHORT ANSWER
1. The Republicans gained control of the Senate for the first time since 1952.
2. The strikes increased tension between the two countries.
3. The Chinese government sent tanks and troops in to clear them out by force; between a few hundred and a thousand demonstrators were killed.
4. AIDS, or acquired immune deficiency syndrome, is the final stage of a deadly disease that was first reported in 1981.
5. President Reagan sent troops there to unseat leaders of a coup that had overthrown the government.

PRIMARY SOURCE
1. obey it
2. to disobey it
3. He is saying that North was not a patriot

as he claimed; that by carrying out unlawful orders he was working against the interests of the United States.

COMPOSING AN ESSAY
1. Answers will vary. Students should give examples of how the arms race increased tensions between the two countries and increased the threat of nuclear war. They should also mention the effects on the economy of the United States; that spending for arms and defense increased the federal budget and took money away from domestic spending. Students should also understand that the United States put tremendous pressure on the Soviet economy through the arms race; the breakup of the Soviet Union may have in part been caused by the huge amounts of money needed to keep building arms.
2. Answers will vary. Students should give examples of positive and negative effects of Reagan's presidency. Positive effects might include the lessening of tensions with the Soviet Union, the strong economy during the 1980s, the general improvement in the attitude of many U.S. citizens about the state of the country, the nuclear test-ban treaty, and the first woman appointed to the Supreme Court. Negative effects might include the huge increase in the budget deficit, which affected the economy after Reagan left office; the Iran-Contra affair; the covert CIA involvement in Central America; the handling of public lands; tax cuts that favored the very wealthy; deep cuts in social programs; and increases in homelessness.

CHAPTER 36

TEST FORM A

REVIEWING FACTS
1. George W. Bush
2. Nelson Mandela
3. Y2K bug
4. Yasir Arafat
5. Los Angeles riots
6. Kosovo crisis
7. Madeleine Albright
8. North American Free Trade Agreement
9. World Wide Web
10. Hillary Rodham Clinton

UNDERSTANDING IDEAS
1. b
2. b
3. c
4. d
5. a
6. c
7. c
8. d
9. c
10. b

TRUE/FALSE
1. F
2. F
3. T
4. T
5. T

PRACTICING SKILLS
1. about $3 trillion
2. about $500 billion

COMPOSING AN ESSAY
1. Answers will vary. Students should explain that the boom created more very wealthy people, very low unemployment, and low inflation. Economists were amazed by this combination. They should say that one of the main causes was the huge rise in the stock market, particularly in technology stocks, and point out that some of the hottest technology stocks were from companies that were not even making a profit.
2. Answers will vary. Students should point out that the primary difference was from where people came: A hundred years ago the majority of immigrants came from Europe, while during the 1990s people came mostly from Asia, the Caribbean, and Latin America. Negative responses included fear that immigrants were taking jobs from native-born residents and lowering wages by being willing to work for

less. Positive responses included that immigrants created new businesses and in some cases were highly skilled workers needed in fields such as high technology.

TEST FORM B
SHORT ANSWER
1. The number of women working outside the home grew by about 30 percent.
2. The Internet enabled people to communicate worldwide, join discussions, and gather information.
3. Thomas-Hill hearings
4. He lowered the deficit by about half.
5. President Clinton was impeached for lying under oath and trying to obstruct justice. He was not convicted.

PRIMARY SOURCE
1. Gore says that the services and information will go into homes, businesses, schools, and hospitals.
2. He says that the world will be united by a seamless web of information.
3. Gore states that the result will be a new information marketplace that provides opportunities and challenges.

COMPOSING AN ESSAY
1. Answers will vary. Students should describe the huge growth in world population and give examples. They should describe how population increases put huge pressures on natural resources and the ability to preserve and protect the environment, create enormous waste problems, cause food shortages and health problems, and generally cause the quality of life to go down. They should identify things that can help, such as massive recycling programs, reducing population growth (one way is by advancing the status of women), being more conscious of urban and semi-urban planning and how food is grown and distributed, and reducing the amounts of fossil fuels and other natural resources that are used.
2. Answers will vary. Students should show how countries compete in economic ways and how world trade can strongly affect the economies of specific countries—that a country can become strong or weak through economic dealings and that one country can essentially "conquer" another without invading with military. Students should point out that like governments, multinational corporations hold tremendous amounts of power and conduct their business worldwide. They should also note that these corporations are less accountable than some governments for their policies and actions.

UNIT 10

TEST FORM A
REVIEWING FACTS
1. Watergate
2. Nicaragua
3. human rights
4. Iran hostage crisis
5. Panama Canal
6. Camp David Accords
7. Gerald Ford
8. China
9. energy crisis
10. Contract with America

UNDERSTANDING IDEAS
1. d
2. d
3. b
4. a
5. d
6. b
7. b
8. a
9. a
10. b

TRUE/FALSE
1. T
2. F
3. T
4. F
5. F

PRACTICING SKILLS
1. bribery and treason
2. the Senate

COMPOSING AN ESSAY

1. Nixon's view of foreign affairs dealt only with what was best for the United States. Whether a policy was immoral or not did not matter; what did was whether or not the policy was good for the United States. He called this realpolitik. Carter, on the other hand, was willing to do things that were not always in the nation's best interest if it meant righting an international wrong. His stance was essentially the opposite of Nixon's. Carter felt human rights and human dignity were always the priority when it came to international relations.

2. Answers will vary. Students should point out that the primary difference was where people came from: A hundred years ago the majority of immigrants came from Europe, while during the 1990s people came mostly from Asia, Latin America, and the Caribbean. Negative responses included fear that immigrants were taking jobs from native-born residents and lowering wages by being willing to work for less. Positive responses include such things as immigrants created new businesses and in some cases were highly skilled workers needed in fields such as high technology.

TEST FORM B

SHORT ANSWER

1. Carter was outraged and demanded that the Soviet Union immediately withdraw their troops. When they did not, he ordered the boycott of the 1980 Moscow Olympics.
2. Clinton was charged by the House of Representatives with lying under oath and obstructing justice.
3. The crisis made Carter look weak and indecisive, which hurt his presidency around the 1980 election. Reagan played off this weakness and vowed to be strong in the crisis, which appealed to American voters. He won the election.
4. Nixon knew the House of Representatives was about to draft articles of impeachment. Rather than go through that ordeal, and knowing the facts of the Watergate case were not in his favor, he decided to end his presidency on his own.
5. The Camp David Accords established peaceful relations between Israel and Egypt, helping stabilize the Middle East.

PRIMARY SOURCE

1. Women continued to lag behind men in terms of salaries.
2. Woman are not encouraged to study lucrative fields, and they lack the sports programs that men have, which can provide scholarships.

COMPOSING AN ESSAY

1. Answers will vary. Students should describe the huge growth in world population and give examples. They should describe how population increases put huge pressures on natural resources and the ability to preserve and protect the environment, create enormous waste problems, cause food shortages and health problems, and generally cause the quality of life to go down. They should identify things that can help, such as massive recycling programs, reducing population growth (for instance, by advancing the status of women), being more conscious of urban and semi-urban planning and how food is grown and distributed, and reducing the amounts of fossil fuels and other natural resources that are used.

2. Nixon's view of foreign affairs dealt only with what was best for the United States. Whether a policy was immoral or not did not matter; what did was whether or not the policy was good for the United States. He called this realpolitik. Carter, on the other hand, was willing to do things that were not always in the nation's best interest if it meant righting an international wrong. His stance was essentially the opposite of Nixon's. Carter felt human rights and human dignity were always the priority when it came to international relations.

3. Arab nations punished the United States for its support of Israel by cutting off oil sales to America. Then OPEC announced it was raising the price of oil. This triggered a rise in the price of gasoline, electricity, and heating oil. Nixon tried to help the situation by calling for energy conservation. He also lowered the speed limit and increased support for the use of nuclear energy to replace oil as the chief energy source.

4. Answers will vary. Students should give examples of positive and negative effects of Reagan's presidency. Positive effects might include the lessening of tensions with the Soviet Union, the strong economy during the 1980s, the general improvement in the attitude of many U.S. citizens about the state of the country, the nuclear test-ban treaty, and the first woman appointed to the Supreme Court. Negative effects might include the huge increase in the budget deficit, which affected the economy after Reagan left office; the Iran-Contra affair; the covert CIA involvement in Central America; the handling of public lands; tax cuts that favored the very wealthy; and deep cuts in social programs.